Positive Perspectives:

Love Your Dog ❤ Train Your Dog

by PAT B. MILLER

Dogwise Publishing
Wenatchee, Washington, U.S.A.
www.dogwisepublishing.com

Positive Perspectives: Love Your Dog, Train Your Dog
Pat B. Miller

Published by Dogwise Publishing
A Division of Direct Book Service, Inc.
403 South Mission Street
Wenatchee, WA 98807
1-509-663-9115, 1-800-776-2665
Website: www.dogwisepublishing.com <http://www.dogwisepublishing.com>
Email: info@dogwisepublishing.com

@2004 Pat B. Miller

Graphic Design: Anderson O'Bryan, Wenatchee, WA
Indexing: Elaine Melnick "The Index Lady"
Photos: Nancy Kearns, Paul Miller, Pat Miller, Nate Woodward, Allex Smith, Simon Thornock

Portions of this book previously appeared in *The Whole Dog Journal*, *The Whole Cat Journal*, and *Your Dog*. Used with permission.

Library of Congress Cataloging-in-Publication Data
Miller, Pat, 1951 Oct. 14-
    Positive Perspectives: the modern guide to successful dog ownership / by Pat Miller.--1st ed.
        p. cm.
Includes bibliographical references and index.
ISBN 1-929242-15-8 (alk. paper)
1. Dogs--Training. 2. Dogs--Behavior. I. Title.
SF431.M552 2004
636.7'0887--dc22

Printed in the U.S.A.

Dedication ❤

To my husband, Paul,
who makes all things possible.

Acknowledgements ❤

Where does one even begin to acknowledge those in your life, human and otherwise, who have supported you to this place in your journey? I could start with Larry and Charlene Woodward and the other good folks at Dogwise, who shared my faith in this project and nursed it to fruition. Of course there is also Nancy Kerns, editor of Whole Dog Journal, whose superb photographs grace the pages of this book, and whose friendship, support and encouragement keep me writing, and with Belvoir, who also gave their blessing to this project. Certainly with professional teachers and peers who have had a positive influence – Karen Pryor, Jean Donaldson, Patricia McConnell, Ian Dunbar, Karen Overall, Judie Howard, Diane Allevato, and too many more to mention. No doubt with family – sisters Meg, Liz, and brother Bill, who share my history and give my life continuity; Mom and Dad – no longer of this world but still and always in my heart; Step-Mom Jan, who is more like a sister to me; and of course, always, Paul.

And finally, for sure, all of my canine companions and teachers, who have shared and continue to share with me the gifts of another world: Flag, Rusty, Pudding, Schmircks, Cinders, Squire, Sandy, Candy, Tempi, Moby, Marty, Brandy, Otis, Watkins, Coby, Caper, Keli, Mandy, Smokie, Josie, Dusty, Katie, Tucker and Dubhy.

Table of Contents ❤

Introduction ❤

Welcome to the world of positive dog training. The fact that you are holding this book in your hands tells me that you are a member of a large and rapidly-growing group of dog owners who are either looking for or are already convinced about using dog-friendly, non-violent approaches to training their dogs. Bravo!

I hope to help you on that journey. I have been sharing my life with dogs for more than 40 years. I've trained my own dogs and have titled several dogs in Obedience and Rally. I've had great fun trying Herding, Canine Musical Freestyle and Agility. When I started training dogs, it seemed that the most people believed the only way to train was by using coercive and sometimes forceful methods. Over time I learned that training can be fun for both my dogs and me and that force wasn't necessary at all. I learned that force could, in fact, damage my relationship with my dogs.

Training is first and foremost about *relationship*. It is also about *success*. A successful relationship has two partners: a happy well-mannered dog and a happy human. Today more and more trainers and owners recognize that the use of modern training techniques based on scientific principles of behavior and learning are the key to success. We realize that in order to create a truly successful dog/human relationship we need to understand these principles and apply them in our training programs.

That is why I've written this book. The information started life as a series of well-received articles for the *Whole Dog Journal, Whole Cat Journal* and *Your Dog*. With the encouragement of my friends at Dogwise Publishing and others, I've re-worked the information into a comprehensive book for the committed owner who wants to have a positive and successful relationship with his/her dog.

While many of the chapters stand-alone and can be used as a quick reference, I recommend that everyone start by reading Part One, *How Dogs Think and Learn* because it forms the basis for all the information that follows. Have a new puppy? Focus on Part Two. Need to learn how to train the basics? Check out Part Three. Need to solve specific behavior problems? Part Four has chapter titles that will guide you to solutions. Part Five contains answers to your questions about alternative veterinary medical care, the best leashes and collars and the very best dog toys in the world.

PART ONE

How Dogs Think and Learn: Key Behavior and Training Concepts

❤ A QUICK OVERVIEW

You will learn that understanding canine behavior is the key to becoming a better trainer. Once you know how and why a dog behaves as he does, training becomes easier and more effective. Properly applied, positive training techniques are more effective than those based on coercion, because they don't risk damage to the relationship the way old-fashioned force-based methods can. Proper management is key to preventing your dog from practicing – and being rewarded for – undesirable behaviors. Positive training and management are simple – but not necessarily easy. The concepts covered in Part One form the basis for all the remaining chapters in the book. You will want to come back to it again and again.

CHAPTER 1 ❤
Ain't Misbehavin': Understanding Your Dog

Not far below the furry surface of your favorite domestic canine companion lurks a mind surprisingly similar to that of his ancestor and current-day cousin, the wolf. We have stretched and molded the dog's plastic genetic material to create hundreds of widely diverse breeds – from the tiny Chihuahua to the giant St. Bernard – all to serve our whims. But our dogs' behaviors and instincts to this day closely mirror those chosen by natural selection to ensure the wolf's survival perhaps more than 100,000 years ago, when the wild canine was first invited to share the warmth and protection of the fires in our ancestors' caves.

The genetics that have enabled the dog to become "man's best friend" come as both a blessing and a curse. The instincts that drive the behaviors we love in our canine companions are the same ones that

Unchecked behavior problems can shorten your dog's life.

make us tear our hair out. For example, the desire to be a member of a social group, or pack, is what makes the dog so amenable to family life and training. It is this same social instinct that in some dogs triggers incredibly destructive "separation anxiety" behaviors when a dog is left alone, behaviors that include non-stop barking and howling, inappropriate urination and defecation, chewing, and self-destructive escape attempts.

When their behaviors and instincts are understood and properly directed, our dogs can be well adjusted, cherished family members. The millions of dogs that are abandoned at animal shelters in the U.S. every year are tragic testimony to how often we fail to do this. Let's look at some examples of how having a better understanding of canine behavior can help prevent this from happening to your dog.

Common Complaints

Dog trainers commonly hear complaints about dogs that bite, attack other dogs, jump up, bark, chase cats, cars or joggers, are shy, or don't come when called. All these activities have a basis in normal, instinctive, survival-based canine behavior. They occur in spite of the owner's training efforts because *often* the dog is rewarded by the unwanted behaviors in some way.

Fortunately, each behavior can be modified, either by figuring out how to make the desired behavior more rewarding than the undesirable one or by managing the dog so he doesn't have the opportunity to engage in the inappropriate behavior. Traditional training methods have often relied on human logic to teach dogs how to behave, by punishing the dog for "bad" behavior. But to our dogs, behavior is neither good nor bad; they are just doing what dogs do, driven by instinct and governed by the consequences of their actions. "Good" behavior is learned behavior. They learn more quickly, effectively and happily if we focus on rewarding the "right" behaviors, and preventing, or to the extent possible, ignoring the "wrong" ones.

Start When They Are Young

Early management and training is the best approach, since it is always easier to prevent an undesirable behavior than it is to correct it. This is not say you cannot extinguish an undesirable behavior in an older dog (see Part Four), but avoiding those behaviors through early training is preferable. For this reason, more and more dog trainers offer classes for puppies as young as eight to ten weeks. Trainers used to recommend waiting until a dog was six months old to start training classes, in part because of the widespread use of "choke chains," which can damage the soft cartilage of a puppy's throat. Now that positive-based training is more widely accepted and available – using a standard flat buckle collar or head collar, and rewards and praise instead of leash-jerk corrections – there is no reason to wait. Owners can take advantage of a puppy's socialization period to teach good behaviors.

The socialization period is a time when puppies in the wild have to learn quickly in order to survive. During the same critical period, *our own* puppies learn which behaviors are acceptable to their human pack, which are rewarding, and which things are safe. While some veterinarians still counsel keeping puppies isolated at home until they are fully vaccinated by age four to six months, enlightened animal-care professionals recognize that there is far greater risk to our dogs' lives (through euthanasia at an animal shelter) if they do not learn to be well-socialized and well-behaved during this vitally important learning period. Many veterinarians now strongly encourage their clients to pursue puppy classes and other controlled socializing activities as long as the pups have received at least two vaccinations and the owner continues to keep up with the necessary schedule of puppy shots.

The Shrinking Violet

Shyness can be genetic, it can result from lack of socialization, or it can be a combination of the two. While the wolf puppy that takes a "no fear" attitude doesn't live long, neither does a wild pup that is so afraid of his own shadow that he doesn't leave the den long enough to find adequate food to eat. Reasoned caution is a good survival skill for all dogs, wild and domestic. But because domestic dogs don't face the same life-threatening forces that wild ones do, genetically shy dogs can and do survive to reproduce, especially when assisted by irresponsible breeders and puppy mills.

While all puppies need to be properly socialized (even the bold ones), it is absolutely imperative to ultra-socialize the genetically shy puppy. Left to his own devices, the shy pup's timid behavior

All puppies, especially shy ones, should be exposed to a wide variety of situations, places, and other people and dogs to build confidence.

will intensify and he will grow up to be fearful, neurotic and dangerous.

With these little shy guys, the flight response is so strong that it is important to be patient. Let the pup initiate the contact with strange people or objects, and reward each contact with an especially tasty treat. *Don't force the pup.* Forced contact will aggravate the fear/flight response and make the shyness worse. But don't coddle him either. Coddling rewards and encourages fear behavior. Be gentle, patient, matter-of-fact and upbeat about helping the shy pup understand and accept the big, scary world.

Come Again?

Puppies, wild or domestic, naturally stay close to other pack members. Again, it's a survival thing: the puppy that wanders away ends up as hawk food. Our eight-week-old puppies usually come running when we call them because they are very dependent and want to be near us more than anything else in the world. We soon believe that they have learned to come when we call them. When they get older and more independent, and start to explore the world on their own, they no longer come when we call. We are convinced that they are being stubborn, ignoring us on purpose.

In fact, they never learned to come when called. Now, if they get reprimanded when they do come back (for not coming when they were called!) they are even less likely to come when we call them, since the consequence for coming is punishment, not reward.

In order to teach a reliable "Come," we capitalize on the dog's desire to be near us and it's instinct to seek rewards. When your pup is a baby and comes to you easily, be sure to reward with treats and praise every time. *Never punish "Come!"* If you have to correct for something (like getting in the garbage), *don't* call her – go to the pup to interrupt the behavior. If she doesn't come to you when you need her to, resist the urge to chase after her. She'll think "chase the dog" is a wonderful game. Instead, turn and run away, doing something to get her attention – like making excited, high-pitched noises, squeaking a squeaky toy, or bouncing a ball. Teaching her to chase *you* engages her prey drive, and takes advantage of her instinct to stay with the pack (you), and her strong desire to be a part of exciting pack activities.

Taking the Bite Out

Of all unwanted behaviors, biting is the least socially acceptable to humans, and the one that most often results in a death sentence for the dog. Yet biting is a totally natural behavior for dogs, both wild and domestic. Wolf puppies and adults bite each other in play and in warning. Very rarely do they bite each other in order to do serious damage. It is vital to the survival of the pack that all members be strong and healthy. It makes no sense for pack members to engage in fierce battles that might result in serious injury. As pups, they learn the importance of bite inhibition by playing with each other. When a pup bites a littermate too hard, the victim yelps loudly and may refuse to play for a while. Thus the biter learns that the fun of play ends when he bites too hard. Over the first five months of his life, he learns to control the strength of his bite. If he doesn't have this opportunity, it is much more difficult for him to learn to use his mouth gently later.

Enter the human. We routinely take the domestic puppy away from his siblings at six to eight weeks, sometimes earlier, effectively eliminating the pup's opportunity to learn bite inhibition. No wonder we end up with shark-puppies who chomp down on our hands, sometimes even drawing blood with their needle-sharp teeth!

Responsible breeders won't release their puppies to new homes until they are at least eight, sometimes ten weeks of age or older. Progressive animal shelters put litters of young pups in foster homes so they can grow and learn from each other, rather than placing them too early. Yet, trusting in the myth that "the earlier you get a pup the more she will bond with you," uneducated dog owners clamor for the six-week-old puppy (or younger). Unethical breeders, uneducated backyard breeders and shelters that lack adequate foster programs may oblige.

Even if adopted at eight to ten weeks, pups need to continue their bite inhibition lessons. The best way for the human teacher to do this is to imitate the puppy's littermates. When a pup bites hard, say "OUCH!" in a loud, high-pitched squeak and remove yourself from the pup's reach for a few minutes. Then return to puppy play. Each time the pup bites too hard, repeat the lesson.

After several repetitions the pup's bite will begin to soften. You can then repeat the lesson at *gradually* decreasing levels of bite intensity until the pup learns not to bite at all. If you try to extinguish bite behavior all at once you will frustrate your puppy's natural biting behavior, and fail at the task. At the same time you are softening the bite you can also direct the puppy's biting toward acceptable chew items. It is virtually impossible for small children to respond properly and consistently to puppy biting, which is why many shelters and responsible breeders discourage families with young children from adopting young puppies.

Adult dog biting behavior is much more serious. Much of wolf body language is designed to avoid an actual fight, again for individual and pack survival reasons. Growls, stiffened legs, stiffly wagging tails, stares, glares and raised hackles are signals intended to warn away a challenger. The majority of bites to humans occur because we misread or ignore the dog's warning signs. This is one reason why children are so often the victim of dog bites – they are even less skilled than adults at heeding a dog's warning – and why it is so important for adults to supervise all interactions between dogs and small children, no matter how trustworthy the dog is believed to be.

A wolf or dog's reaction to a possible threat is either to stand ground and fight, or flee. Individual canines usually have a preference for one reaction style over the other. Most dogs that prefer to stand and fight will still give warnings. If they are ignored, a bite often follows. A dog who prefers flight will try to escape the threat rather than challenge it, but if the escape route is cut off – when a dog is cornered, restrained or tied up – a bite often follows.

Most dogs signal their intent to bite before they do. The signal may be obvious, or very subtle. Most bites occur because someone misreads or ignores the dog's warning signs.

The more a puppy is socialized before the age of five months, the fewer things are ultimately perceived as threatening, and the less likely it is that a bite will occur in the adult dog.

Jump Back, Jack!

All creatures instinctively seek rewards. In order to take advantage of instinct-driven behaviors, we just need to figure out how to make the behavior we want more rewarding than the one we don't want, and then continue to reinforce the "right" behavior until it is a programmed response.

Wolves, of course, don't have much opportunity to jump up on people. They do greet each other face-to-face – sniffing noses and licking faces. Our dogs jump on us in their greeting ritual to try to reach our faces (and will often lick our faces if we let them), to demand attention, and because when they are puppies we pick them up and cuddle them, teaching them that "up" is a very rewarding place to be. When they jump up they are self-rewarded simply by touching us. Everything we do to get them off of us also rewards them. We look at them. Eye contact is a reward! We push them away. We touch them. That's a reward! We tell them to get off. We speak to them. That's a reward too! A sturdy, rambunctious dog can view even the forceful technique of "kneeing him in the chest" as an invitation to play.

If, instead, we ignore the behavior we don't want – in this case by turning away from the dog, and stepping away so he isn't even self-rewarded by touching us. Then reward the behavior we do want by waiting for the dog to sit, then turning to him and giving him a treat, along with the greeting and attention he wants. He will soon learn that he gets rewarded by running up to us and *sitting*, rather than jumping.

The Thrill of the Chase

The wolf would not survive without a strong prey drive. The lives of pack members depend on their ability to chase, catch and kill things that run away from them. Our dogs have retained a

Puppies and small dogs are irresistible, but they must be taught not to jump up on people. The same behavior with an 80-pound dog is not so cute.

very strong prey drive. In many cases, we use this instinctive behavior to our advantage. The intense herding behavior of the Border Collie is a modified prey drive with a strong inhibition for the killing part of the process. Many of the terriers, hounds and sporting dogs were bred to pursue and kill or retrieve other animals. We encourage prey drive in our pets to this day, with mutually enjoyable games of fetch the Frisbee™, stick, dumbbell and tennis ball.

Small wonder then that some dogs are driven to chase cats, joggers, bicycles, cars, and other fast-moving objects. This is such a strong drive in some dogs that it is difficult, if not impossible, to eliminate. Prevention is mandatory for your dog's own safety. Dogs who are allowed to run loose to chase cars tend to have short lives. Dogs who chase cats, joggers and kids soon get in trouble with neighbors and animal control. Dogs who chase livestock get shot. With a real commitment to a long-term training program we can teach our dogs to pay attention and respond to us even in the presence of an enticing prey-distraction, but a dog with a strong prey-drive will always chase if given the opportunity, and must always be securely confined when not under the owner's immediate control.

Hark, a Bark

Barking is also a natural behavior. In fact, when Lassie barks to warn us of an intruder, or to tell us that Timmy has fallen in the well, she's a hero. But if she barks at the mail carrier, the stray dog in the yard, or when Aunt Emma knocks on the front door, we yell at her to "Shut up!" It is a wolf's job to alert other members of the pack to anything out of the ordinary, and when Lassie barks at the mail carrier, she's just doing her job. How is she supposed to know when we want her to alert us and when we don't? Some dogs may well think that "Shut up" is just our way of joining in the barking! A better way to respond is to acknowledge the intruder and thank Lassie for doing her job. Then tell her that you have everything under control, with a "Good girl, that's all, quiet." Using a positive-reward approach, you wait for the barking to stop, and reward the silence with a treat while you say "Good dog, quiet."

The dog who barks non-stop in the backyard is a different matter. Non-stop barking is often a sign of a dog who is bored and lonely. She is isolated from her human pack and expressing her natural desire to rejoin the social order. The obvious solution is to bring the dog into the house and let her be part of the pack. Crate training (teaching the dog to sleep in a wire kennel or airline crate) is an excellent tool to help incorporate the dog into the family without risking damage to antique furniture and Oriental carpets. Dogs are meant to live with others and isolating a dog in the yard is a form of extreme mental cruelty and should not be permitted.

Endless Possibilities

Most dog behaviors are connected in some way to that genetic package of instincts handed down from the wolf. All dog behavior, if properly managed, can be turned into something positive. Dogs that dig can find truffles in France. Dogs that climb and jump fences are great candidates for agility training. The hound that always runs off with his nose to the ground can learn to track and do Search and Rescue. Dogs that chase can fetch golf balls. Their potential is limited only by our creativity.

The next time your dog does something you don't like, stop and think before you yell. He's not being bad – he's being a dog. What instinct is driving his behavior? How can you work *with* his instincts instead of against them to modify his behavior into something positive? It's worth the time it takes to figure it out and apply it to his training. You'll end up with a happier dog. You'll be a much happier dog owner. The incredibly rewarding bond that is created between the two of you will guarantee that your dog never ends up in the ranks of the homeless hounds at your local humane society.

CHAPTER 2 ❤
Just Rewards: The Key to Training

The key to having a well-mannered dog is to consistently reward the behaviors you want your dog to do. If you reward and reinforce your dog for coming when called, for example, you will avoid the common problem that many owners face of having their dogs run away from them. Another key is to make sure you don't inadvertently "punish" your dog's desirable behaviors. If you focus on these two concepts, you will minimize many of the problems that you might otherwise encounter with your dog. Sometimes finding the "right" reward can be a bit of a challenge. The following example illustrates this key concept.

Skip and Carla

The trim, middle-aged lady strode briskly down the rubber mat in the training center, her black Labrador Retriever bouncing happily at her side. She came to a smooth halt, and Skip sat promptly next to her, in perfect heel position. "Yes!" I thought to myself, and then winced as Carla reached down and enthusiastically patted Skip on the head. Skip jumped up and backed away from his human.

"Carla," I said softly. "You just punished him for sitting straight." Carla's face fell. "Darn it!" she exclaimed. "Why can't I remember that!"

Wait a minute...since when is patting a dog considered punishment? Ever since

Skip let us know by ducking his head and backing away from Carla's hand that he didn't enjoy being petted. All the other Labs that Carla had owned and trained throughout her life had *adored* being touched as a reward. Carla petted her dog for being good without even thinking about it – it was a well-conditioned response. Unfortunately, since Skip didn't like being touched, every time she did it to *him,* she was actually punishing him, decreasing the likelihood that he would perform that perfect sit again!

A dog's decisions in life, and his resulting behaviors, are based on whether a particular behavior yields something he likes (a reward), or something he doesn't like (a punishment). Training is simply a matter of managing the rewards and punishments in a thoughtful manner. But you have to know your dog and be aware of his likes and dislikes – and your own behavior to make "training" work for you.

Rewards and Punishments

In the 1950's, behavioral scientist B.F. Skinner developed a number of principles that are applicable to all living things with a central nervous system. He found that animals are likely to repeat behaviors that are enjoyable/rewarding to them, and not likely to repeat behaviors that result in something unpleasant (punishment). Neutral stimuli – things that don't matter to the animal – don't have an impact on behavior one-way or the other.

Skinner demonstrated that humans could use these simple principles to modify an animal's behavior. Rewards are the most reliable way to deliberately increase an animal's offered behaviors; conversely, punishment decreases those behaviors.

❤ THE FOUR PRINCIPLES OF OPERANT CONDITIONING

Behavior scientist B.F. Skinner developed the following behavior principles in the 1950's, and asserted that they were applicable to all living things with a central nervous system. Trainers Keller Breland, Marian Breland Bailey, and Bob Bailey were among the first to apply the principles in the real world, building a successful business using Skinner's work for a wide spectrum of purposes from pigeons and dolphins carrying military messages, dogs and other animals acting in television commercials, and marine mammals performing at places such as Sea World™, to chickens playing tic-tac-toe at boardwalks and fairgrounds.

In recent years, the Baileys turned their talents toward teaching dog trainers, joining with luminaries such as Karen Pryor to educate trainers and move the dog training industry toward a more scientifically based, positive profession. By applying these principles creatively and judiciously, you can teach your dog to do just about anything he is mentally and physically capable of:

1. **Positive reinforcement**. The dog's behavior makes something good happen. "Positive," in behavioral terms, means something is added. "Reinforcement" (i.e. "reward") means the behavior increases. So, for example, when your dog sits, you feed him a treat. His behavior – sitting – made something good happen, something was added – the treat. As a result, your dog is more likely to offer to sit again, so the behavior increases. Positive trainers use positive reinforcement a lot. Dogs who are positively reinforced learn to think and to offer behaviors that we like in order to get rewarded.

2. **Positive punishment**. The dog's behavior makes something bad happen. Positive means something is added, punishment means the behavior decreases. For example, when your dog jumps on you with muddy paws you knee him in the chest, hard. He gets off. His behavior – jumping up – made something bad happen; something was added – your knee in his chest. As a result, your dog is more likely to think twice before jumping on you again. Positive trainers do **not** use positive punishment very much, if at all. Positive punishment can work and does with many dogs, but dogs who are positively punished may learn to fear the punisher, can become aggressive, may simply shut down in training, and are often reluctant to offer new behaviors for fear of being punished.

3. **Negative punishment**. The dog's behavior makes something good go away. Negative means something is taken away, punishment means the behavior decreases. Back to our jumping up example. When your dog jumps up on you with muddy paws you turn your back on him and step away. As long as he keeps jumping up you keep stepping away. When he stops jumping and has four paws on the floor, or even better, sits, **then** you reach down to pet him and feed him a treat. His behavior – jumping up – made something good – your attention – go away. Then you followed with positive reinforcement; his behavior of sitting made something good happen – you paid attention to him. Positive trainers **do** use negative punishment as a non-violent means of providing a negative consequence for an unwanted behavior.

4. **Negative reinforcement**. The dog's behavior makes something bad go away. Negative means something is taken away, reinforcement increases the behavior. Some trainers use a shock collar to teach their dogs to come when called. They call the dog, and push the button, holding it down and causing the dog to experience an unpleasant sensation until the dog has returned to the trainer. When the dog reaches the trainer, the button is released. The faster the dog returns, the quicker the shock stops. The dog's behavior – coming quickly when called – makes the bad thing, the shock, go away. Positive trainers may use a limited amount of gentle negative reinforcement in the form of mild physical pressure, but generally consider shock collar training to be unacceptable.

We use these behavioral principles in dog training with great success.

We have seen that the practical application of "rewards" and "punishments" varies from dog to dog, even though the definition doesn't. A reward is anything a particular dog likes. A punishment is anything that dog doesn't like (think of Skip, who doesn't like to be touched).

Giving this water-loving Golden Retriever permission to jump into the lake is a high-value reward for this dog – however it would be an ineffective reward for many dogs.

We frequently use food treats as our reward in training, because we can almost always find *some* food that a dog will value highly enough that it can serve as an irresistible reward, but food is not the *only* reward available to us. Remember, a reward is anything a dog likes. It could be a scratch behind the ear, verbal praise, a game of tug o' war, a chase after a stick or tennis ball, a walk on leash, a car ride, permission to jump up on the sofa, the

cue to run an agility course, the release from a "wait" to run out into the yard, permission to go jump in the lake, or the signal to round up a flock of sheep.

When the average inexperienced dog handler hears the word "punishment," he generally thinks of overt forms of physical punishment, such as smacking, pinching, or kicking the dog, or jerking on the leash. I do not recommend or use physical punishment, as it endangers the handler, damages the relationship with his dog, and can destroy the dog's enthusiasm for training. Fortunately, physical punishment is not the only way to eliminate an unwanted behavior.

Remember, behaviorists define the word "punishment" as anything that causes an animal to *decrease* a certain behavior. So, in the case of Skip, the Lab who didn't like being touched, a pat on the head after he performed a straight sit was enough to make him *stop* performing those straight sits.

"Positive trainers" – people who have made a commitment to train without the use of pain, fear, force, or intimidation – often use certain forms of "punishment" (in the behavioral sense) to accomplish their training goals. For example, when a dog who craves physical contact and attention jumps all over the trainer, she will turn her back on the him and step away, removing both her attention (eye contact and interaction) and the possibility of physical contact with the dog. These are the rewards that the dog is seeking by jumping up. When the dog's jumping behavior keeps resulting in the loss of something he wants badly, he will stop jumping – especially when this "punishment" is paired with the "reward" of attention, treats and petting for sitting quietly.

What actually constitutes a punishment or reward to any given dog, then, is an individual matter; in behavioral terms, context is everything.

Unintentional Training

Training, therefore, is the intentional use of rewards and punishments to purposefully manipulate or shape a dog's behavior. What is sometimes difficult to remember is the fact that dogs are learning all the time, whether or not we are paying attention. People are often mystified as to why their dogs do some of the things they do, or fail to do what the people want them to do.

It's actually pretty simple. Dogs do what works for them; they don't continue to repeat a behavior unless they get something out of it.

Dogs do things that we consider "inappropriate behaviors," because they are fun, they feel good or they taste good. From a dog's perspective, behaviors that are unacceptable to us, such as getting in the garbage, chasing cats, or sleeping on the sofa, are just plain fun!

Frustrated owners frequently say to their trainers, "He *knows* he's not supposed to do that! I punish him when he does, but he still does it. Why?" Sometimes, the enjoyment the dog gets from the behavior outweighs the owner's "punishment." A dog who is highly aroused by the experience of chasing a cat over the backyard fence may not care a bit about getting yelled at for it.

In other cases, the "punishment" may actually be rewarding to the dog. For example, a boisterous Labrador who gets yelled at, hit or even kicked for jumping up on his owner may not have any clue that the yelling, hitting, and kicking are supposed to be punishment. To dogs who *crave* attention and *love* physical contact with people, this rough treatment is simply an invitation to play an enjoyable (rewarding) game.

Also, dog owners may fail to realize that they often unthinkingly punish a dog for doing the right thing. If you do this frequently enough, you will inadvertently "train" your dog to *stop* offering the behaviors you want.

Consider the woman whose dog is enjoying a good romp with some canine pals at the dog park. It's time to leave, so she calls her dog to her. He immediately leaves his play pals and races to her. "Good dog!" she exclaims, and snaps his leash on, taking him from the park. In her view, the verbal praise was ample reward, and leaving the park has no connection to the recall. But here's how the dog sees it: "Mom called, I came, and the fun's over. When I come to Mom, a bad thing happens – the fun stops." He is likely to think twice about coming the next time she calls while he is playing with friends!

Many people have lots of trouble training their dog to come reliably when called. Perhaps they haven't given enough consideration to what happens to the dog *most of the time* after he does come. It doesn't take a canine Einstein to realize that coming when called is a bad idea if something "bad" consistently happens to him immediately afterward – say, he gets stuffed into the basement or locked away from all the guests in the kitchen, or tossed outside in the cold rain.

Training may also break down when the reward just isn't valuable enough to motivate the dog to bother trying to get it. You must program an automatic response to the "come" cue with a high value reward in the absence of enticing distractions before you try to apply it in the face of dashing squirrels. Few dogs will leave a squirrel hunt in order to come and earn a piece of dry kibble! Many positive trainers advocate using a variety of enticing rewards and mixing them up. Then the dog is never sure how big the "payoff" for his good behavior will be, he just knows it will be good.

If you doubt that mixing small rewards (such as verbal praise, a pat, or a piece of dry kibble) with larger rewards (such as pieces of fresh meat, chasing a ball, or being released to run free) is a powerful motivator, consider the slot machine. As long as it pays out a mixture of no rewards, small rewards, and only an occasional jackpot, human gamblers will continue to sit there and pull the handle, long past the time that it makes sense to do so!

A Positive Click

Clicker training is an informal trainers' term for "applied operant conditioning," that is, training with positive reinforcement, with the addition of a word or sound that marks the instant of a behavior you want to reward. A clicker is a handy training device that when squeezed makes a sharp, quick sound that the dog can associate with a specific action and a reward.

I will be discussing and recommending the use of clicker training frequently

Tools of the trade: an inexpensive clicker and a ready supply of delicious treats – something the dog will be motivated to work for.

during this book, so let's take a minute here to review what clicker training is all about. The clicker trainer uses treats (or something else the dog values) to reward the animal for a desired behavior. The Click! sound serves as the marker signal, or bridge, that gives the animal instant feedback about what behavior is desired. The animal quickly learns to offer the desired behavior again, in order to hear the Click! and get the treat. It is easy for the average dog owner to use, because it is not a system that requires an excessive amount of practice and skill; it only requires an open mind.

1. Start with the clicker in your pocket. The sharp Click! of the clicker startles some dogs. If you put it in your pocket at first it will muffle the sound until Buddy has a chance to associate it with the positive reinforcement of the treat. Once you are sure he is okay with the sound, you can hold it behind your back for a few clicks, then hold it in front of you to Click! and treat as you continue training. If your dog seems unduly frightened of the clicker you can use the softer Click! of a ballpoint pen, a mouth Click! or just use a verbal "Yes!" as your reward marker.

2. "Charging" the clicker, also known as "conditioning the dog to the reward marker," simply means teaching him that the Click! sound *always* means that a treat is coming. In order to charge the clicker, all you need to

do is Click! the clicker, pause for a half-second, then feed Buddy a treat. He doesn't have to do anything at all to earn the Click! at this point, as long as he isn't doing something you *don't* want to encourage (such as jumping up on you). After six to twelve repetitions, most dogs begin to make the connection between the Click! sound and the treat.

3. Now if you consistently Click! and treat every time he does a particular behavior, such as sit, he will learn that he can *make* the Click! happen, just by sitting, which is exactly what we want. This part of the process generally takes less than fifteen minutes. Once Buddy learns that *he* controls the Click! he will offer behaviors in order to make the Click! happen, and we are ready to have fun with it.

By withholding the Click! and treat until the dog tries a new variation on an old behavior, one can "shape" a new one.

Random Acts of Reinforcement

Having a variety of rewards in your training tool kit gives you greater flexibility and allows you to train your dog without always having a huge supply of treats in your pocket. A good training program moves toward variable reinforcement once the dog is reliably performing a new behavior. Instead of clicking and giving the dog a treat *every* time he performs the behavior, you occasionally skip a click and praise the dog instead, then ask for the behavior again and click the next one. Gradually increase the variation and length of the reinforcement schedule, remembering that randomness is important.

If you simply keep making your dog work harder and harder for a click, he's likely to quit on you. If you vary the reinforcement schedule, like a Las Vegas slot machine, he can't predict when you will pay off. Will I get a click this time? This time? This time? Click! Just as people will continue inserting quarters, your dog will keep offering behaviors with enthusiasm, sure that the *next* one will hit the jackpot.

To maintain his enthusiasm as you gradually lengthen the reinforcement schedule, use other rewards to let him know he's still on track. I frequently use "Good dog!" or "Yes!" as praise *after* I click and treat, so that my dogs associate the same warm fuzzy feeling of getting a food reward with the verbal praise. Then, when I use the verbal praise even without the click and treat, they still have the same classically conditioned response from the association of praise with food, and it makes them feel good. Thus, "Good dog!" becomes a useful reward even without food.

Other rewards may create more of an interruption in the training game. If you use a toy as a reward, you have to stop and let your dog play with it for a while. This can work really well to amp him up on the enthusiasm scale, especially for a dog who is ball crazy or loves to tug. It *doesn't* work well when you want to do a lot of repetitions of a particular behavior in a row. If you toss the ball every time he responds to your "down" cue, it will take you a long time to do a half-dozens repetitions. It *does* work well as a reward for an extended behavior, such as heel. A ball-crazy dog can learn to heel with perfect attention for long stretches in anticipation of the ball-chase that happens at the end.

Timing is Key

It is vitally important to a successful training program to understand what your dog likes and doesn't like, and to use those rewards and punishments effectively. In order to be effective, consequences – good or bad – must be delivered in close proximity in time to the behavior you are trying to influence.

Say your dog tips over your kitchen garbage can while you are away at work. If you reprimand him when you get home from work, hours after the garbage raid occurred, it only teaches your dog that you are sometimes unpredictable and dangerous when you come home. No matter how "guilty" he looks when you scold him, he makes no connection between your behavior of yelling at him and his behavior of getting in the garbage hours earlier. Your perception of his apparent guilt-stricken conscience, manifested in his lowered head, lack of eye contact, and slinking along the baseboards, is a faulty interpretation of his classic canine body language attempts to quell your wrath, *whatever the cause.*

Behaviorists agree that a reward or punishment must be delivered in close time-proximity, preferably one second or less, to the behavior you are trying to increase or decrease. This is a pretty small window of time, and underscores the value of using a clicker or other reward marker (or no-reward marker) to mark the instant of desired (or inappropriate) behavior. If you say "Oops!" the instant your dog jumps up and you turn away, you are teaching your dog a no-reward marker – or conditioned punisher – which you can use to communicate to your dog which behavior it was that made the good thing go away (negative punishment). If you Click! or say "Yes!" the instant your

dog sits, he will come to understand that the *sit* earned the reward, even if it takes several seconds for you to get the treat into his mouth, and even if he gets up from the sit before you manage to deliver the treat.

Back to Carla and Skip

Carla and I had a long discussion about how to continue with Skip's training. We identified two options. Using desensitization, we could teach Skip that having Carla pat him on the head really was a reward, by consistently pairing her touch with an off-the-charts treat reward, using gentle contact at first, then increasing in intensity until he learned to associate vigorous patting with "really good stuff." Carla made a commitment to doing this for the long term, as she really wanted Skip to enjoy her touch.

We also initiated a short-term approach of modifying *Carla's* behavior, agreeing to use positive reinforcement and negative punishment with *her.* Every time Skip sat and she didn't reach down to pat him, Carla earned a reward, perhaps a quarter, a piece of chocolate, or a dog toy. Every time she forgot and reached down to pat him, I stepped out of the training room without a word, for a period of time from 30 seconds to three minutes. It worked beautifully, and in short order, Skip was sitting happily in perfect heel position when Carla halted, without fear of being punished for his good behavior.

CHAPTER 3 ❤
Trainer or Trainee: Who is Training Whom?

Is your dog training you? Don't laugh; in fact, it's pretty common. Many clients come to me complaining of behavioral problems with their dogs. Upon exploring the problem, we discover that the training roles have been reversed and in an attempt to stop an undesirable behavior the owner actually has been reinforcing it! Let's explore this common problem, and then analyze how it happens and how you can avoid it.

Scruffy, an Australian Cattle Dog, had his owner beautifully trained to open the door to let him in or out whenever he barked – every 20 minutes or so, all day. Lots of dogs have turned their

Who is walking whom? It may be that these dogs are training their owner to let them pull, making a mutually enjoyable outing a rather one-sided experience.

humans into on-call petting machines by teaching them to reward an endearing nudge of the nose or tap of the paw with a placating scratch behind the ear. Not until the barking, nose-nudging or paw-tapping gets annoying does the owner try to make the dog stop, and by then it's too late – the dog fully expects the owner to respond appropriately and gets upset when the human doesn't perform the desired behavior.

Anytime you and your dog are together, one of you is training the other. Dog-human relationships are generally most successful when the human is the trainer and the dog the trainee – at least the majority of the time! You need to be aware when your dog is doing something to try to modify *your* behavior, and only cooperate if you are sure it's a behavior you want to encourage. If not, you must ignore the dog's behavior so he stops trying to get you to perform (behaviors that aren't rewarded in some manner will go away) and be sure to reward an incompatible behavior in its place. Rather than petting your dog when he nudges you, make it a point to pet him when he is sitting or lying quietly at your feet.

This is easiest to do when your dog first offers a behavior. Behaviors that are well established are harder to extinguish than embryonic ones. Scruffy had long ago discovered that if his owner had any thoughts of *not* letting him out, all he had to do was bark louder and longer and she would eventually give in. This creates a very long schedule of reinforcement for the pet owner. If you are going to try to make an established behavior go away by ignoring it, you may have to ignore it for a very long time. It becomes a test of stamina – both yours and that of the dog!

You may even have to suffer through an "extinction burst." Sometimes, shortly before the dog finally gives up, he will try *really, really hard* to get you to perform – barking louder, poking harder with his nose, or digging unmercifully at you with his paw. If you could read your dog's mind during this temper tantrum, you might hear him saying, with much irritation, "Darn you, you stupid human! You *know* how to do this behavior; we've worked on it for years! Why are you being so stubborn?"

Caution: If you give in during an extinction burst, realize you are creating a very long reinforcement schedule and rewarding a very strong exhibition of the behavior. This will make it even harder to stop the next time you try!

In the long run, it's much easier to make it a point to be aware of what your dog is trying to teach you, and to be sure you are the trainer more often than you are the trainee.

CHAPTER 4 ❤
Good Management: A Trainer's Secret Weapon

Dog owners ask me questions all the time, in person, on the phone and on-line, about how to stop their dogs or puppies from doing something. The variations are virtually limitless:

❤ **How do I make him stop stealing food from the counter?**

❤ **How do I stop him from peeing on the carpet?**

❤ **How do I keep her from chewing up my shoes? (or books, or furniture, or toys)**

❤ **How do I stop him from chasing deer? (or cats, or bicycles, or joggers, or livestock)**

❤ **How do I keep him from roaming the neighborhood?**

❤ **How do I stop her from nuisance barking when she's outside?**

❤ **How do I stop him from jumping up on the windows and scratching the woodwork?**

❤ **How do I keep him off the furniture?**

❤ **How do I stop her from getting in the garbage?**

I normally answer these questions with an explanation of how to resolve the presented behavior problem, but every once in a while I am sorely tempted just to answer the question with a succinct, "Don't let him do it!"

As absurdly simple as this seems, behavior management is, in fact, the appropriate answer in probably better than 75% of the questions I am asked by dog owners. *Management is the key* to resolving the vast majority of behavior problems people face with their dogs, and even more important, it is the key to preventing those behaviors from ever occurring in the first place! Proper management is not hard to understand, but it does take a significant commitment on the part of the owner in terms of planning and implementation. If you take the time and make the commitment, the benefits of proper management are huge!

Managing Unwanted Behaviors

In many cases, management is necessary while the dog learns a new, more appropriate behavior. In others, management simply replaces unrealistic training expectations. I offer my clients a three-step formula for reprogramming or preventing unwanted behaviors:

1. Rephrase. That is, identify what you want the dog *to* do instead of what you want him *not* to do. In all the behaviors described above, the owner is asking how to get the dog to stop doing something rather than how to get the dog to do something.

2. Manage. Figure out how to *prevent* the dog from being rewarded for the unwanted behavior. This is actually the *easiest* part. Behaviors that are rewarded are reinforced – in other words, the dog is more likely to do them again. Chasing a cat is very rewarding to a dog – he gets a big adrenalin rush, and the cat runs away – what fun! Every chance your dog gets to chase a cat increases the likelihood that he will chase (and maybe eventually catch) the next cat he sees. If you don't want him to be rewarded by chasing cats, prevent him from doing it.

3. Train. Figure out how to consistently reward the dog for the desired behavior identified in Step #1. This is often the hardest part. Each of the training programs for the behavior challenges listed above could be a full-length chapter of its own.

Let's take a look at some of the behaviors listed above and see how they can be addressed by our three-step formula, with particular focus on the management aspect:

❤ **How do I make him stop stealing food from the counter (or table, or coffee table)?**

Rephrase: "How do I get him to only eat things that are in his bowl or on the floor?" Dogs are opportunistic eaters by their very nature. They are morally incapable of "stealing" food. A dog in the wild who eats food when and where he finds it is smart – and much more likely to survive than one who passes food by just because it happens to be above eye level.

Counter surfing is one of the easiest problem behaviors to manage. Simply put the food away!

Manage: Clearly, the food that he finds on counters tastes good and is very rewarding. Prevent him from being rewarded for counter-surfing.

Management tools: A) Doors: if food must be left out, shut the dog in another room so he doesn't have access to it. B) Cupboards and the refrigerator: put food away – *never* leave it out as an invitation to counter-surf. C) Crates, pens, baby gates, leashes and tethers: use other reasonable means of restraint to prevent his inappropriate access to food. D) Exercise: tired dogs tend to be well-behaved dogs.

Train: Teach him a positive "Off!" or "Leave It!" cue and consistently reward him for ignoring food on the counter and for keeping all four feet on the floor around food-laden counters and tables.

❤ How do I stop him from peeing on the carpet?

Rephrase: "How do I teach him to go to the bathroom outside?

Manage: Prevent him from being rewarded for peeing on the carpet. A full bladder causes discomfort. Urinating relieves that discomfort. Urinating on the carpet is more rewarding for an unhousetrained dog than suffering the discomfort of "holding it" until he can go outside.

Management tools: A) Take the dog outside so frequently that his bladder is never full to the point of discomfort (every hour on the hour, at least at first). B) Keep the dog under close supervision so you can notice when he is acting restless (a sign that he has to eliminate), and take him outside quickly, before he has a chance to pee on the carpet. C) Keep the dog crated (see Chapter 8) or penned, or tethered (only tether if you are home – see Chapter 15) if you can't

supervise him closely to prevent him from being rewarded by peeing on the carpet when you're not paying attention. Keeping his crate – his den, as it were – unsoiled is more rewarding to most dogs than relieving even a moderately full bladder.

Train: Implement a full housetraining program that includes going outside with him regularly and rewarding him with praise and a treat immediately after he goes to the bathroom in the appropriate toilet spot (see Chapter 7 for complete details).

❤ How do I keep her from chewing up my shoes? (or books, or furniture, or baby's toys)

Rephrase: How do I get her to chew on her *own* things and *only* her own things?

Manage: Prevent her from being rewarded for chewing on inappropriate objects. Things like shoes, baby toys and furniture have a nice firm-but-giving texture that feels good (is rewarding) to a dog's teeth and gums, especially to a puppy or young dog who is teething.

Management Tools: A) Pick up non-chew objects when the dog is in the room. B) Remove her from the room when non-chew objects must be left within dog-reach (put her in a crate or pen if necessary). C) Supervise the dog closely and distract her attention from inappropriate objects. D) Tether or leash her in the room with you to prevent her access to non-chew objects. E) Exercise her a lot; tired dogs tend to be well-behaved dogs.

Train: Provide her with irresistible chew-objects and interactive toys such as stuffed Kongs (see Chapter 37), Buster Cubes, Roll-A-Treat Balls, and other safe items. If she is given the opportunity to chew only acceptable items she will eventually develop a strong preference for chewing on these things, and your personal possessions will be safe.

❤ **How do I stop him from chasing deer? (or cats, or bicycles, or joggers, or livestock)**

Rephrase: "How do I teach him to ignore fast-moving objects?" or "How do I teach him to respond when I ask him to stop?"

Manage: Don't let him have the opportunity to be rewarded for chasing, and don't have unrealistic training expectations. Do not expect to be able to train a dog who has a strong prey/chase instinct to "not chase" in the absence of direct supervision. This includes many of the herding breeds, terriers, hounds and sporting breeds.

Management Tools: A) Fences: solid physical fences of sufficient height are great tools for thwarting chasing behaviors. B) Doors: keeping him safely confined indoors except when directly supervised can go a long way towards preventing rewards for chasing.

C) Leashes and long lines: ideal for preventing chase rewards. (*Note: I do not ever recommend tying/chaining a dog as a routine method of outdoor confinement.* D) Exercise: tired dogs tend to be well-behaved dogs.

Train: Teach your dog a very reliable recall. Train him to drop to a "Down" at a distance. Teach him a solid "Wait" cue that will pause him in mid-stride, even when he is in chase mode (see Chapter 14).

Baby gates are a cat's best friend. Dogs are denied the thrill of the chase when cats know they don't have to run.

❤ **How do I stop him from roaming the neighborhood?**

Rephrase: "How do I keep him safe at home?

Manage: Use appropriate physical means to keep him safely confined at home and make sure he never experiences and reaps the rewards of the "joy" of running loose in the neighborhood. I occasionally have potential clients call and ask me how to train their dogs to stay on their property without a fence. This is an unrealistic training expectation, and I *never* accept such a training assignment. I don't believe it can be done safely and humanely. For most, if not all dogs, there are stimuli that are strong enough to induce them to break through the shock of an electric fence collar, to say nothing of a simple boundary-training program.

Management tools: A) Fences: solid physical fences of sufficient height are great tools for thwarting roaming. B) Doors: keeping him safely confined indoors except when directly supervised can go a long way towards preventing rewards for roaming. C) Leashes and long lines: physical restraint tools are ideal for preventing roaming rewards. D) Neutering: lowering your dog's testosterone level can be a very effective way of eliminating one very strong reward for roaming (see Chapter 32). E) Exercise: tired dogs tend to be well-behaved dogs.

Train: Teach your dog a very reliable recall. Train him to drop to a "Down" at a distance. Teach him a solid "Wait"

cue that will pause him in mid-stride, even when he is in chase mode. And then never leave him outdoors alone, unfenced and unsupervised.

❤ **How do I stop her from barking when she's outside?**

Rephrase: "How do I keep her quiet when she's outside?"

Manage: Dogs usually become nuisance barkers because they are bored, lonely, over stimulated, or convinced that their job responsibilities include 24-hour sentry duty.

Management tools: A) House confinement: most dogs who are nuisance barkers spend entirely too much time outdoors, which contributes to boredom, loneliness, over stimulation and the perception that their job duties include constant sentry duty. B) Crates and pens indoors: if necessary, they can help manage the dog's behavior while indoors. C) Exercise: tired dogs tend to be well-behaved dogs.

Train: Teach her a positive interrupt – a gentle "Thank you, quiet!" followed by a reward to acknowledge her for notifying you of something you should be aware of, and to let her know that you have everything under control so she can stop barking. Use this judiciously; do not expect it to work for a bored, lonely, over stimulated dog who is kept outside in the back yard all day and/or all night.

❤ **How to I stop him from jumping up to look out the windows?**

Rephrase: How do I teach him to be calm about outside stimuli at the windows?

Manage: The easiest way to manage this behavior is to either block the dog's view from the outside stimuli, or provide him with the means to see out the window without having to jump up on the windowsill.

Management tools: A) Shades or drapes to block the dog's view of the outside. B) Closed doors that keep him out of the room in question. C) Move the sofa up against the windows so he can look out to his heart's content without having to jump up on the woodwork. (Of course, this isn't an option if you are trying to keep him off the furniture, unless you put his *own* sofa next to the window…)

Some dogs enjoy seeing what's going on outside. You can help relieve their boredom by providing them with a safe observation point.

Train: Teach him using a positive interruption and consistently reward him for turning his attention to you when there is something happening outside his window.

❤ **How do I keep him off the furniture?**

Rephrase: How do I teach him to sleep on his own bed?

Manage: Control the environment to prevent him from being rewarded for getting on the furniture. The sofa is comfortable, so lying on it is its own reward.

Management tools: A) Place boxes or upside-down chairs on the furniture to prevent his access. B) Lift up sofa and chair cushions so there's no flat surface for him to lie on. C) Close doors to prevent his access to rooms with forbidden furniture in your absence. D) Use crates and pens to prevent his access to forbidden furniture in your absence. E) Provide him with his own very comfortable furniture to lie on.

Train: Consistently reward him for lying on his own very comfortable furniture.

❤ **How do I stop her from getting in the garbage?**

Rephrase: How do I convince her to keep her nose in appropriate places?

Manage: This is a behavior where management is critically important. You would be wise to never put extremely tempting garbage such as meat scraps, pork chop bones and turkey carcasses in any garbage can that is easily accessible to your dog, no matter how well mannered she is.

Management tools: A) Garbage cans with tightly closing lids that seal tempting odors in and curious noses out. B) Cupboards or cabinets (complete with baby-proof latches) that close securely and protect garbage cans from marauding moochers. C) Closed doors to prevent the dog's access to rooms with raidable garbage cans. D) Exercise because tired dogs tend to be well-behaved dogs.

Train: You can teach your dog a positive "Off!" or "Leave It!" (see Chapter 13) with garbage cans, and for a dog who is very motivated by garbage, you will still want to use management to prevent him from being rewarded for garbage play in your absence.

Many dogs are unable to resist the temptation to sniff at or snack from a kitchen garbage can that is left out without a lid.

Training Yourself to Manage

We could keep going – this list truly is endless – but you should be getting the idea by now. Any time you're faced with a behavior challenge, just apply these three simple steps: Rephrase, Manage, and Train. Then design your action plan for managing and/or modifying the inappropriate behavior.

My all time favorite management solution was the Peaceable Paws client in Carmel, California, who asked me to teach his Australian Shepherd-mix to stop drinking out of the toilet.

"It would be far easier," I said, "to teach *you* (the supposedly more intelligent species) to close the toilet lid or shut the bathroom door, than it would be to train *him* not to take advantage of a constantly fresh water source. In fact, he's probably trying to figure out how to train *you* to stop peeing in his water bowl!" This is one of those cases where it makes much more sense to implement a simple management technique than to expend the energy required training the desired behavior.

He got the message. When I visited the house for our next appointment, the bathroom door was securely closed.

PART TWO

Puppy Training and Housetraining

❤ **A QUICK OVERVIEW**

In Part Two the focus will be on the training and management skills that you need to make the first few months of your puppy's life with you as problem-free as possible. Training and management lapses during this stage often result in the puppy being surrendered to a shelter if he becomes an out-of-control adolescent. Preparing for and choosing the right dog are major parts of the equation for successful dog keeping. Your first few weeks with your puppy set the stage for a lifetime of joy and companionship; starting off on the right paw with good supervision as well as those all important housetraining and crating skills. While the focus is on puppies in this section, the information applies equally well to adolescent and adult dogs as well. Finally, I will take look at the products, tools and toys that will enhance your positive training and management program.

CHAPTER 5 ❤
Pre-Puppy Preparation: Before You Get Your Dog

The Miller five-dog pack consists of two mixed-breed and three purebred dogs – a Scottish Terrier, a Pomeranian, and an Australian Kelpie. Of the purebreds, one was found as a stray, one was adopted from an animal shelter, and one was rehomed from a friend who could no longer keep her.

I get several calls every week from people asking me to refer them to a breeder. But it has been well over 20 years since we purchased a dog from a breeder, and I'd wager that I'll go to my grave without ever purchasing another. Good breeders can be found and if you are looking for a dog with a certain type of breeding then this can be an option. However, decades of work in animal protection have made me painfully aware of the easy availability of any breed of dog your heart might desire.

Acquiring a Dog

The fact is both mixed breeds and purebred dogs are everywhere. You can find them at shelters, in rescue groups, free in the newspaper, running loose in the streets, for sale by breeders and, unfortunately, in pet stores. There are pros and cons to acquiring your next family member from any of these sources; you can find good dogs from any one of them, and conversely you

can find dogs with minor to severe health and behavior problems from each. Much of the dog breeding industry seems to subscribe to the "caveat emptor" philosophy. The average dog owner is very much on her own when it comes to acquiring a new canine companion, and she'd best be very wary, indeed. Let's examine the good, the bad, and the ugly of each source of purebred dogs.

The Pros and Cons

BREEDERS

If you have any intention of showing your dog in the conformation, or "breed" ring, your dog must have registration papers. If you want to be *successful* competing in the breed ring, you must have a *very good quality dog* with papers. There are good breeders who sell good quality dogs and bad breeders who sell unsound and unhealthy dogs. Both sell puppies with papers. Sadly, many irresponsible breeders abound, so take the time to find a good one – it's worth the effort.

After more than 30 years of experience working in and around animal shelters – and seeing untold thousands of mixed-breed *and* purebred dogs euthanized for lack of homes – I have developed a pretty stringent definition of a "responsible" breeder. In my opinion, an ethical breeder produces puppies solely for the purpose of improving the breed, not to make money.

In a good breeding program, sire and dam are thoroughly screened for any health problems known to be common to that breed, and pairings are based on a complete awareness and understanding of how one dog's qualities complement the other's. Dogs of questionable temperament or health are *never* bred, and dogs of breeding quality are shown and titled in at least one competitive canine sport to demonstrate that they have brains as well as beauty.

The conscientious breeder provides extra nutrition for the dam before and during pregnancy to ensure that she and the puppies are all healthy, and doesn't hesitate to seek whatever veterinary care is recommended during gestation, whelping and puppy development, including vaccinations, worming and microchipping.

Once the puppies are born, they are kept in a clean environment and socialized to the extreme – beginning at about 4 weeks of age (or sooner) – in order to avoid any possibility of behavior problems related to the puppies' unfamiliarity with other people and the world around them. Good breeders begin training their pups before they place them in new homes – giving them a head start on good manners and helping them to be comfortable in crates and away from the pack even before they leave their littermates for good.

A conscientious breeder screens new homes carefully, and does not just sell puppies to the first buyer who arrives with check in hand. She educates buyers about all aspects of the breed, not just the warm-fuzzy qualities.

Good breeders don't sell puppies before the age of 8 weeks despite a buyer's pleas, and have pet-quality pups spayed and neutered prior to placement (juvenile spay/neuter techniques now allow 8-week-old puppies to be safely sterilized – see Chapter 32). They might insist on visiting the buyer's home to inspect, and may refuse to sell a puppy to a home that doesn't have a safely fenced yard, or a good pet-owning track record.

A good breeder rarely sells two pups to the same buyer, knowing full well what a difficult challenge it is to raise two baby dogs together without behavior complications. Good breeders also rarely advertise in the newspaper, since they have taken care to have prospective buyers for any pups they produce *long* before the actual breeding takes place, and they *never* sell to pet stores. Finally, a responsible breeder makes a commitment to *always* take back *any* pups that she has produced at *any time* during that dog's life, if the new owners must give them up for any reason whatsoever.

As you might imagine, it can be somewhat difficult to find breeders who meet these admittedly stringent criteria. If more breeders were responsible, there wouldn't be so many purebred and crossbred dogs available from other sources, such as shelters and rescues. A breeder who does anything less is actively contributing to the serious problem of pet overpopulation in this country.

On the positive side, a truly good breeder is a treasure. She produces healthy puppies of exceptionally good quality, provides a valuable education to those fortunate enough to purchase from her, is a wonderful resource for her buyers once the puppies have gone home, and becomes a lifetime friend to her puppies and their new families.

Of course, breeders are not the *only* source for purebred dogs, and purebred dogs don't *have* to be registered in order to compete in many canine sports. Many organizations offer competitions and titles for mixed-breed and unregistered purebred dogs – they are more interested in performance than pedigree. Even the American Kennel Club, the biggest stickler for "purebred-only" policies, will issue "Indefinite Listing Privileges" to dogs who appear to be purebred, even if registration papers are not available. A dog with an ILP number may enter most AKC-sanctioned competitions, such as obedience and agility. They may not compete in the conformation, or "breed" ring.

So, read on to learn more about additional sources for purebred dogs!

ANIMAL SHELTERS

Most people are astonished to discover how many purebred and crossbred dogs and puppies end up in the kennels of our nation's animal shelters. Over the past three decades I have visited shelters around the country at every conceivable opportunity, and not once did I fail to find at least one, more often several, purebreds of various breeds and ages available for adoption.

There are lots of good reasons to adopt shelter dogs. First, you may well save a life. At many shelters, adoption dogs have a limited time to find a home before the specter of overcrowding forces animal care staff to make euthanasia selections. You might also save money. Many adoption fees include a complete package of vaccinations, license, ID tags, and spay/neuter that cost far less than the price of the actual services from a private veterinarian – not to mention the initial cost of a puppy from some private sources.

There are wonderful dogs at shelters. While some end up there because of serious behavior problems, most do not. Some have minor, easily addressed behavior or health issues that the previous owner couldn't be bothered to fix, while many have no problems at all. They may simply have wandered off and their owners didn't care enough to come look or pay impound fees. Still other "perfect" pooches get left at shelters simply because their owners are going through some lifestyle change that doesn't include Fido.

You do need to be careful when adopting from a shelter. If your local shelter has a deserved reputation for harboring distemper and parvovirus germs, you will want to range farther afield and find one with a good disease control program to adopt from. Also, some shelters do a better job than others at screening their canine adoption candidates and matching them to appropriate homes. You may need to be a pretty good evaluator all on your own – or enlist the help of your favorite dog trainer – to find the shelter diamonds in the rough.

The best shelters offer breed match-up services. You can go in and get approved as a prospective adopter and be put in their files for a particular breed. When a dog of your chosen breed comes in looking for a home, they can call you to come see it. It may take a little patience to wait for the right dog to come along, but it's well worth the satisfaction of knowing you have given a shelter dog a second chance at life.

BREED RESCUES

In the last decade, animal rescue groups have gained high visibility for their work. Today, there is a rescue group for every breed imaginable as well as for crossbreeds and mixed-breeds, and there are rescue groups in every community. A search on the Internet for Dog Breed Rescue offers thousands of possible sources.

Rescue dogs come from a variety of sources; including shelters, breeders, private homes, Greyhound racetracks, and law enforcement actions against puppy mills and hoarders (animal collectors).

Like shelters and breeders, rescue groups also run the continuum from very good to very bad. Good rescue groups offer dogs for adoption who are fully vetted, already spayed and neutered, and evaluated for behavior problems. They make full disclosure of any known or anticipated behavior challenges, and screen prospective adopters to ensure the best possible placements. A good rescuer is an expert in her breed, and well fitted to make sure *you* are prepared to appreciate and manage the idiosyncrasies of your chosen breed.

Beware of rescuers who get caught up in the hoarder syndrome. Kindhearted animal lovers who do rescue work are sometimes unable to recognize when their responsibilities have come to outweigh their resources. Steeped in their mission to save lives, they may end up rescuing more animals than they can care for, or take in animals who require far more rehabilitation than they, or the average adopter, are able to provide. Hoarder syndrome is a recognized psychological condition. If you come across such a person in your search for the dog of your desired breed, you will be doing her, the animals in her care, and her community, a great service by reporting her to authorities so she, and the animals, can get the help they need.

Be prepared to pay an adoption fee for your rescue dog. Good rescue groups, like good shelters, make a significant commitment of resources to rehabilitating and placing the dogs they rescue. They are largely dependent on donations, and your adoption fees will help defray some of their operating and animal care expenses.

NEWSPAPER ADS

Good breeders do not advertise in local newspapers. They don't have to. Backyard breeders and puppy millers *do* frequently advertise in the newspaper, and are not a recommended source for your new family member.

You can, however, find your ideal dog in the paper if you are careful, and if you can resist the temptation to fall for the first furry face you see. Look for a private owner who must place an individual dog or pup for some reason – usually a lifestyle change, or a sober realization that the addition of a dog to the family was an unfortunate mistake. Be sure to take the time to evaluate the dog thoroughly before you take him home, and have a clear understanding with the owner about your ability to return him should he not work out for you.

PET STORES

I said that there were pros and cons about every source for purebred dogs.

The only positive aspect of purchasing a puppy from a pet store is that you are essentially paying to rescue that doggie in the window – and that's a good thing for that individual pup. However, while some people are perfectly happy with their pet store purchases, the risks related to buying pet store puppies so greatly outweigh the single good that I urge you to *never* even let the thought cross your mind.

For starters, when you purchase a pet store puppy, you are supporting the horrendous puppy mill industry. Every dollar you spend to rescue that beguiling face in the window goes to produce, market and sell more puppies who often are raised in substandard conditions. By "freeing up" that puppy's cage, you, in essence, place the pet store's order for more puppies, to be produced by mothers who are nothing more than breeding machines to the puppy farmer. In dog training terms, you are reinforcing this behavior! Pay no attention to the store manager's reassurances that their puppies come from "responsible breeders." *No responsible breeder sells puppies to pet stores*. None.

Every breed of dog is burdened with the potential for specific diseases or medical conditions; genes transmit the potential for hip displaysia, heart defects, cancer, etc. The parents of pet store puppies are unlikely to have had any screening for hip displaysia, eye problems, or any of the other myriad of genetic defects common to various dog breeds, so the chances are far greater that your pet store pup will suffer from one or more of these debilitating defects in his lifetime. The puppies and their parents may have missed out on some important health care practices, such as routine worming and vaccinations. Some may even grow up to bear very little real resemblance to the breed you are seeking.

The sooner people stop buying pet store puppies, the sooner pet stores will stop selling them, and the sooner puppy mills and other irresponsible breeders will start going out of business.

Finders Keepers

Of course, you could always buy into the "No two alike" Pat Miller philosophy of dog keeping. With this guide, and no preconceived idea of who we want our next dog to be, we are always open to the delightful miracle of the next serendipitous canine discovery. If we had our hearts set on a particular breed, we would have missed the opportunity (after an unsuccessful search for his owners) to keep Dubhy, our 18-month-old piano-playing, skateboard-riding Scottish Terrier who wandered into our family last winter and has amused us with his no-fear attitude and Gaelic sense of humor ever since. Nor would we have had the joy of sharing our lives with Josie for the last 15 years, the wonderful Terrier mix who crossed our paths during a cockfighting investigation in San Jose many years ago, and who has been my teacher and guide on our positive training path ever since.

❤ THE TOP FIVE CAVEATS OF PUREBRED DOG BUYING

1. Research your breed carefully to avoid common breed problems. Because of the smaller gene pools that make up purebred dogs, they are more likely to suffer from serious genetic defects than are crossbreeds and mixed breeds. For a comprehensive list of genetic problems common to various breeds of dogs, visit the Association of Veterinarians for Animal Rights (AVAR) website at: www.avar.org and click on "Dog Disease Guide."

2. Hold your breeder to a high standard. Buying a puppy from a less-than-responsible breeder encourages that breeder to continue making contributions to the pet overpopulation problem. If you do buy from a breeder, be sure to buy from a good one.

3. Don't fall into the "fad breed" trap. Learn about the breed that appeals to you – don't get a Jack Russell because Wishbone and Eddie are cute, a Border Collie because your kids loved "Babe," or a Siberian Husky just because you liked "Snow Dogs." All three of those breeds can present above-average challenges to the novice dog owner.

4. Watch out for "breeder deals." Unscrupulous breeders often try to unload their unsold adolescent pups who are now beyond the "cute" stage, or their "used up" breeding stock, with some story about how the dog was a show prospect who didn't quite make it, and he's willing to give you a really good deal. In fact, these dogs are often very poorly socialized, have had no training whatsoever, and are a real liability to the breeder, who should be paying **you** to take the dog off his hands. If anything the breeder tells you sounds "hinky", it probably is. If you do take one of these breeder deals, be prepared to invest in the services of a good behavior consultant.

5. Avoid your own unreasonable expectations. Not every Collie can grow up to be a Lassie. If your German Shepherd pup's ears never stand tall like they are supposed to, your Bichon Frise never makes it to Madison Square Garden, or your Australian Kelpie is afraid of cows, will you love her despite her flaws, and fulfill your commitment to love and keep her until death do you part?

CHAPTER 6 ❤
Starting Off on the Right Paw: A Case Study With Buddy the Lab Puppy

Getting puppy training right will certainly make your life as a dog owner easier. Habits and behaviors start early, and you have a window of opportunity during the dog's first few months of life to establish patterns of behavior that will last a lifetime. Let's take a look at the steps I took to train an exuberant Lab puppy for one of my clients as a way of illustrating the kinds of challenges you may encounter. If you follow the steps and techniques in this case study you will have come a long ways towards raising a puppy who is content and well mannered.

Buddy the Lab Puppy

The first time I saw Buddy he was a tiny tan morsel nestled in his owner's arms; a perfect pudge of a yellow Labrador retriever puppy – eight weeks old, fat, round and chunky with a shiny black button nose, warm brown eyes and milk-sweet puppy breath. His owner, Tena, had carried him into my training class to hand him over to me for three weeks of in-home-board-and-train.

I generally don't recommend that an owner send an eight-week-old puppy to a trainer for boarding and training. This is an important learning and bonding

It is critical to your puppy's development – and your sanity – to start off on the right foot.

period for dog *and* owner; it is usually more beneficial for the two to learn together. But Buddy's owners had made some big mistakes in the two weeks they had owned their new puppy.

First, they had purchased him at the age of six weeks, depriving him of a very important two-week period of education and socialization with his mother and littermates. Puppies taken away from their litters at this tender age often have problems with being mouthy (biting too hard on human skin) because they missed out on the chance to learn bite inhibition from their mother and siblings. Unless they are given ample opportunity to socialize with other puppies or gentle adult dogs as they grow up, "only" puppies can become canine social nerds, failing to learn appropriate body language and other canine social skills. Puppies taken away from their litters too soon often grow up to be aggressive to other dogs.

The owners' second big mistake was adopting a six-week-old puppy two weeks before going on a three-week vacation. They had belatedly realized the folly of putting a very young pup in a commercial kennel for three weeks, and had begged me to take him. I agreed, reluctantly. I am not set up to do boarding, and have long resisted adopting a puppy myself because of the huge commitment of time and energy that they require. However, I, too, was reluctant to see Buddy spend these important formative weeks in a kennel, and his owners were willing to pay a considerable sum for the privilege of keeping Buddy at my home. Buddy was coming to stay for three weeks.

My class was just concluding. I dismissed my students and walked outside with Tena to discuss last-minute details.

"Put him down," I urged her. "Let him walk."

She gently placed him on the ground and he toddled along behind us as we strolled down the driveway. Suddenly he stopped and sat in the middle of the road. We continued on, and when we had gone about 15 feet she turned back to him.

"What are you doing?" I asked her.

"Going back to get him," she replied.

Big mistake number three – Buddy was already training her to do what he wanted!

"Nope," I said. "Leave him."

"Leave him?" There was a note of panic in her voice.

"Leave him," I insisted. "He'll come."

We kept walking, Tena glancing nervously over her shoulder every three steps. Sure enough, we hadn't gone another fifteen feet when Buddy jumped up and came galloping after us. My first lesson for Buddy (and for Tena!) was a success – we were the leaders, and it was *his* job to keep up with us.

I reassured Tena that Buddy would be fine. She bid him a reluctant good-bye, got in her car and drove away. I used a treat to lure Buddy into the crate I had brought with me, put him in my van and headed home.

Coming Home

"Home" had been prepared for Buddy's arrival. I had put down a plastic tarp in the living room, covered it with a thick layer of newspaper and set up a puppy pen on top of it. A variety of enticing chew toys awaited Buddy's needle-sharp baby teeth: a Kong stuffed with cream cheese, a bleached marrow bone filled with peanut butter, a Goodie Ship™ with freeze-dried liver jammed into the holes, a Roll-A-Treat Ball™ full of tasty kibble, a couple of Vermont Chew Toys™. We were ready!

We would use the "umbilical cord" approach to puppy management. Buddy would at all times either be in his pen, in the safely fenced and puppy-proofed yard with my dogs, on a leash with me, or under my direct supervision in the house. We would thus avoid a common mistake of novice puppy owners – giving the puppy too much freedom. The first few weeks of puppyhood are a critical time. If the pup's early behavior is well managed, he will never learn to chew the furniture, climb on the counters and urinate in the back bedroom. Through the judicious use of puppy pens, fenced yards, crates, adult dog baby-sitters, leashes and direct supervision, we avoid unwanted behaviors that are much easier to prevent than they are to unteach.

Three Weeks With Buddy

I arrive home with Buddy and introduce him to the Miller pack. I know none of our four dogs will hurt him, but I also know that they won't tolerate obnoxious puppy behavior. As he charges through the front gate he is greeted by Josie, our then 11-year-old Terrier mix and pack leader. Josie promptly lets out a fierce throaty growl that knocks Buddy onto his back. From Tucker, the 75-pound Cattle Dog mix and Katie the 45-pound Australian Kelpie, all the way down to Dusty, the eight-pound Pomeranian, each of the four Miller dogs lets Buddy know in turn that they will brook no misbehavior.

I take Buddy inside and put him in the pen, where he promptly begins to cry and shreds the newspaper. This is where puppy owners often make another huge mistake. If I heed his cries and relent, letting him out of the pen, he learns an important lesson – crying gets him what he wants. Instead, by ignoring him, I will teach him that crying is not a useful behavior. If I "Click!" (see Chapter 2) a clicker and treat him when he stops crying, he will learn to be quiet even faster. I ignore Buddy's cries, and within 15 minutes he finally gives up and settles down for a nap.

I start Buddy's housetraining from day one, teaching him a verbal cue to go to the bathroom and rewarding him for eliminating. At 11:00 p.m. I wake Buddy and take him outside on his leash to a pre-designated area. As he squats, I tell him "Go pee!" When he is done,

I "Click!" and feed him a treat. After a short wait he also deposits feces, also accompanied by my "Go pee!" followed by a "Click!" and treat. We will do this every two hours throughout each day for the next three weeks, giving him lots of opportunities to do it right, and never giving him the chance to "make a mistake" in the house.

If I made the common novice-owner error of just putting him outside by himself, he could eliminate anywhere he chose. He might not even go to the bathroom at all, especially if I give him a treat when he comes back in. If "coming in" is the behavior that gets rewarded with a treat, he might as well skip the bathroom step!

Having other dogs to play with outside can also distract him from his bathroom purpose – he may be having so much fun playing that he forgets to stop and eliminate. By going out with him, I teach him to relieve himself in the exact spot I want him to use, and I make sure he actually eliminates. If he doesn't, I bring him back inside and return him to his crate for a while, then try again.

By rewarding him immediately after he goes, I make sure he knows what he is getting rewarded for. The "Click!" from a clicker gives him a clear message about which behavior is getting rewarded, even if the treat arrives a few seconds later. We will be using the "Click!" a lot with Buddy over the next few weeks. When Buddy is done going to the bathroom,

I lead him into the bedroom and toss a treat into his crate.

"Go to bed," I urge as he pokes his nose into the crate, looking for the treat. A gentle nudge to his tail pushes him into the crate, and he is ready for bed. Within three days he will voluntarily go into his crate upon hearing the verbal cue, "Go to bed." He has had a long, exciting day and is ready to sleep. He cries for a few minutes, but when I continue to ignore him, he curls up and sleeps through the night without a further peep.

The Routine

The following days fall into a routine that centers on Buddy. We wake at 5:30 a.m. to a dry crate, and rush outside for his morning bathroom ritual, and then come back inside for breakfast in his puppy pen. The day consists of lots of trips in and out, interspersed with three meals, and several short training sessions. Within two days he is galloping into his pen at the "Go to your pen" cue, ready for his meal. He quickly learns to run up to me and sit for a "Click!" and treat instead of jumping up. We accomplish this in less than a day by turning our backs when he jumps up – ignoring the behavior we don't want – and clicking and rewarding him with a treat when he sits. By Day 4 he offers a sit for every possible occasion.

He also learns to sit quietly in order to be released from his pen. When I approach

Buddy spends all unsupervised time in the house in his crate or a pen, set up on a tarp covered with newspapers. There's no way to get in trouble or make a mistake in here.

the pen gate he must sit in order for me to proceed. If he jumps up, I turn away. When he sits, I start to open the gate. If he gets up, I turn away again. He quickly realizes that the sooner he sits and stays sitting, the sooner the gate opens. If he gets up before I release him, I close the gate again. I don't even have to ask him to sit – he *chooses* to sit because that gets him what he wants – out! He is learning to control his own behavior without being nagged by me to do the "right" thing. This is a key element of positive reinforcement training – teaching the dog to take responsibility for his own behavior rather than always being told what to do.

On Day 3, after just one session with the clicker, he learns to lie down on a verbal cue. We start by "luring" him down with a treat without even using the word "Down," then "Click!" and treat him when he does it. Once he does the "Down" behavior smoothly, we add the word to tell him what he is doing, *as he does it,* still clicking and treating for each "Down." After a dozen or so repetitions, I ask for the "Down" first, then lure with the treat, followed by "Click!" and reward. It only takes a couple of dozen repetitions for Buddy to understand that the word "Down" means the same thing as luring "Down" with the treat, and he is soon dropping like a rock to the floor on the verbal cue alone.

As expected, because he was removed from his litter early, Buddy is excessively mouthy. When I offer him a treat, he chomps down on my hand. His sharp little teeth hurt! I consciously resist the impulse to punish him for the pain he inflicts on me – instead I begin to teach him to soften his uninhibited bite. I offer the treat in my closed fist, and suffer the discomfort of his teeth until I feel his bite begin to gentle. As soon as the bite softens, I say "Gentle," then I "Click!" tell him "Take it!" and give him the treat. He soon learns that he doesn't get the treat until he is gentle with his mouth. Although I see progress within a few days, it takes the entire three weeks to get him as soft with his mouth as I want him to be.

A Constant Watchful Eye

Anytime Buddy is given house freedom he requires direct supervision. He wants to eat everything! Distracting him with the Chew Man toy only lasts as long as I play with him. We work on increasing his self-control. I sit on the sofa and ask him to "Down" at my feet. At first I "Click!" and reward him just for the down. Then I gradually increase the length of time between the cue for "Down" and the "Click!" and reward. ("Gradually" means a few seconds at a time!) By the time Buddy returns to his owners, he will lie quietly at my feet for as long as a half-hour.

We walk on leash to the mailbox every morning to get the newspaper. He is overcoming his tendency to sit and wait to be picked up, and is beginning to walk nicely by my side. I "Click!" and reward him *a lot* whenever he walks with me, and stop and stand still if he pulls on the leash. He soon learns that pulling does not get rewarded – the more he pulls, the longer it takes him to get where he wants to go.

Encouraging Good Behavior

On Day 4 the newspaper is lying on the ground. Buddy grabs it in his mouth. Having spent the last three days taking

forbidden items away from him, I have to stifle my immediate instinct to take it out of his mouth. This is a *good* behavior to encourage! I allow him to carry the paper proudly back to the house, where I trade him for a treat. From that morning on, he fetches the newspaper every day.

Finally! Buddy has found something that he is allowed to pick up and carry around; bringing the newspaper into the house is a behavior to be encouraged.

It is possible to completely inhibit a dog's natural retrieving tendencies by punishing him every time he puts something in his mouth. I encourage Buddy to pick up, play with and fetch appropriate play toys. I use the words I want him to learn. "Fetch" when he runs to get the toy that I throw, and "Give" when he brings it back.

Of course, he doesn't know what "Give" means until I teach him. He is reluctant to unclamp his tiny jaws from his favorite chew toy, so I offer to trade him for a treat. Bingo! He lets go of the toy as I say "Give," and I "Click!" and reward him with the treat for his good behavior. We use this same method to get him to give up a forbidden item, and thus avoid teaching him to play keep-away by chasing after him when he has something he shouldn't. We try to keep inappropriate objects off the floor and out of his reach, but he always seems to be able to find something he is not supposed to have!

By the beginning of the second week I am looking for new challenges for Buddy. He loves to splash in his water bowl, so we buy a baby's swimming pool and teach him to play in the water. He is hesitant at first, but within a few days he is leaping into the pool to fetch his toys. He accompanies me to my "Dog Days of Summer" lecture at the Santa Cruz SPCA, acting as my "demo" puppy for the "Puppy Stuff" lecture. His quick response to the clicker wins several converts over to the positive reinforcement method of dog training. I also take him with me to do a television show promotion for the lecture series, and on T.V. we demonstrate clicker training and puppy behavior management tools such as the Kong™ stuffed with cream cheese.

We spend the third week polishing his behaviors and preparing to return him to Tena. He has added "Come," "Stay," "Off," "Relax" and "Touch" to his repertoire. He sits and downs promptly on cue, and walks nicely on a leash. He goes into his pen and stays there without protest, sleeps through the night in his crate without a sound, and is allowed much more house freedom, although still with supervision. He can last six hours in his pen without soiling his papers, and in three weeks has only had one accident in the house.

I am exhausted. It takes so much work to raise a puppy! It is no small wonder that so many dogs end up at animal shelters – there are far too many puppies who never get the attention they need to become well-behaved canine citizens.

In preparation for returning Buddy to Tena, I review all that he has learned in three weeks. I recognize that there is an inherent satisfaction in shaping a puppy's behavior, watching him explore the world, and teaching him to be a good canine citizen. And while I look forward to the relief of returning Buddy to his owners and having my own household return to normal, I worry about whether his people will keep up with his training and behavior management. I realize that I will miss this bright little guy with his boundless enthusiasm for life and learning.

Epilogue

Buddy's owners were quite pleased with the results of his stay at "Camp Miller," and signed him up for one of my Peaceable Paws puppy training classes. Buddy and I were delighted to see each other when he arrived for class, where he was handled by his owner's son, seven-year-old Mark. Buddy and Mark graduated from puppy class with honors.

CHAPTER 7 ❤
Minding Your Pees and Cues: Housetraining Success!

The term "housebreaking" grates on my sensibilities like fingernails on a blackboard. What is it that we are supposed to break? This term is deeply rooted in the force-based philosophy of dog training, and immediately gives new dog and puppy owners the wrong mind-set about the process of teaching their dog to urinate and defecate in appropriate places. We are house*training*, not house*breaking*, I gently remind my human students and fellow dog trainers when they slip and use the old-fashioned phrase. *Breaking* implies punishing the pup for pottying in the wrong spot. *Training* focuses the client on helping the puppy do it right.

Three-Step Formula For Training Behavior

Housetraining is simple. You don't give your puppy the opportunity to make mistakes. You do give him plenty of opportunities to do it right. Simple, however, does not necessarily mean easy. It means making a commitment to manage your pup's behavior 24 hours a day, until he is old enough to be trusted with his house freedom for increasingly long periods of time.

Until your puppy is several months old and consistently eliminating outdoors, you must keep her either in a crate, on a leash, or under your direct supervision.

I teach my clients a basic three-step formula for training or changing a behavior. By applying each of these steps you can get your dog to do just about anything that he is physically and mentally capable of, including housetraining.

STEP 1:

Visualize the behavior you *want*. Create a mental image of what you want your puppy to do and what that looks like – in this case, to consistently and reliably go the bathroom outside in his designated toilet spot. You need to be able to imagine how this looks in order to be able to train your pup to do it. If you utilize all your brain cells envisioning your puppy making mistakes in the house, you won't have the creativity you need to help him do it right.

STEP 2:

Prevent him from being rewarded for doing the behavior you don't want. A reward doesn't have to come from you in order to be reinforcing to your dog. It is very rewarding to a puppy with a full bowel or bladder to relieve the pressure in his abdomen. If you give him the opportunity to go to the bathroom in the house, that will feel good to him, and he will keep doing it when he has the opportunity. It will eventually become a habit, and then his *preference* will be to eliminate in the house. Step 2 requires you to manage your pup's behavior so he doesn't have the opportunity to be self-rewarded by going to the bathroom in the house.

STEP 3:

Help him do it right and consistently reward him for the behavior you *do* want. This is the step that often gets skipped. You need to go outside with Spot and reward him when he performs. If you toss him out in the back yard and don't go with him, you won't know

if he went to the bathroom or not. Coming back in for a cookie may be more rewarding to him than relieving his bladder, so he waits by the back door, comes in, eats his cookie, and *then* pees on the rug.

You'll notice that none of the steps involve punishing the puppy for going to the bathroom in the house. Old-fashioned suggestions like rubbing his nose in his mess or smacking him with a rolled-up newspaper are inappropriate and abusive. They teach your pup to be fearful of relieving himself in your presence, and are very effective at teaching him to pee behind the bed in the guest room where you can't see and punish him. Besides, it is much easier to teach him to go to the bathroom in one *right* place than it is to punish him for going to the bathroom in an almost infinite number of *wrong* places. If you do "catch him in the act," simply utter a loud but cheerful "Oops!" and whisk him outside to the proper place. Remember to treat the "oops" spot thoroughly with an enzyme-based cleaner designed to remove all traces of animal waste, such as Nature's Miracle™. Finally, if you really feel you *must* make use of that rolled up newspaper, smack yourself in the head three times while repeating, "I *will* supervise the puppy more closely, I *will* supervise the puppy more closely, I *will* supervise the puppy more closely!"

The 8-week housetraining program described below is the one that I provide to my clients for an 8-week-old puppy. Many dog owners are amazed by how simple housetraining can be, as well as by the fact that their dogs can be trained to go to the bathroom on cue, in a designated spot. If you are starting with an older pup or an adult dog, you may be able to accelerate the timeline, since an older dog is physically able to "hold it" for longer periods than a very young pup. If, however, at any point in the program your furry friend starts backsliding you have progressed too quickly. Back up to the previous week's lesson.

You will need a properly sized crate; a collar and leash; treats; poop bags; time and patience. A puppy pen, tether, and fenced yard are also useful. For more information on using these tools, see Chapters 8, 9 and 15.

An 8-Week Housetraining Program

WEEK 1

Acclimate your puppy to his crate on his first day in your home, off and on all day (see Chapter 8). While you do this, take him outside on his leash to his designated potty spot every hour on the hour. When he obliges you with a pile or a puddle, tell him "Yes!" in a happy tone of voice (or Click! your clicker), and feed him a small treat.

Pick up his water after 7:00 pm to prevent him from tanking up before bed (later if

The crate is a key part of successful housetraining – however do not leave your puppy in a crate all day. If he is forced to eliminate in the crate his "clean den" instinct may be broken.

it is very hot), and then crate him when you go to sleep.

Most young puppies crate train easily. The crate should be in your bedroom so your baby dog is not isolated and lonely, and so you can hear him when he wakes up and tells you he has to go out. *Do not* put him in his crate on the far side of the house. He will feel abandoned and lonely and cry his little heart out, but worse than that, you won't hear him when he has to go and he will be forced to soil his crate.

A successful housetraining program is dependent on your dog's natural instincts to keep his den clean. If you force your puppy to soil his crate you break down that inhibition and make it infinitely harder to get him to extend the "clean den" concept to your entire house.

When he cries in the middle of the night, you *must* get up (quickly), put him on his leash and take him out to his potty spot. Stand and wait. When he starts to go, say "Go potty!" or "Do it!" or "Hurry up!" or whatever verbal cue you ultimately want to use to *ask* him to go to the bathroom. If you consistently speak this phrase whenever your pup starts to urinate or defecate, you will eventually be able to elicit his urination or defecation, assuming, that is, that he has something to offer you at the moment. Being able to put his bathroom behavior on cue is an added bonus of this method of housetraining, and a very handy one when you're late for a date, or it's pouring rain or freezing cold outside!

As soon as your pup has finished "doing his thing," tell him "Yes!" in a happy tone of voice and feed him a treat, praise him, tell him what a wonderful puppy he is. Then take him in and put him back in his crate. No food, no play, and no bed-cuddling. If you do anything more than a perfunctory potty-performance in the middle of the night he will quickly learn to wake you up and cry for your attention.

First thing in the morning, take him out on leash and repeat the ritual. If you consistently go out with him, on leash, you will teach him to use the designated spot for his bathroom. If you just open the door and push him out, he may well decide that two feet from the back door is far enough, especially if it's cold or wet out. For the first week or so, if his bladder is too full to make it safely out the door, you can carry him out, but by the end of the second week he should be able to walk to the door under his own power.

Now you can feed your puppy and give him his water bowl, but be sure to keep him right under your nose. If you have to use the bathroom, he goes with you. If you want to sit down to eat breakfast, he's on his leash under your chair, or tethered by his pillow. Ten to 15 minutes after he is done eating, take him out again, repeat your cue when he does his thing, and "Yes!" treat and praise when he is done. Also take him out immediately upon the completion of any exuberant play sessions, and whenever he wakes up from a nap.

For the rest of the day, take him out every hour on the hour for his potty ritual, as well as 10 to 15 minutes after every meal. The remainder of the time he must be under your direct supervision, or on a leash or tether, in his pen or in his crate, *every second of the day.* Judicious use of closed doors and baby gates can keep him corralled in the room with you, but you still need to watch him. If Spot starts walking in circles or otherwise looking restless, toss in an extra bathroom break.

"But wait!" you cry. "I work all day, I *can't* take him out every hour on the hour."

Ah, yes, that is why housetraining is simple but not always easy. "Home alone" pups are more likely to end up stuck out in the back yard, where they get left for convenience sake as the housetraining program drops lower and lower on the priority list. If you haven't yet acquired your pup and you aren't going to be a stay-at-home dog parents, seriously reconsider the possibility of adopting an older dog who is already housetrained and who may be in desperate need of a home.

If you already have your pup, you will need to either find a skilled and willing puppy daycare provider, or set up a safe, puppy-proofed environment with wall-to-wall newspapers or pee pads, and recognize that your housetraining program will probably proceed more slowly. You *cannot* crate him for the eight to ten hours a day that you are gone. You are likely to destroy his den-soiling inhibitions, cause him to hate and fear his crate, and possibly trigger the onset of separation anxiety.

When you *are* home, be extra diligent about your housetraining protocol, and as your pup starts to show a preference for one corner of his papered area you can start slowly diminishing the size of the covered area. You will eventually have to add the step of teaching him not to go on papers at all, which is one of the reasons

many trainers don't recommend paper training. You are, in essence, teaching him that it *is* okay to go to the bathroom in the house, and then later telling him that it is *not* okay.

WEEK 2

Continue crating Spot at night. Some pups are sleeping through the night by Week 2. Others need nighttime breaks for at least a few more weeks. During the day, continue to take him out immediately upon waking, 10-15 minutes after each meal, and after play and naps.

You can now begin teaching him to associate "getting excited" behavior with going out to potty. This will eventually translate into *him* getting excited to let

Dogs have their preferences, but it's useful if your dog can eliminate on cue wherever it is most convenient for you.

you know he has to go out. If you want him to do some other specific behavior to tell you he has to go, such as taking a bow, or ringing a bell hung from a door handle, start having him do that behavior before you take him out.

By now, you should be able to tell when your puppy is just about to squat in his designated place. Say your "Go pee!" cue just a second or two before he starts, so that your verbal cue begins to precede, rather than follow the behavior.

Stretch his bathroom excursions to 90 minutes apart, and start keeping a daily log – writing down the time, whether he did anything outside, and if so, what he did. Make note of any housetraining mistakes – when and where they occurred. While an occasional "Oops!" may be inevitable (we are only human, after all), if you are having more than one or two accidents a week you are not supervising closely enough or not taking him out enough. The log will help you understand your puppy's bathroom patterns over the next few weeks, and tell you when you can start trusting him for longer periods.

WEEK 3

Crate your puppy at night. I keep my dogs crated at night until they are at least a year old, and until I am totally confident that they can be trusted to hold their bowels and bladder and keep their puppy teeth to themselves. During the day, try stretching your pup's bathroom

intervals to two hours, still remembering to take him out after all meals, play sessions, and naps.

Continue to keep your log, to make sure Spot's housetraining program is on track. This is especially helpful for communication purposes if two or more family members are sharing puppy-walking duties.

Also continue to encourage the desired bathroom signal behavior before you take him out, and to use your bathroom cue outdoors, prior to the actual onset of elimination. Over the next few weeks, the verbal cue will begin to actually elicit the behavior, so that you can bring his attention to the business at hand when he is distracted, when you are in a hurry, or when you are in a new place where he isn't sure he is supposed to pee.

By the end of this week, your puppy should be leading you on his leash to the bathroom spot. Look for this behavior as an indication that he is making the connection to the designated spot that you want him to use.

WEEK 4

Crate Spot at night. Assuming all is going well, stretch daytime intervals to three hours beyond meal, play and nap trips. Go with him to his fenced-yard bathroom spot *off-leash*, to confirm that he is going there on his own, without you having to lead him. Continue to keep your daily log, and reinforce your "outside" and "bathroom" cues.

WEEKS 6-8

Keep crating at Spot night. Gradually increase the time between bathroom breaks to a maximum of four hours, including meals, play and naptime. You still need to go out with him most of the time, but you can occasionally send him out to his bathroom spot in his fenced yard all on his own, watching through the door or window to be sure he goes to his spot and gets the job done. By this time, accidents in the house should be virtually nonexistent. As long as the program is progressing well, you can begin phasing out your daily log. As your pup continues to mature over the next eight months, he will eventually be able to be left alone for up to eight hours at a time, perhaps slightly longer.

At that point, you can break out the champagne and celebrate – you and your puppy have come of age!

❤ 10 HOUSETRAINING TROUBLESHOOTING TIPS AND REMINDERS

1. If your housetraining-program-in-progress relapses, back up a week or two in the process and keep working from there. If that doesn't resolve the problem promptly (within a day), a trip to the vet is in order, to determine if there is a medical problem, such as a urinary tract infection, that is making it impossible for your pup to hold it. The longer you wait, the more ground you have to make up.

2. If your pup has diarrhea, not only is it impossible for him to comply with housetraining, he may also be seriously ill. Puppies can dehydrate to a life-threatening degree very quickly. Contact your veterinarian immediately.

3. If your paper-trained pup refuses to go on anything other than paper, take a sheet of newspaper or pee pad outside and have him go on that. Each subsequent trip, reduce the size of the fresh sheet of paper or pad a tiny bit until it is gone.

4. If your dog's inhibitions against soiling his den have already been damaged, you may need to remove his bedding from his crate. It is possible that his bedding is now his preferred surface. Try the bare crate floor or a coated metal grate instead, and set your alarm to wake you up at night as often as necessary to enable you to consistently take him out before he soils his crate.

5. Neutering your male dog between the ages of eight weeks and six months will minimize the development of assertive territorial leg lifting. Already existing territorial leg-lifting can be discouraged as part of a complete housetraining program with the use of "Doggie Wraps," a belly band sold for this purpose through various pet supply catalogs and outlets.

6. If at any time your reliably housetrained dog begins having accidents in the house, have him examined by your veterinarian in case there is a physical cause.

7. Remember that drugs such as Prednisone can cause increased water intake, which causes increased urination. If it is not a medical problem, evaluate possible stress factors and return to a basic housetraining program.

8. Vigorous exercise can also cause excessive water intake and subsequent urination, as can a medical condition known as polydipsea/polyurea, which simply means drinking and urinating too much.

9. When Spot has learned to eliminate on cue, start asking him to poop and pee on various surfaces, including grass, gravel, cement and dirt. Dogs can easily develop a substrate preference – grass, for example – and may refuse to go to the bathroom on anything but their preferred surface. If you are ever in a location where there is no grass, your dog could be in trouble.

10. If your situation is such that your dog must constantly be asked to wait to go for longer periods than is reasonable, consider litter box training. Lots of people do this, especially those with small dogs and those who live in high-rise apartments. This also resolves the surface-preference problem.

CHAPTER 8 ❤
Crate Training Made Easy:
For Puppies AND Older Dogs

Some twenty-plus years ago I got a new puppy. Keli was an Australian Kelpie, a herding dog, acquired by the Marin Humane Society to be my Canine Field Agent, partner and assistant in my daily duties as an Animal Services Officer. Being selected for this model program was a huge honor and responsibility. I was determined to do everything right in caring for and training my pup.

I had recently heard about a new technique in puppy-raising, called crate-training, where you put your dog in a small fiberglass airline kennel at night, and whenever you had to leave him alone. I was skeptical. Put Keli in a cage? It sounded cruel! Still, determined to provide cutting-edge care for my pup in this cutting-edge program, I decided to try it. After all, Keli would be with me most of the time in the animal services truck, so we were really only talking about nighttime crating. Unconvinced but willing to try, prior to bringing Keli home I purchased a crate and set it up in my bedroom.

When I brought my ten-week-old red Kelpie puppy home, I braced myself for the two most trying challenges of puppy raising: housetraining and chewing. I was about to be pleasantly surprised. The first night in her crate, Keli cried for a few minutes – typical first-night-away-from-home puppy behavior – then curled up and went to sleep.

At 2 a.m. she woke me with her insistent puppy crying. She was telling me she needed to go out – NOW! I got up, took her out to pee – which she did immediately – then returned her to her crate and went back to bed. After another perfunctory period of puppy protest she went back to sleep. When I woke up the next morning her crate was clean. I didn't have to worry about stepping in – or cleaning up – puppy piles or puddles, and thanks to the boundaries of the crate, there were no chewed up shoes or electrical cords. My skepticism started to fade.

Two nights later it vanished completely when I went to put Keli in her crate and found Caper, my three-year-old Bull Terrier mix, already curled up on the soft pad in Keli's airline kennel. Caper looked up at me and thumped her tail several times, clearly saying, "These are cool, Mom! Please can I have one of my own?" I went out the following day and bought Caper her own crate, and I've been a crate convert ever since.

Home Sweet Crate

The crate is a sturdy plastic, fiberglass, wood, metal or wire box just big enough for a dog to stand up, turn around and lie down in comfortably. It can be used with the door open, at the dog's convenience, or with the door closed, when mandatory confinement is called for.

Dogs who have positive crate experiences when they are young almost always voluntarily hang out in their crates whenever they have the opportunity to do so.

When the crate is properly introduced using positive training methods, most dogs love them. Dogs are den animals and a crate is a modern den; a dog's personal portable bedroom that he can retire to when he wants to escape from the trials and tribulations of toddlers and other torments. He can take it with him when he stays at boarding kennels, and when he travels with you and sleeps in hotels and motels.

Owners love crates because they generally make housetraining a breeze

and prevent damage to the house, furnishings and personal possessions. They can give a new puppy-owner peace-of-mind when Baby Buddy has to be left home alone. They can be used for a positive time-out when visitors tire of Buddy's antics, or when he insists on begging at the dinner table.

The crate is also a great tool for convincing owners of back-yard dogs to bring their hounds into their homes where they belong. By bringing the dog indoors but keeping him confined, at least at night, hesitant owners can ease their fears about total mayhem and ruined rugs while at least partially integrating the deprived dog into the family.

Not A Prison

A crate is not a place of punishment. Never force your dog or puppy into a crate in anger. Even if he has earned a time-out through inappropriate behavior, don't yell at him, throw him in the crate and slam the door. Instead, quietly remove the dog from the scene and invite him into his crate to give both of you an opportunity to calm down.

Nor is a crate appropriate for long-term confinement. While some puppies can make it through an eight-hour stretch in a crate at night, you are sleeping nearby and available to take him out if he tells you he needs to go.

During the day, a puppy should not be asked to stay in a crate longer than two to four hours at a time; an adult dog no more than six to eight hours. Longer than that and you risk forcing Buddy to eliminate in his crate, which is a very bad thing, since it breaks down his instinctive inhibitions against soiling his den. As mentioned before, dogs who learn to soil their dens can be extremely difficult, sometimes nearly impossible, to housetrain – a common behavior problem for puppies from unclean puppy mills and other less-than-responsible breeders.

Training Do's and Don'ts

Most puppies, and the majority of adult dogs, can be crate-trained with relative ease. Remember that the crate should be just large enough for your dog to stand up, turn around and lie down comfortably. He doesn't need to be able to play football in it. If you want to get one large enough

Make sure you increase the size of the crate as your puppy grows. This crate is far too small for this dog even for the shortest period of time.

for your puppy to grow into, block off the back so he has just enough room, and increase the space as he grows. Cover the floor of the crate with a rug or soft pad to make it comfortable and inviting, and you're ready to begin training.

Start with the crate door open, and toss some irresistibly yummy treats inside. If your dog is hesitant to go in after them, toss the treats close enough to the doorway that he can stand outside and just poke his nose in the crate to eat them. If you are training with a clicker or other reward marker, each time he eats a treat, Click! the clicker or say "Yes!" if you are using a verbal marker (see Chapter 2).

Gradually toss the treats farther and farther into the crate until he steps inside to get them. Continue to Click! each time he eats a treat. When he is entering the crate easily to get the treats, Click! and offer him a treat while he is still inside. If he is willing to stay inside, keep clicking and treating. If he comes out that's okay too, just toss another treat inside and wait for him to re-enter. Don't try to force him to stay in the crate.

When he is routinely entering the crate to get the treat without hesitation, you can start using a verbal cue such as "Go to bed" as he goes in, so that you will eventually be able to send him into his crate on just a verbal cue.

When he happily stays in the crate in anticipation of a Click! and treat, gently swing the door closed. Don't latch it! Click! and treat, then open the door. Repeat this step, gradually increasing the length of time the door stays closed before you Click! Sometimes you can Click! and reward without opening the door right away.

When your dog will stay in the crate with the door closed for at least ten seconds without any signs of anxiety, close the door, latch it, and take one step away from the crate. Click! return to the crate, reward, and open the door. Repeat this step, varying the time and distance you leave the crate. Don't always make it longer and farther – intersperse long ones with shorter ones, so it doesn't always get harder and harder for him. Start increasing the number of times you Click! and treat without opening the door, but remember that a Click! or a "Yes!" *always* gets a treat.

It's a good idea to leave the crate open when you aren't actively training. Toss treats and favorite toys in the crate when your dog is not looking, so he never knows what wonderful surprises he might find there. You can even feed him his meals in the crate – with the door open – to help him realize that his crate is a truly wonderful place.

If at any time during the program your dog whines or fusses about being in the crate, *don't let him out until he stops crying!* This is the biggest mistake owners make when crate training. If you

let Buddy out when he is fussing, you will teach him that fussing gets him free.

If, however, he panics to the point of risking injury to himself, you must let him out. You may have a dog with a separation anxiety challenge. A crate is generally not recommended for dogs with separation anxiety, since they tend to panic in close confinement. If you believe your dog has a separation anxiety problem, stop the crate training and consult a behaviorist or a trainer who has experience with this behavior.

Instead of letting your dog out when he fusses or whines, wait for a few seconds of quiet, then Click! and reward. Then back up a step or two in the training program until he is again successful at the task you've set out for him. When your dog is doing well at that level again, increase the difficulty in smaller increments, and vary the times rather than making it progressively harder. For example, instead of going from 5 seconds to 10 to 15, start with 5 seconds, then 7, then 3, then 8, then 6, then 4, then 8, and so on.

Maintaining Success

Sometimes dogs and often puppies can do the whole crate training program in one day. Some will take several days, and a few will take weeks or more.

Once your dog is crate trained, you have a valuable behavior management tool for life. Respect it. If you abuse it by keeping him confined too much, for too long a period of time, or by using it as punishment, he may learn to dislike it. Even though he goes to bed willingly and on cue, reward him often enough to keep the response happy and quick. Keep your verbal "Go To Bed" cue light and happy. Don't ever let anyone tease or punish him in his crate. (Kids can be especially obnoxious about this. Watch them!)

Keli quickly learned the "Go to bed" routine. It wasn't long before I didn't even have to use the verbal cue – when I emerged from brushing my teeth in the bathroom she was already curled up in her crate for the night. I could count the number of housetraining mistakes she made in her lifetime on one hand, and the number of things chewed inappropriately on the other. Over the years, through multiple moves, a divorce, and countless trips to dog-sitters' homes her crate was a constant in her life. If she were able to speak today, in her typical herding-dog control-freak fashion, she would insist that every dog be given the opportunity to enjoy the many benefits of crate training.

Many dog owners have discovered that dog crates can serve double duty – safe havens for your canine pals and sturdy end-tables for you!

CHAPTER 9 ❤
The New Dog Owner's Hope Chest

Blushing brides used to come to their new marriages with a hope chest and a trousseau – a collection of the basic necessities for setting up a new household. It occurred to me that dogs should come to their new homes with a trousseau too – containing everything dog and owner need to lay the foundation for a successful lifetime relationship. I put my mind to the task, and came up with the following collection of items that should be in every new dog owner's hope chest.

Management Tools

CRATES

The crate is your dog's den, her safe haven, her very own private spot, and when you travel, her home away from home. When properly introduced using positive methods, most dogs love their crates.

The crate is an indispensable behavior management tool; it facilitates house-training and prevents misbehavior by keeping your dog safely confined when you're not there to supervise. It allows you to sleep peacefully at night and enjoy dinner and a movie without worrying about what the pup is destroying. Regular

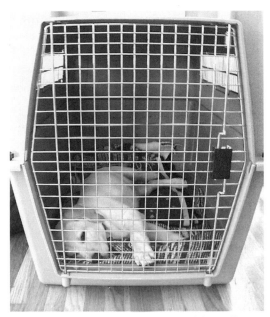

Your dog should love her crate and be willing to spend a reasonable amount of time in it if you use it properly. Remember, however, while cheerful time outs are okay, it's not to be used as part of physical or angry verbal punishment.

crates come in either wire or plastic/fiberglass models. Once a dog is crate trained, one of the collapsible portable crates is also a very handy accessory and can be used while traveling.

TETHERS

A training and behavior management tool, not for long term restraint or outdoor "chaining," the tether is a short (about four feet in length) plastic-coated cable with sturdy snaps at both ends. One end is snapped onto an eyebolt screwed into a wall or beam in a convenient, comfortable place.

A dog can chew the plastic coating off of a cable, but can't chew through it (thus rewarding himself for his efforts).

Tethers are intended to temporarily restrain a dog for relatively short periods of time *in your presence*. They should not be used as punishment, or to restrain a dog for long periods in your absence. A tether can be used as an aid in a puppy supervision and housetraining program, and as a time-out to settle unruly behavior. The tether is also useful for teaching your dog to sit politely to greet people, and to help her learn long distance "Downs." See Chapter 15 for more details on using tethers as training devices.

PUPPY PEN/EXERCISE PENS

The puppy or exercise pen is another useful management tool. It expands the "den" concept of a crate to a slightly larger area, giving your pup more room to stretch her legs, but still keeping her in a safe, confined area.

Most pens found on the market are collapsible and portable, made of plastic or wire, and usually consist of six or eight two-foot wide panels anywhere from two to four feet high. For lively pups who can scale the pen fence (usually Jack Russell Terriers), some pens come with a wire top.

Set the pen up in your living room or den, and plop the pup in it when you want to give her the freedom to move around but don't want to have to keep your eye on her every second. Tarps and newspapers can protect rugs and floors from pups who aren't yet fully housetrained, and the relatively small space will still help promote a pup's clean den instincts. The pen is also an alternative for pups who must be left home alone for longer periods than they can "hold it" in a crate.

Two Italian Greyhounds in a pen where they are kept safe but have more room to roam than in a crate.

SEAT BELTS

Nothing makes me hold my breath like the sight of an unruly dog bouncing around the seats of a moving vehicle. I have included a seat belt in our trousseau as an alternative to the crate for safe canine car travel. Some dogs don't crate well, some cars are too small to accommodate crates, and some owners just like to let their dogs look out the windows. Slipping your dog into a harness and using one of the many car restraints that fasten to your car's seat belts will keep her safe, and safely away from the driver. Remember that airbags can be hazardous to dogs, especially small ones; the back seat is the best bet for the traveling hound.

Canine seat belts keep a dog from interfering with the driver or jumping out a window. They also minimize the chance of both of you being injured in an accident.

Training Tools

LEASHES

A leash is a must-have for the hope chest. No matter how well trained your dog, there are times when she must be leashed, such as walking down a busy street, in the vet hospital, and anywhere in town where a leash law is in effect.

Bright-colored designer nylon leashes are appealing and fine for the trained

dog, but can burn your skin if your dog pulls. Plain leather and cotton canvas are softest on your hands, and the best choice for a dog-in-training's basic leash wardrobe. The "hands-free leash" is a nifty innovation, especially if you have strollers to push, bags to carry, or just want your hands free while you walk with your pal. Retractable leashes have limited application; they should only be used in wide-open spaces, away from other dogs and people, *after* your dog has been taught to walk politely on a leash. Chain leashes aren't even worth discussing.

COLLARS AND TAGS

Your dog's collar is like a wedding ring – the endless circle that symbolizes your never-ending relationship. You show your love for your dog by giving her a collar (and using a training method) that won't inflict pain – a basic flat or rolled nylon, cloth or leather collar fastened with a snap and buckle. Of course, you must also attach an I.D. tag and license to the collar – her ticket home should she ever be separated from you.

CLICKERS

Cheap, small, ridiculously simple, the clicker is my nomination for the best beginning-of-the-century training tool. This insignificant-looking gadget has led the dog training profession into the modern world of humane, positive training.

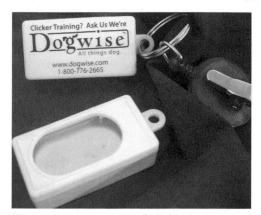

Two common varieties of clickers.

Properly used as a reward marker, the clicker significantly enhances your communication with your furry friend, speeds up the training process, and helps your dog learn how to think. It won't take up much room in the hope chest, but it will hold a prominent place in your dog training tool kit.

TREATS/REWARDS

A clicker, of course, is nothing without its accompanying reward. You can never have enough rewards in the trousseau! I use treats as the primary reward to pair with the clicker because most dogs are food motivated, and because they can quickly eat a small tidbit and get back to the training fun.

The best treat is whatever your dog loves best, and the best trainers work with a smorgasbord of treat options so that an extra special treat is always available to motivate the stressed or distracted dog, or to reward an extra special accom-

plishment. The list of possible treats is endless, and includes everything from Cheerios™, carrots and pretzels to hotdogs, string cheese and roast beef. Treats have calories too so be sure you reduce your meal sizes proportionally.

There are a wide variety of healthy treats available from various pet supply companies.

Other rewards may include tugging on a tug toy, chasing after a tennis ball, running out the door into the back yard, a walk around the block, a word of praise or a scratch behind the ear, as long as your dog likes those things.

LONG LINES

One of the greatest training challenges for some dog/owner teams is making the transition from "come reliably when called in a safe, controlled area" to "come reliably when called regardless of where we are or what other exciting things are happening." The long line is an ideal training tool to help you meet this challenge.

Enjoying an outing with a dog on a long line.

Long lines are simply long leashes – I have seen models from 10 to 50 feet – that are lightweight but strong, and made with various nylon, cotton or poly fabrics. The key is finding one that's comfortable in your hand, preventing you from getting rope burns while making it easy for you to maintain your grip.

With a long line, you can prevent your dog from being rewarded for the inappropriate behavior (running off into the woods), while waiting for her to offer you the appropriate behavior (returning to you) so you can Click! and reward her with a very high-value treat. This, of course, is the tried and true recipe for successful positive reinforcement training – rewarding the behaviors you want and prevent your dog from being rewarded for the behaviors you don't want.

HEAD HALTERS

Not all dogs need a head halter, but for those who do, it's a valuable addition to the chest (see Chapter 36 for more details).

Head halters come in a few different styles, but they all share the trait that makes them work so well to prevent a dog from pulling. They are worn on the dog's head (similar to a horse's halter), where he lacks the power to pull. Pressure on the head halter – when the dog pulls – actually turns the dog back toward you. Halters should not be confused with muzzles, as they do not prevent a dog from opening his mouth to pant, drink, or take a treat.

The determined puller who doesn't respond well to leash training, the big strong dog in the hands of a not-so-strong owner, and dogs with aggression challenges, are all good candidates for the head halter.

Toys

No trousseau would be complete without a wide variety of interactive toys, tug toys, chase toys and chew toys. The perfect toy for your dog depends a great deal on individual canine and human preference, but here are a few that we would bring to our new relationship.

KONGS

If I could only put one toy in our hope chest, it would be the Kong™. The Kong is the sturdiest, most versatile toy we have encountered in a lifetime of dog relationships. It's a chew-resistant (not chew-proof) rubber, beehive-shaped toy with a hollow center, a small hole at one end and a larger hole at the other. The Kong can be used "plain" as a toy, but makes an irresistible treat for any dog when stuffed with kibble or treats that are held in place with something healthful and edible like peanut butter, cream cheese, or yogurt.

The popular, versatile Kong.

I have yet to find a dog who couldn't be enticed to enjoy a properly stuffed Kong. Among other things, it can serve as a chase toy, a crate pacifier, a puppy distracter, a stress reducer, an energy diffuser, a hide-and-seek object, and a barking alternative. You can throw it, stuff it, freeze it, float it, hide it, and hang it. It comes in several sizes to meet the needs of all size dogs, and several colors; the black Kongs are the toughest, for super-chewer dogs.

BALLS

Balls and dogs go together like peanut butter and jelly. The variety of balls available ensures that there are plenty for every play style and jaw strength.

My favorites include the Bully Ball™ – very sturdy, great for dogs who like to push balls around with noses and paws; the Goodie Ball™ – small, with a ridged hole in the middle to hold a dog treat; the Karlie Action Ball™ – a sports ball inside a sturdy nylon strap with rope tugs; the Jolly Ball™ – rugged polyurethane with a handle – good for dogs who like to lug their ball around with them; the Zap Ball™ – flashing lights and wonderful electronic noises; and the Kong ball – a very sturdy basic red rubber ball. There are tons more balls, of course; even the humble tennis ball keeps many dogs happy and well exercised. There's no excuse to not have at least a couple of balls in the toy box!

INTERACTIVE TOYS

These are toys that require your dog to *do* something to make the toy work. They are designed to keep your dog's brain, mouth and body occupied productively rather than destructively.

Topping this list are the Buster Cube™ (a hollow cube with a hole in it) and the Roll-A-Treat Ball™ (a hollow sphere with a hole in it) that you fill with your dog's breakfast kibble and let him push around the floor to make the treats fall out. Another great new interactive toy is the PitBall™ – a circular plastic rim within which the ball-obsessed dog can pursue the object of her obsession to her heart's content without worrying about losing it under the sofa. Keep your eyes open for other interactive toys to add to the hope chest. The more you keep your dog's mind and body occupied the better behaved she'll be, and the more solid your relationship.

FETCH TOYS

I suspect that as long as dogs have had relationships with humans, humans have been throwing things for dogs to fetch. Dogs who love to fetch never seem to tire of the game, and a new fetch toy is cause for celebration. There are fetch toys that float, for the Mark Spitz's of the canine world; fetch toys that fly, for the Ashley Whippet wannabes; rubber fetch toys; wooden fetch toys; and for dogs with tender mouths, plush disc-shaped fetch toys.

TUG TOYS

Contrary to some trainer's opinions, I believe that tug-of-war, played with proper rules, is a *great* game. Most dogs love to play tug, it's a good way to use up excess energy indoors on a rainy day, it can help teach your dog good mouth manners, and it provides a productive outlet for those family members who want to play rough physical games with Fido.

The right tug toy is an imperative accessory to safe tugging – long enough to keep teeth far away from skin, inviting for the dog to put her teeth on *her* end of the tug, and with a comfortable handle

on the other end so the human player can keep his grasp and win the war most of the time (an important tug rule).

Dog and Home Clean Up

GROOMING

Of course, every new bride comes to her new home with a well-equipped toilette, and your dog should be no different. Make sure you leave space in one corner of the hope chest for combs, brushes, shampoos, scissors, clippers, cotton balls, toothbrushes, nail trimmers, grinders, and whatever other grooming accessories your dog might need. The vast array of different grooming tools can be confusing, so be sure to find the right ones for your particular dog. If you're not sure, ask your local groomer, veterinarian or dog trainer for grooming tips.

CLEANING

In long-lasting relationships, partners accept their loved ones' imperfections. Let's face it, we love our canine companions, but they can be messy! Dog hair, poop and pee and occasionally blood and vomit are facts of life in the dog-owning household, and the wise human is prepared to deal effectively with these doggie by-products. Clothes brushes, extra-strength vacuum cleaners, enzyme-based waste removers and sturdy poop bags and scoopers are dog-owning necessities. Funny, our dogs don't seem to have any trouble accepting our *human* imperfections!

Educational Materials

The best dog owners I know find room in their hope chests for extensive libraries, from obscure dog training volumes to the current best-selling videos. Here is my suggestion for inclusion in the trousseau.

TOP 10 BOOKS

- *Your Outta Control Puppy,* by Teoti Anderson

- *The Culture Clash*, by Jean Donaldson

- *The Good Little Dog Book,* by Dr. Ian Dunbar

- *The Other End of the Leash*, by Patricia McConnell Ph.D.

- *The Power of Positive Dog Training*, by Pat Miller

- *The Dog Whisperer*, by Paul Owens with Norma Eckroate

- *Natural Health for Dogs & Cats*, by Richard H. Pitcairn, DVM, PhD, & Susan Hubble Pitcairn

- *Don't Shoot the Dog*, by Karen Pryor

- *Circles of Compassion*, edited by Elaine Sichel

TOP 8 VIDEOS

- *Click & Go*, by Deborah Jones Ph.D.

- *Clicker Magic,* by Karen Pryor

- *Take A Bow, Wow*, by Virginia Broitman & Sherri Lippman

- *Dogs, Cats & Kids*, by Dr. Wayne Hunthausen

- *Dancing With Your Dog*, by Sandra Davis

- *Click & Fetch*, by Deborah Jones Ph.D.

- *Click & Fix*, by Deborah Jones Ph.D.

- *Puppy Love*, by Karen Pryor

The Intangibles

Just like a marriage, the dog-human bond relies on intangibles to make the relationship work. You may not be able to physically place them in your hope chest, but if you bring kindness, compassion, patience, forgiveness and understanding with you to the relationship, you and your dog should share a lifetime of love and happiness.

PART THREE

Basic Training

❤ A QUICK OVERVIEW

Think of Part Three as basic training, a summer camp for dogs and their owners that gets results from positive methods. You and your dog enter the camp as relatively blank slates and come out an accomplished canine good citizen team with a foundation of the skills you and your dog need to live a happy life together. You can use the techniques in this section with either puppies or older dogs, or as a refresher for your already-trained canine pal. Keep training sessions fun. Only work as long as you and your dog are having a good time and meeting with success. Five to fifteen minutes for most dogs, longer if you are both loving it!

CHAPTER 10 ❤
Living With Humans 101:
The Top 10 Things Every Dog Should Know

There are certain basic behaviors that all dogs need to know if they are going to survive in human society. Generally, the dogs who are likely to live happily ever after in their original homes are those who are regarded as "good" by their owners. Before we go into basic training skills in detail, let's review the kinds of things your dog needs to learn. This will serve as a handy skill list but it also may give you – the new dog owner – a bit of a reality check; after all, it's *you* who will be taking responsibility to make sure your dog learns all these things!

While some (or all!) of the Top 10 Things might seem overly elementary to an experienced and responsible dog owner, many of the dogs I see in training classes – and animal shelters – lack many of the following skills. Certainly, a committed canine caretaker is willing to manage or overlook some of her dog's shortcomings; we are not perfect, nor should we expect our dogs to be. However, the less you have to manage or overlook, the more pleasant life will be for the both of you in the long run.

OK – let's get started and see how you and your dog are doing. Keep track of the Top

Ten Things that you and your dog have successfully mastered together. If you can do all of them, then congratulations! You and your canine pal are well on your way to a lifetime of happiness and good times together. If you had to answer no on some of them, you might want to get to work and help your dog become an even better companion for you.

#1 How to Live and Play With Humans

This may seem like a pretty broad topic. It is, in fact, the foundation of many of the ones that follow. Specifically this means that your dog needs to accept that many human rules simply make no sense from a canine perspective. For example, humans have this incredibly bizarre habit of leaving food around uneaten. Really good food! Large chunks of prey animal, right out in plain view on the kitchen counter or on the coffee table. What creature in his right mind would not eat high value food when the opportunity presents itself?

Yet, humans do just that, *and* they expect their dogs to do the same. Although this exceptional example of canine self-control is often taken for granted, the dog who leaves the roast beef sandwich unmolested on the coffee table when his human takes a potty break in the middle of the Rose Bowl Parade deserves to be held in high esteem by his human caretaker.

Other examples of bizarre human rules include a taboo on drinking water from the freshest water source in the house (a fountain that humans call a toilet) and an expectation that their dogs not perceive an open door as an open invitation to dash through.

Our dogs also must adapt to what probably seems to them to be very odd human play behavior. Dogs play with tooth and claw – jumping up, biting, body-slamming – while most humans want their canine playmates to keep their teeth to themselves, and to refrain from jumping up and body-slamming, even in play, unless expressly invited.

Dogs are capable of learning these eccentric human rules, and they learn best when their humans understand that it is a dog's nature to eat available food, drink fresh water, go through openings at will, and roughhouse in play. In each of these cases, proper management – not allowing the dog to be rewarded by the natural but undesirable behavior – and consistent reinforcement for alternative behaviors can get the job done (see Chapter 4).

#2 How to Accept Intimate Contact From Family, Friends and Relative Strangers

Throughout your dog's life, you will expect him to happily accept being touched and handled by all sorts of people: family, friends, strangers on the street, children in the schoolyard, veterinarians, groomers, and more. Dogs, however, do not come already programmed to love attention and touch. While some seem more naturally inclined to like human contact than others, all dogs must be socialized – ideally from a very early age – and taught to accept, even enjoy intimate touch. Even something as apparently innocuous as a pat on the head is foreign to a dog's natural instincts and non-verbal communication style.

The best puppy raisers begin an intensive socialization program starting when pups are four weeks (or even younger), by exposing them to gentle handling and touch from an increasing number and variety of humans as the days and weeks pass. Handling ears, touching paws, examining teeth and private parts should all be accompanied by rewards – treats, toys, praise – so the pup comes to believe that humans and human touch make very good things happen. This concept should be instilled in his little dog brain well before he reaches the advanced age of four months.

Dogs who are stressed by human contact are far more likely to bite, and bite seriously, at some point in their lives. If your dog missed that all-important socialization period between four weeks and four months, you will need to work hard to make up for lost time. You can probably improve his willingness to accept contact, but he's not likely to be as social as he could have been. A strong commitment to a program of counter conditioning and desensitization is in order, and you may need the assistance of a behavior and training professional to maximize your success.

#3 How To Share

In the dog world, possession is generally nine-tenths of ownership, and even a small, lower-ranking pack member can often successfully fend of other dogs' threats to her food and other valuable objects. Dogs will share with each other, but only when they choose to. You probably expect your canine family members to share happily and willingly, each and every time you decide that what's hers is yours. Resource guarding is, in fact, a relatively common behavior with dogs, ranging from mild tension when folks are playing with the dog's food bowl, to serious aggression with potential to maim.

You can start early in a puppy's life to insure against food guarding, by teaching her that your approach is *not* a threat to her possessions, but actually brings more good stuff. When she's eating, approach her bowl and drop several high value treats, one at a time, into her bowl. When she has something she shouldn't, trade her for something better, instead of chasing her around in anger, scaring her and putting her on the defensive. If she consistently gets something wonderful when you approach, and rarely loses the good thing she has, she will not resort to resource guarding – she won't need to!

If your dog is already a resource-guarder, seek the help of a qualified positive professional to help you work with it. This is a dangerous behavior, and one that should be addressed by someone who is confident and capable (see Chapter 24).

#4 When and Where To Go Potty

Dogs come genetically programmed not to soil their own dens, so this is one human rule that makes pretty good sense to them. They may wonder why we insist on living in such *large* dens when small ones are so much cozier, but once they realize that the *whole house* is a den, housetraining usually comes along with relative ease.

The trick is to manage the dog's behavior through crates, pens, tethers, leashes, and direct supervision, so he doesn't have the opportunity to get in the habit of using any part of your house/den as his bathroom. Meanwhile, take him outside frequently and consistently enough so that he gets in the habit of relieving himself outdoors.

Remember, it's a much simpler training challenge to teach him to go in *one right spot* than it is to teach him not to go in an almost infinite number of *wrong* spots (see Chapter 7).

#5 How to Be Alone

To a wild dog, "alone" is synonymous with "danger." A puppy, especially, is at high risk for being eaten if he is left without the protection of the pack. Although they are thousands of years away from their wild ancestors, many of our domestic dogs still experience a residual anxiety when they are left alone. In extreme cases, dogs can develop a condition known as separation anxiety – the equivalent of a panic attack when left alone – and can cause great damage to their environment and injury to themselves. While crates can be used with some destructive dogs to safely contain them while unattended, crating is rarely a solution for unfortunate dogs with separation anxiety, as close confinement can send them into a panic frenzy.

To prevent separation anxiety, accustom your new puppy or dog to being left alone gradually during the first few days he is with you, perhaps crated or tethered while you move around the room, occasionally returning to him when he is calm and

quiet. Calm departures and returns will also help him learn to be matter-of-fact about your comings and goings.

When this procedure causes him no discernible stress, begin stepping out of the room – for just a few seconds at a time, then longer and longer as he shows that he can handle it. Avoid returning to him when he is fussing. If he learns that fussing makes you return, you will teach him to fuss harder and harder until he develops a full-blown anxiety attack when you are out of sight.

If your dog has mild signs of separation anxiety, the above program can also work, although it may take longer than a few days. If your dog has a serious anxiety condition, you will probably need the assistance of a professional, and perhaps anxiety relieving drugs, to see improvement (see Chapter 23).

#6 When and Where to Use Teeth

There are lots of uses for a dog's teeth, and all of them are acceptable, if properly directed. Dogs eat the meals you give them with their teeth; obviously that's okay. The best way to keep dogs from eating what they shouldn't is to manage their behavior to prevent access and reward for counter-surfing, and to train a positive "Leave it" exercise.

Dogs also chew with their teeth. This, too, is normal behavior, and it behooves you to provide your pup with plenty of appropriate chew objects (a stuffed Kong being my favorite) while he is developing his chewing preferences. Once he zeroes in on suitable chew objects and matures past the experimental puppy stage, your own personal possessions should be reasonably safe. For this reason, I keep all new dogs crated when I can't supervise until they are at least a year old, gradually giving them increased house freedom as long as they show me they can handle it.

Dogs play with their teeth. Since canine teeth on human skin is generally an unacceptable behavior, I redirect that play-bite urge to tug 'o war toys, complete with rules designed to make it a safe and rewarding game for both tug partners. Dogs should be free to engage in tooth-play with other dogs, as long as both dogs are willing participants.

And finally, dogs bite aggressively with their teeth. There are rare circumstances when this is acceptable behavior – for trained protection and police dogs, and for the untrained family dog who wisely bites a criminal intruder – but most companion dogs need to not bite humans if they want to live happily ever after. The best way to accomplish this is to go back to the socialization work of Top Thing #2 above.

Most aggression is caused by stress. A good socialization and positive training program reduces the number of things

that might cause a dog to be stressed, thereby decreasing the likelihood that he will ever bite. All dogs are capable of biting, however, no matter how well socialized, if the situation is stressful enough. Which is why the extreme stress generated by a stranger's attack can cause even a very well-socialized and well-mannered dog to bite – as well he should!

#7 How to Come When Called

A very reliable recall is the key to a dog's supervised freedom outdoors. While I would never counsel you to just open the door and turn your dog loose, if your dog has a solid "come when called" you can have him with you off-leash in many suitable outdoor environments – gardening in your yard, hiking on dog-legal trails, playing in dog parks – without worrying that an errant deer will entice your dog into the woods and beyond your control. Very reliable recalls don't happen all by themselves. It takes a lot of training to end up with a dog who will turn his back on Bambi bounding across the meadow and return to you at a happy gallop instead.

One of the keys to achieving this milestone in dog training is to manage your dog so he doesn't have the opportunity to take off and romp in the woods with you screaming at him to come back. This means keeping him on a long line – and training him in the face of ever-increasingly-enticing distractions – until you know his recall is rock solid.

It takes an average of three years to train a dog to come to you in the face of extreme distractions. This means some dogs will get it sooner, and some will take longer, but plan on three years. Remember, that's three years of committed *training,* not just three years of sitting around waiting for the dog to get older (see Chapter 12).

#8 How to do an Emergency WHOA!

No matter how well trained, no dog is perfect. Even the most rock solid recall may someday fail, and when it does, you'll be glad to have an emergency brake.

I like to train a long-distance "Down" for emergency stops. Many dogs, while unwilling to turn their backs on their chase object and return to you, will happily drop to a down position, as long as they can keep their eyes glued to their prey. Once the prey is out of sight, the dog's arousal decreases, and she is willing to return to me when I call her.

I also teach a "Wait" cue, which can stop a dog in her tracks, but she's still standing, which makes it more likely that she will pick up the chase again before I can get her to return to me.

Some trainers use "NO!" or "STOP!" in a loud roar to stop a dog from whatever

behavior she is engaged in, including chase. This can work, but my preference is to tell the dog to do something, rather than nothing.

#9 How to Walk Politely on a Leash

Walking on leash, along with other important good manners behaviors such as "sit to greet people," can greatly enhance your enjoyment of your canine companion's presence. If he walks happily on a leash by your side instead of dragging you down the street, and politely greets people he meets on his outings, you are far more likely to take him places with you. The more places you take him the more socialization and exercise he gets, the better behaved he is likely to be. The better behaved he is, the more likely you are to take him places, proudly, as a well-loved and full-fledged member of your family (see Chapter 16).

#10 How to Play and Live With Other Dogs

You may only have one dog, so what's the difference if he gets along with others? For one thing, dogs are naturally social animals. You can enhance the quality of your dog's life if you socialize him with other dogs and provide him with opportunities to play with his dog pals, at dog parks, doggie day care, or arranged play-dates in his own back yard. A day of dog-play will eat up his excess canine energy and leave you begging for more play outlets. A tired dog is a well-behaved dog.

In addition, when you take your four-legged family member out in public, he will inevitably encounter other canines. If he is well socialized to dogs, he can handle these encounters with equanimity. Dogs who don't know how to act around other dogs may become fearful, or overly excited – both of which can lead to aggression. Either way, if your dog acts out around other dogs you are likely to limit his exercise and socialization, which can give rise to other behavior problems, including destructive behavior and aggression.

Time to Tally Up

So, how'd you and your dog do? If you can honestly say you and your dog can do nine or ten of these behaviors, you have reason to be proud of the work the two of you have done together, and the relationship you share.

If there are a lots of things your cannot yet do, better get a move on! The next several chapters will give you the skills

If you scored well on this test, you and your dog deserve high-fives!

to master these ten important tasks. Even if *you* are comfortable working around the gaps in your dog's knowledge, his lack of social or behavioral graces may be a source of friction between you and your roommates, spouse, or neighbors. Why not improve relations between the species and teach him a few more vital skills? He'll be far safer and more welcome in human society if you do.

CHAPTER 11 ❤
Sit Happens!

Sitting on cue is one of those basic behaviors that every dog should know. Happily, it is an absurdly simple behavior to teach. In fact, I remind my students that their dogs already *know* how to sit – it's just the "doing it on cue" part that we have to work on!

Nowhere, perhaps, is the difference between positive and compulsion training more beautifully obvious than with the "Sit." A considerable part of the first session of many compulsion classes is spent teaching owners how to *force* their dogs to sit by jerking, pushing and manipulating various body parts. I spend *my* first night of class talking with my students, explaining how (and why) we train our dogs without using force. Meanwhile my demo dog for the night, an obstreperous, untrained dog provided by one of my students, a dog whom I have never met before – emphatically *offers* sit, after sit, after sit. Magic? Not really – just an application of the positive reinforcement elements of operant conditioning, a training technique that teaches a dog to voluntarily offer the behaviors that we want.

Magic Markers - A Quick Review

As we have already established, the key to positive training is remembering to notice and reward the dog when he does something right. A dog sits dozens of times a day, all on his own. If we make it a point to reward him a good percentage of the time when he does, he'll do it even more, because *all living beings repeat behaviors that are rewarding to them.* This is why so many dogs jump up on people. We tend to ignore dogs when they're sitting quietly, and pay attention to them when they jump up. Thus, they get rewarded for jumping, so they jump more.

A quick review of clicker training is in order here as it is a great tool to teach the sit (see Chapter 2 for more details). Remember that a reward marker is a word or a sound that tells the dog the instant he has done a desirable behavior. Clickers are commonly used as reward markers because the Click! sound is so distinctive and consistent. You can also use the word "Yes!" as a back-up reward marker or a "mouth click," the click of a ballpoint pen, or any other short, consistent and distinctive word or sound, for those times when you don't happen to have a clicker handy, or for the occasional dog who is afraid of the clicker sound. The Click! or "Yes" is a *promise* to your dog that a treat is forthcoming. Every Click! earns a treat.

OK – now let's take a look at my first-night demo dog and see how the reward marker works in teaching the sit.

I begin class by introducing myself and talking about the philosophy of positive dog training. While I do that, I also have the demo dog's leash in my hand. I test his response to the clicker by clicking it in my pocket to muffle the sharpness of the sound. Then I feed him an irresistible treat. I click and treat several more times and then, assuming he doesn't react badly to the sound of the clicker, I bring it out of my pocket and continue the clicks and treats while I talk. Usually, it takes no more than a half-dozen treats to convince my demo dog to rivet his attention on me.

Once this happens, I stop the consistent flow of treats, and hold one up near my chest. Often, the dog will try to jump up for the treat. If he does, I simply whisk the treat out of sight and turn away, without making eye contact or paying him any attention. Eventually he will sit, because it's easier to look up at me (and the treat) when he's sitting. The instant he does, I Click! and treat.

It takes most demo dogs less than three minutes to become sitting machines, offering sit after sit in order to make the Click! happen and earn the treat reward. This is the secret of the "magic marker." The dog learns that *he* makes the Click! happen. Trainers jokingly call this the "Helen Keller moment." Once we open that door, the dog is ready for training.

On Cue

Although the class listens to my comments while I work with the designated demo dog, they also watch his miraculous transformation from out-of-control to sitting at my feet, paying rapt attention to me. His behavior, more than any words I could speak, underscores the effectiveness of positive training.

I take a moment to point out that I have not yet *asked* the dog to sit. With positive training, we get the behavior first, *then* we add the verbal cue. There is no point in using a word to ask the dog to do something when he has no idea what it means. Once we know we can get the dog to offer the behavior, then we add the word so that he can start to make the association between the word and the behavior.

This is easy with the sit. I take a step backwards. The dog gets up to follow his newfound treat machine. I stop, and he sits to make the Click! happen. As his bottom touches the floor I say, "Sit!" then Click! and treat. I am telling him – in verbal shorthand – that the behavior he just did is called "Sit." I repeat this several times, and then start saying, "Sit" just *before* he sits. By watching his body language, it's easy for me to predict when he is about to sit. Now I am teaching him that the "Sit!" sound precedes his sit behavior. I still click and treat every time. I suggest to the class that an uneducated observer would think that

Begin your session by freely handing out tasty treats after each "Yes!" The puppy begins to associate the reward marker (Yes!) with the treats.

The puppy's full attention is now riveted on the trainer. She then stops the flow of food. The puppy waits and wonders if he will get another delicious morsel.

Finally he gets tired of craning his neck to look up. He sits for a more comfortable view. Immediately the trainer says "Yes!" and delivers a treat. He is on his way to learning how to sit!

the dog was responding to the verbal sit cue, when he's really not. I am *predicting* the dog's sit behavior with the word. He does not yet understand that the word is his prompt to sit.

We test this assertion. I ask him to sit at a time when his body language tells me he is not about to sit – he is distracted, sniffing the floor, or looking away from me. Lo and behold, he doesn't sit! I explain that he has not "refused" to sit on cue – he simply didn't understand the slightly different context. I don't nag at him with several repetitions of the "Sit" cue. Rather, I get his attention, and when I can see that he is ready to sit, I say the word. He promptly responds. The class gets the message.

Downhill From Here

Teaching the "Down" is not quite as easy as the sit. Dogs are less likely to "offer" the down in a training session. Once again, a food-treat motivator comes in handy. You can lure your dog into a down, without using force, by putting a treat in front of his nose and moving it slowly toward the ground. Lots of dogs will follow the lure easily and end up in a perfect down on the first try. Click! and treat!

Some dogs won't however. They may not understand what we want them to do, so they stand up when you try to lure them down. Some dogs are reluctant to lie down because they feel more vulnerable in the down position. In these cases you can shape the behavior. Shaping means breaking the final desired behavior into small steps and clicking and rewarding the dog repeatedly at each step along the way. Here is one way to shape the down:

1. Have the dog sit facing you. Hold the treat in front of his nose and move it two inches toward the ground. Click! and treat. Repeat several times until he shows no sign of trying to stand when you move the treat.

2. Have the dog sit facing you again. Hold the treat in front of his nose and move it five inches toward the ground. Click! and treat. Repeat several times until he shows no sign of trying to stand when you move the treat. If he does get up, say "Oops" in a cheerful tone of voice, and try again. If he consistently gets up, go back to two inches, and when he can do two inches without getting up, try *three* inches. When your dog has trouble with the transition from one step to the next, make the steps even smaller.

3. Keep moving the treat closer to the floor until your dog's nose is touching the ground. Now move the treat away from his nose along the floor, toward you, a few inches. Click! and treat when he follows it with his nose.

4. Gradually move the treat farther and farther away from his nose, clicking and treating as he follows

The trainer teaches the puppy to lie down by luring him down from a sit with a treat. She says "Yes!" and gives him a treat as he makes a forward and down motion.

The trainer "shapes" the puppy's movement into a proper "Down" by waiting for him to lower himself further and further before he gets a "Yes!" and treat.

Highly motivated by food, this puppy learns the Down exercise VERY quickly. "Fading" the lure will take a little longer.

without getting up. If he gets up, "Oops" and start over with the sit again. Eventually he will move one paw forward as he follows the lure. Click! and treat, then continue to lure him with the goodie until he is all of the way down. Click! and jackpot! – give him several treats, one after the other, while you tell him what a wonderful dog he is.

Bingo – you've done it! Or rather, the dog has done it. Once. Fortunately, it's usually much easier the second time. Keep practicing until he will lie down for you easily when you lure him, and then start adding the verbal cue, "Down," *as* he does it. Remember, we're not asking Bingo to "Down" yet, we're telling him that the behavior he is doing is called "Down."

As soon as your dog has had an opportunity to hear the word *with* the behavior – a half-dozen times or more – you can use the word first, then lure to help him lie down.

Fading The Lure

Now comes the real challenge. Getting your dog to lie down on the verbal cue *without* the lure. You must "fade" the lure, that is, reduce his (and your) dependence on the treat to get the "Down."

Have your dog sit facing you, and hide the treat behind your back. Say "Down" in a cheerful tone of voice. He probably will sit there and look at you, since he

doesn't know what the word means yet. Give him several seconds to think about it, then put the treat in front of his nose and lure him down. Click! and treat. Then do it again.

Watch him closely when you say "Down." If he looks at the ground, or makes a tentative motion as if to lie down, it's almost as if he's asking you if that's what he's *supposed* to do. Tell him "Good boy!" and quickly lure him the rest of the way down for a Click! and treat. If you encourage his tentative movements, you can speed up his response to the verbal cue.

Another way to fade the lure is to use smaller and smaller motions toward the ground with the treat until you're not moving it at all. Or, motion toward the ground with an empty hand (the same hand you have been holding the treat with in the past), Click! when he goes down and feed him the treat from your *other* hand.

How quickly you accomplish the verbal down depends on both dog *and* you. I have seen dogs go down on a verbal cue in as few as three repetitions, and I have had students who are still relying on the lure at the conclusion of a six-week class. Timing and persistence are important here. If you constantly forget to pause after the verbal cue before you lure, Bingo will focus on the lure, and won't learn the word. If you are committed to fading the lure, he'll get it.

One of the more intriguing aspects of positive training is that there is no "one right way" to do things. If one way doesn't work, you can try something else. If luring your dog from a sit doesn't work, try it from a stand. This method works best if you move the treat forward (away from you) and under his chest as you lower it toward the floor, to fold him back into a down. Another approach is to sit on the floor with your knee raised and lure him under your leg, so he has to lie down and crawl to follow the treat. This can also work with a stool or low coffee table, depending on the size of your dog.

The Training Formula

Remember that the more complex a behavior is, the more likely it is that you will have to shape it. The better you are at breaking the behavior into small steps, the easier it is for your dog to understand what you want. Once he figures out that *he* makes the Click! happen, you can use the same basic training formula to teach *any* behavior. Figure out how to get the behavior, Click! it, and put it on cue. Simple. Not always easy – but simple.

The most valuable aspect of this training method is that it teaches the dog *how to learn*. This is a skill that the two of you can rely on for the rest of his training career, whether for formal competition, or to perform new tricks to impress your friends. His ability and interest in learning behaviors that please you will also help make him a more enjoyable housemate and companion.

CHAPTER 12 ❤
Come: Achieving Total Recall

Caper was a Spuds McKenzie-style Bull Terrier mix – white with a rakish black eye. She spent the first 18 months of her life running free in the small California coastal community of Bolinas, where resident dog owners eschewed leashes and threw bottles at trucks driven by animal services officers. As happens all too often with dogs who are given too much freedom, the energetic terrier got into trouble. She nipped a small child who tried to play with her on the beach. I adopted Caper upon her release from bite quarantine at the Marin Humane Society more than 20 years ago, and immediately enrolled her in an obedience class.

Caper excelled in class despite the fact that in those days I was still using compulsion-based methods. It seemed to me at the time that the vigorous yanks that I applied to her leash and choke collar didn't dampen her enthusiasm for training in the slightest. When we ventured into the obedience competition ring she was always in the ribbons.

Her recall in the ring was superb. On the judge's instructions, I would leave her in a sit-stay, march to the opposite side of the ring, wait for the judge's signal, and then issue the clarion call, "Caper, come!"

Caper would rocket across the ring and slam her compact, muscled body into an unerringly straight sit at my feet, gazing into my eyes with adoration and anticipation. My next command invariably sent her into another faultlessly straight sit at heel position to complete the exercise – a picture-perfect show-ring recall.

Outside of the ring, however, the picture wasn't quite so perfect. If Caper was within 40 to 50 feet of me, my "Caper, come!" command worked 98% of the time. If she was farther away, however, the word "Come," more often than not, only served to lend wings to her heels as she fled directly away from me on some compelling Bull Terrier mission. Was it a coincidence that our show-ring recall was also performed at a distance of approximately 40 to 50 feet? I doubt it.

I stumbled over a solution to Caper's recall problem totally by accident. I acquired an Australian Kelpie, a breed with intensely strong herding instincts. Whenever Keli the Kelpie heard the note of hysteria in my "Come!" command that meant Caper was running off again, she would charge after the errant terrier on her lightning fast Kelpie legs and forcefully herd her back to me. Problem solved.

This, however, is not the solution I would use now, and it's certainly not the one that I offer my clients today for teaching their dogs a reliable "Come."

"Come" Is A Four-Letter Word

"Come" is perhaps the most important behavior we can teach our dogs – and the most difficult one. The average dog owner spends far too little time teaching "Come" as an exercise. We tend to use it mainly in real life, when we *really need* the dog to respond, and then we get upset if he doesn't. When does the average dog owner usually call her dog? When the dog is doing something he's not supposed to do – something that is infinitely more fun and rewarding than returning to his human.

"Let me see," ponders Rover for a tenth of a gigasecond. "Chase the deer or go back to my person, who sounds like she's mad at me, and who is probably going to put me in the car and take me home? Roll in the dead squirrel or go back to my person? Eat horse poop or go back to my person?" The person loses every time. To make matters worse, she starts to use an angry tone of voice when she calls Rover, and "Come" quickly becomes a four-letter word. Rover learns, like Caper did, to run away from his person when she uses the bad "Come" word.

There is a much better way. If we condition Rover to respond to a "Come"

cue that means "wonderful things are happening here," even if the "wonderful thing" isn't *really* as good as eating horse poop, prior positive conditioning *can* triumph over the allure of tasty horse poop, running deer and dead squirrel perfume.

We want our dogs to think that "Come!" is the best thing in the whole world. We do this by teaching a positive association with the come cue, and by making sure that the consequences of coming are *always* positive. We *never* punish Rover for coming to us, and we never resort to intimidation and threats to *make* Rover come to us.

Punishment is anything that Rover doesn't like. This means that if Rover

From the dog's point of view, promptly approaching people when they call can be a risky proposition. To teach a reliable response to the request "Come!" we must help our dog associate only good things with the appropriate cue and behavior.

doesn't like having his nails trimmed, don't call him to you, evil nail clippers in hand, then nab him for a manicure when he arrives. If you do, you've punished him for coming, and he will be a bit more leery about coming to you the next time he is called. If Rover stays in the back yard while you are gone all day at work, but he'd really rather be in the house, calling him to you and tossing him in the back yard just before you leave for work is punishment.

Of course, you *do* need to trim his nails, and perhaps you *do* need to put him in the yard when you leave, so what are you supposed to do? You have several choices. You can call him to you, do something very fun for 10 to 15 minutes, and *then* say, "Oh, by the way, as long as you're here, let's trim your nails." This way, the "bad thing" is far enough removed from being called that he won't make the association between the two. If you do this too often, however, there is a danger that he may start to realize that bad things *often* follow being called, especially in a certain context, such as your preparations to leave for work.

You can walk up to Rover wherever he happens to be, feed him a treat, take hold of his collar and proceed to trim his nails. However, if you do this too often with negative things, he will learn to move away when you approach. The most elegant solution is to convince him that nail trimming and going in the back yard are wonderful things, so that calling him

to you to do those things is a *good* thing, not a bad thing. If you make it a point to go out in the yard and play with Rover before you leave, he will think going in the yard is wonderful. If you gradually desensitize Rover to the nail clippers with yummy treats, he may never *love* having his nails trimmed, but at least it will seem better to him than bad. Meanwhile, you need to teach Rover to come on cue as a fun game, totally separate from doing negative things. Here's how:

The Short-Distance, Low-Distraction Come

Start with short-distance recalls in a low-distraction environment such as a quiet room in the house where you are by far the most exciting thing happening. Have a handful of over-the-top tasty treats that Rover doesn't get during regular training sessions, such as squeeze cheese, string cheese, bits of roast beef, baby food, or anything else that will really make Rover's eyes light up. With Rover just a few feet away from you, say his name in a cheerful tone of voice. When he looks at you in response to his name, *run* backwards several steps and say the word "Come!" also in a very happy voice. The message implied by your tone should be, "Hey, we're having a party over here, and *you're* invited!" Be sure to *run* away from your dog. Running triggers a dog's chase instincts and increases your attraction potential to Rover several-fold over standing boringly still.

Sandy starts out working with Happy in a quiet, enclosed room, free of distractions. As Happy approaches, Sandy offers a treat.

As soon as Rover starts moving toward you, use a reward marker that has already been paired with food, such as the Click! of a clicker, or the word "Yes!" You are marking the behavior of coming toward you, and letting Rover know that moving toward you has earned him a reward. This will also enhance the "Come," since Rover is likely to hurry faster toward you to get his treat after he hears the clicker.

As Rover approaches, stop moving, and tell him what a wonderful dog he is. If he sits easily for you, lift the treat as he arrives at your feet. Do not *ask* him to sit. If he sits, great! Feed him the treat and tell him he's fantastic. If not, go ahead and give him the treat anyway, and tell him he's wonderful. It's nice if our dogs sit when they come to us. It parks them briefly, so we can restrain them if necessary, and it is also much better than coming to us and jumping up. If sitting is a challenge for Rover, however, and we get into a sit-struggle when he

comes, then we are punishing him for coming, and come is no longer positive and fun. If Rover doesn't sit easily, give him the treat just for coming, and make a mental note to work on sit as a separate exercise.

Medium To Long Distance, Low-Distraction Come

When Rover is happily playing the short-distance come game with you, gradually start increasing the distance between you and Rover when you call him. Remember to mark the desired behavior – coming toward you – with a Click! or "Yes" *as he is coming toward you*, to encourage him to keep coming for his treat reward. Be sure to use lots of enthusiastic praise as well, to keep the party attitude.

Gradually, Sandy is able to call Happy from greater and greater distances across the closed room. Only good things happen to Happy when he comes on cue.

The Round-Robin Come

Now that Rover thinks that "Come" is a fun thing, you can include friends and family in the training game. Have several people in the room, each with a clicker and a handful of equally tasty treats. Take turns calling Rover, in no particular order. Each person Clicks! and treats Rover as he arrives, then another person calls him. *Note: In a group setting, if one person calls Rover, other people need to ignore him if he comes to them instead. No eye contact, no petting, no treats, no talking to him. He'll quickly learn that only the person calling him has any rewards.*

Adding Mild Distractions

Here's where most people start to lose the training game. Rover comes beautifully in the house, therefore, he knows what "Come" means and he is trained to come when called – right? Wrong! He is beautifully trained to come when he is called, *in* the house, *if* there is nothing more interesting around. Now we have to teach him to come in other places, even when there's other good stuff happening.

Sandy introduces a mild distraction into the environment. Happy can't resist a glance at the toys the man is playing with, but he proceeds to Sandy anyway.

For this part, put Rover's leash on. You are not going to jerk him with it, you are just going to use it to prevent him from being rewarded for going somewhere else when you call him. Start small. Have a friend moving around in the room while you practice short-distance recalls. Each time you change the rules of the game, go back to short recalls and gradually increase the distance. Instruct your friend to ignore your dog if he approaches her instead of coming to you. When Rover responds to your "Come" cue even with mild distractions, drop his leash and start increasing the distance, until he will romp to you across the room, even with another person, a ball, a cat, or a child in his path. When he will do this, you're ready to take the show on the road.

Adding Major Distractions

Until now, we've been working indoors. Outdoors is a whole new ballgame. There are all kinds of wonderfully enticing things for Rover to pursue outdoors. Great things to smell, eat, see, chase, roll in. You are going to have to work very hard to make yourself more interesting than the nearest dead squirrel. Arm yourself with your tastiest treats, and go back to square one – short distance recalls on-leash. If you've done your homework well in less distracting environments, Rover will catch on quickly, and your progression to longer distance and Round-Robin recalls will happen much faster than your initial training. As you increase the distance, use a long-line to prevent Rover from getting rewarded by the unanticipated appearance of a distraction that is beyond his training level.

Advanced Recall Challenges: The Premack Principle

The greatest challenge of "coming-when-called" is the reality that there will always be *something* out there that is more enticing than whatever we can offer Rover. In order to overcome this challenge, we use the Premack Principle, which teaches Rover that in order to get the wonderful thing at location "B," he has to come to us first at location "A". That is, if he wants to chase the squirrel up a tree, he comes to us *first* when we call him, *then* we let him go chase the squirrel.

You can teach your dog the Premack concept through controlled exercises. Start by having a friend stand with Rover, 20 feet away from you. The friend has a handful of yummy treats, and lets Rover sniff and lick her hands, *but does not give him any treats*. Call Rover to you. It may take a while for him to decide that he's not going to get any treats from your friend. That's okay. Just keep calling him in your happiest party voice. If necessary, squeak a squeaky toy, jump up and down – do whatever you need to do to get Rover interested in you. When he starts to come to you, Click! and feed

him treats when he arrives. Your friend should follow behind him, and give him *her* treats after he eats yours. He gets a double reward for coming to you – your treats *and* her treats. When he will do this exercise easily, he's ready for the advanced Premack challenge.

Empty a can of cat food (or something equally tempting) on a plate, and set it

The Premack Principle is a fantastic, advanced exercise for teaching "Come." The man has wonderfully tasty treats – but if Happy approaches him, he covers the treats. Sandy calls Happy in her usual chirpy voice and Happy passes by the man.

Sandy rewards Happy with a special treat when he comes to her – and then leads him to the man's treats for another reward.

off to the side. Have your friend kneel behind the plate with a bowl that she can use to cover the plate. Show Rover the plate of cat food, then put him on a sit-stay about 20 feet from the plate. Walk 20 feet away from Rover in a different direction so that you, the plate (and your friend) and Rover form the points of an equilateral triangle. Now call Rover. If he comes to you, great!! Good boy, Rover!! Click! treat, and then run with him over to the cat food and let him have a healthy mouthful. If he heads for the plate first instead, have your friend cover the plate with the bowl to prevent him from eating the food. Keep calling him until he gives up on the cat food and comes to you. Good boy, Rover!!! Click! treat, and run back with him to the plate for a mouthful of food. Keep practicing until he figures out that the *only* way to get the cat food is to come to you first. Now you and Rover are starting to achieve a really reliable recall!

A Few Final Recall Tips

If you are working with a dog like Caper, who already has a negative association with the word "Come," you might want to switch to a new recall word. Some dog owners use "Close" or "Here." You can use any word you want – it doesn't have any meaning for Rover until we associate it with the "Come" behavior. Just be sure to keep the *new* word positive, or you'll be looking for yet another one.

Make a real commitment to teaching your dog a positive "Come." It doesn't happen overnight. In fact, it can take some dogs two or three years to learn to come reliably in the face of the most enticing distractions – *if* you work at it. Remember it doesn't happen all by itself.

Meanwhile, don't put your dog in a situation where his lack of reliable recall can endanger his life. That is, don't take him off leash in places where he can run away and get into trouble, like I foolishly did with Caper. I was extremely lucky that Caper never got into serious trouble when she ran off, and I was fortunate to find a serendipitous solution to Caper's recall challenge.

Caper has long since died – of old age, not from a failed recall, thank goodness. I would love to have her back again, to show her how much fun "coming when called" can be, but of course, I can't. I'll just have to make it up to her through all of my current and future dogs, through all of my clients' dogs who come to me for training, and through you, who can teach *your* dogs positive, reliable recalls. Let the recall games begin.

CHAPTER 13 ❤
Off: Teach Your Dog to Leave It Alone

When they fill out their evaluation forms at the end of a six-week course, my Peaceable Paws clients frequently name the "Off" exercise as one of the most useful behaviors they have taught their dogs in class. "Off" means: "Whatever you are paying attention to right now, I want you to leave it alone." It can be applied to the roast on the counter, the tray of hors d'oeurves on the coffee table, the dead skunk beside the trail, the neighbor's cat darting across the back yard, or 93-year-old Aunt Martha. It's one of my favorite exercises for watching a dog's brain at work as she grasps the concept of "leave it alone." Best of all, its fun and easy. You can do the exercise all in one session if your dog is an "Off" whiz, or it may take several.

The Ten Step Program

Here is my ten step program for teaching a reliable "Off" cue.

1. Hold up a highly desirable "forbidden treat object," such as a cube of freeze-dried liver, so your dog can see it. When she shows interest, say "Off!" in a cheerful tone of voice and place the object on the floor. Be sure to use a pleasant tone, not an intimidating one. You are giving her information, not scaring her away from the treat.

2. Quickly, before she can grab it, cover the treat with your foot. Let her dig, claw, bite, and lick to her heart's content. Wear sturdy old shoes – do not do this with bare feet, or your shiny Sunday best. Do *not* repeat the "Off" cue. Just wait.

Say "Off!" then place a high value toy or treat under your foot.

3. Sooner or later she will lose interest in the forbidden object, or be distracted. The *instant* she looks away from your foot, Click! the clicker (or say "Yes!") and reward her with a treat *of equal or greater value* from your hand. Do *not* feed her the treat under your foot.

Reward the dog when he looks away from the toy.

4. If she eats the reward and immediately goes back to digging at your foot, wait until she looks away again, then Click! and reward. Keep doing this until she is no longer paying any attention to the treat under your foot. Use a high rate of reinforcement (lots of Clicks! and treats) until she realizes that it is more profitable to "not look" at the treat under your foot.

5. If she eats the reward and does not immediately go back to your foot, Click! and reward her so she quickly figures out she does not have to repeatedly try to get the object and then stop, in order to make the Click! happen. Your goal is to get her to leave it alone completely, not keep going back to it.

6. After several repetitions, pick up the forbidden object, show it to her again, say "Off" and place it on the floor, again covering it with your foot. Each time you start the exercise fresh by picking up the object and placing it on the floor, say "Off" one time, and only one time. Do *not* keep repeating the "Off" cue if she keeps trying to get it from under your foot. You want her to understand that once you say "Off!" it means *forever.*

7. When she is beginning to understand that she should leave your foot alone, uncover the treat slightly. Be prepared to cover it again quickly with your foot if she dives for it! Keep clicking and rewarding her for looking away from it, until she will leave it alone even when it is uncovered. You will be amazed by how quickly she learns this.

8. As she becomes more reliable about leaving it alone with your protector-foot nearby, gradually move farther and farther away from the treat until you can stand three to four feet away and she still honors the "Off." Err on the side of caution. If you progress too quickly and she grabs the forbidden object, you must back up in the training program and repair the damage done by her getting rewarded for the exact *opposite* of our behavior goal.

See how far you can move away from the toy or treat while the dog still honors the Off.

Buoyed by his successes, the dog now happily passes the toy on the ground and focuses on his trainer.

9. When she is reliably honoring the "Off" with you standing four feet away, attach the leash to her collar, set up the "Off" with the forbidden object on the floor, and move three feet off to one side. Keep the leash just barely taut but not tight, so you can restrain her if she moves toward the treat. Now call her to you. She should honor the "Off" cue and come to you rather than lunging forward to get the treat. When she does, Click! and Jackpot! (give a handful of treats, one by one, as an extra big reward). If she moves toward the treat, simply restrain her with the leash – don't say "No!" or repeat the "Off" cue. Just wait for her to give up and turn back to you. Then Click! and treat.

10. Now you can apply this to real life. With your dog on leash, walk past piles of treats you have laid out on the floor, or other natural enticements, such as a bowl of chips on the coffee table. As soon as she makes eye contact with the enticement say "Off" *one time* in a cheerful tone of voice and stand still, restraining her, with the leash short enough that she can't reach the object. Wait until she gives up and turns back to look at you. Click! and reward. Repeat until she understands that "Off" applies to real-life encounters. When she will reliably and routinely honor the "Off" cue without even tightening the leash, you are ready to try it off-leash.

On your first off-leash attempt, use relatively boring enticements such as a pile of dry cookies, and be sure to have wonderful rewards to give her when she turns back toward you in response to your cue. Warm her up on-leash, then take off the leash and give it a try. Be confident and visualize success, so you don't tense up near the item, and she'll likely reward you with a perfect performance.

CHAPTER 14 ❤
Wait a Bit, Stay Awhile

Have you ever watched Open Obedience competition at a dog show? If so, you may have been impressed by the long sits and downs, where all of the dogs do a group Sit-Stay for three minutes with the owners out of sight behind a barrier or in another room, and a Down-Stay for a full *five* minutes with the owners nowhere to be seen.

If you struggle to get your dog to stay in the car when you open the door, you may find these show ring achievements downright awe-inspiring. As you should! It *is* awesome to see a dozen or more dogs sitting shoulder to shoulder amidst all the distractions of a dog show, stoically awaiting their owners' return. It takes a serious commitment to training to accomplish this feat.

Fortunately, teaching your dog to stop leaping out of open car doors, dashing out the front door when visitors open it, or getting too far ahead of you on an off-leash trail, are attainable goals for any dog owner who is willing to make a commitment of a few minutes a day to the training project.

Wait A Minute!

Where many people might ask their dogs to "Stay," I use the cue "Wait," saving the "Stay" cue for a different situation. To my dogs, "Wait" means "Pause," and "Stay" means "Don't move from the position you're in until I tell you it's time to get up." If I'm getting out of my car I use the "Wait" cue, since what I really mean is "Don't jump out of the car," not "Freeze and don't move until I return."

If I use the word "Stay" in this scenario, I damage my dog's understanding of the stay cue and behavior. Dogs can only learn *one* meaning for a particular cue. Humans can understand that the word "Down" might mean lie down on the ground, get off the sofa, don't jump on me, or go down the stairs. Dogs can't make those distinctions.

Most owners actually mean "Wait" when they say "Stay." Think about it. When you leave your home all day while you go to work, do you say "Stay!" as you walk out the door? You don't *really* want him to sit frozen by the door all day, do you? You are really asking him to pause long enough for you to get out the door, not "Sit right there until I return."

You can, of course, continue to use "Stay" to mean "Wait" and use a different word, like "Freeze" for his formal "Stay." Whichever cue you choose, remember to be consistent and use each cue for its specifically intended behavior. Otherwise you risk muddling both cues in the dog's mind.

Teaching The "Wait"

I have my dogs "Wait" every time they go in and out a door to the outside world. This gives me a great opportunity, at least a half-dozen times a day, to remind them to defer to me, thereby reinforcing their good manners. It's also a great safety reminder. An open door is *not* an open invitation to go charging out into the big wide world.

He needs practice at waiting once the tailgate is down. Her owner uses a verbal cue for "Wait" as well as a hand signal. She also dispenses treats liberally for success.

Teaching your dog to "Wait" is best accomplished in small increments. Blue has learned to "Wait" until her owner lowers the tailgate, however...

One of the easiest ways teach the "Wait" behavior is by using a door, preferably a door that your dog *wants* to go through, one that opens to a safe, enclosed yard, garage, or other room. Most dogs are eager to go outside. It usually means a romp in the yard, a walk on the leash, or a ride in the car. You can use this to your advantage by teaching your dog that *calm* behavior – sitting at the door – not pushy behavior, gets the door to open.

Put your dog on a leash, stash a healthy supply of treats in your pocket, and have your reward marker handy, such as a Click! or the word "Yes!" Walk up to the door and ask your dog to sit. Click! and treat. Move your hand halfway to the doorknob. If he's still sitting, Click!, treat, and tell him he's a good boy. If, however, he gets up when you move your hand halfway to the door, say "Oops!" and have him sit again. Now reduce the challenge. Move your hand *four inches* toward the doorknob. If he's still sitting, Click! and treat. If he gets up when you move, try moving just two inches. When you find the increment of motion that doesn't cause him to get up, work at that distance for several repetitions, clicking and treating each time. Then try moving your hand a little farther. Click! and treat him for not getting up. Do several repetitions at each increment until you can reach all the way to the doorknob without your dog jumping up. Don't forget to praise him in addition to the clicks and treats!

Now jiggle the knob. Click! and treat for sitting. If he gets up, say "Oops!" have him sit and repeat the step, but do a smaller jiggle. When you find the level of knob-jiggle where he can succeed (where he stays sitting), do several repetitions of that. Then gradually increase the amount of jiggle, clicking and treating for each repetition.

Next you get to open the door – but only a crack. Click! and treat your dog for staying in the sit position. If he gets up – you guessed it – "Oops!" close the door and try again, with a smaller crack this time.

By closing the door when he makes a mistake and gets up, you are using negative punishment – making the *good* thing go away. The more eager he is to go out, the quicker he will realize that the way to get the door to open is to *keep sitting*. Once he has learned the "Wait" you can fade the use of the Click! and treat. Since what he *really* wants is to go through the door, you can sometimes give him a life reward just by telling him to go out.

Some dogs will "get it" in just one session. Others will need to practice over a period of several days or more, depending on their energy level and attention span – and yours. Any time you feel you or your dog getting frustrated in a training session take a break, after doing one easy, fun behavior that you both like so you end the session on a happy note.

Adding The Cue

In positive training, you add the verbal cue only *after* you know your dog will do the behavior, not before. This is because you want him to associate the word with the *right* response, not the wrong one. When your dog will remain sitting as you open the door, you can add the "Wait" cue. In essence, you are telling him that the behavior he is now doing is called Wait.

Other Applications For "Wait"

When your dog understands "Wait" in one situation, you can apply it to others. Practice in the car so he also understands that an open car door is not an invitation to jump out. You'll be amazed at how nice it is to have a moment or two to pocket your keys, or even tie your shoes before you invite your dog to jump out of the car. You'll also appreciate being able to use "Wait" to ask your dog to pause if he is wandering too far ahead of you when you on an off-leash outing. Or about to follow the wrong person out the gate at the dog park.

"Stay" Is Different

I teach my dogs the formal "Stay" behavior for those instances when I absolutely need them to remain frozen in their places. For example, when I walk down my driveway in the morning to get the newspaper, my dogs accompany me, but only to a point 20 feet from the end of the drive. I don't want them to go near the main road, so I tell them "Down," and then "Stay." For their own safety, they must remain where they are, not follow me to the road.

Other useful applications include putting your dog on a Down-Stay when the

Blue's owner chooses a quiet location for teaching her dog to "Stay." Blue is easily distracted, so her owner works at a close range and SLOWLY builds the duration of the "Stay."

neighbor boy rides by on his skateboard, or when a delivery person comes to the door.

I should mention that "Stay" is a much more challenging exercise than "Wait." It takes more focus and concentration for both you *and* your dog. You have a greater responsibility when you ask your dog to stay; once you give him the stay cue, you can't forget and go off to start dinner or work on the car.

Consider This

Until the advent of positive dog training, "Stay" was taught by punishing the dog, sometimes severely, for moving out of position. While many dogs did learn reliable stays by this method, they also often learned to associate the return of their owners with fear and pain.

Before you begin teaching your dog a positive stay, it's important to recognize that "Stay" has three elements – duration, distraction and distance. Duration is the length of time the dog remains in place, distraction is the reliability of the dog's stay in the presence of distractions, and distance is the distance you can move away from your dog. *It is critically important to work on the length of time first, then distractions, before you work on distance.* If your dog won't do a reliable stay, with distractions, when you are standing in front of him, it is wholly unreasonable to expect him to do it when you are across the room.

The most common mistake people make in teaching "Stay" is advancing too quickly. If you ask your dog for too much, he's likely to make a mistake, and you may be sorely tempted to correct him for "breaking" the stay. Remember: you want him to *succeed* so you can reward him for doing the right thing. You can use negative punishment here if necessary (dog's behavior makes a good thing go away), but it's more effective to create positive opportunities to Click! and treat.

Positive Stays

Start by asking your dog to "Sit." Tell him he's a good dog, then hold up a treat. After one second, feed him the treat (calmly, so he doesn't jump up), then use a release word (see below) and encourage him to get up. (I'll talk about release words in just a moment.) You can praise him for getting up, but don't Click! the release, since it's the stay behavior that you want to reinforce and reward. When he will stay for several seconds at a time you can add the verbal stay cue in a pleasant tone of voice *while he is staying*. Owners tend to want to say "Stay" harshly, as an order. Remember that you aren't trying to intimidate your dog into staying; you are using the word as a cue for a behavior.

Note: There is an art to positioning the treat for the "Stay." You need to either hold it directly under Buster's nose so he can nibble on it – essentially luring the stay – or far enough away that he realizes it's not worth trying to lunge for it. If you hold it in the "danger zone" – usually about 6" – 24" inches in front of his nose – he will probably get up to eat it, either because he thinks you are trying to lure him into a stand, or because the treat is close enough that the temptation is too great.

Cue For Release

The release word is a cue that means "get up now, the stay is over." Lots of people use the word "Okay," and the only problem is that it's a word used frequently in conversation. I *do* use "Okay" as my release word, and this means I have to be careful. If my dogs are on a down-stay at the beach and I turn to my husband and say, "Okay, let's eat our picnic lunch now," whoops... there go our dogs!!!

I have heard a variety of other release words used, including "All Done," "You're Free," "Break Time," "Get Up," "Release," "Free Dog," "At Ease." You can use just about any word or phrase you want; your words mean nothing to your dog until you give them meaning.

Gradually Increase The Difficulty

When your dog is staying for one second in the Sit-Stay, extend the time to 2 seconds. Then increase the stay to 4, then 7 seconds. Then 10. Vary the longer stays with shorter ones so your dog can't guess how long you will ask him to stay each time. If you're not good at estimating time by counting in your head, you can use a stopwatch or have someone else count for you. Don't use a timer – the dog will start releasing himself when he hears the "Ding!"

As the stays get longer you can Click! and reward *during* the stay, then remind him not to move, with another verbal "Stay" cue, since your dog may think the Click! ends the stay. Reward with treats several times during the stay, then release him *before* he decides to get up on his own. *Remember, you want him to succeed.*

If your dog *does* get up before you release him, whisk the treat behind your

The key to teaching "Stay" to a young, distractible, high-energy dog like this is to progress VERY slowly, with LOTS of reinforcement (VERY yummy treats and praise). If your dog makes lots of mistakes on the "Stay" you are asking for too much, too soon.

back. This is the negative punishment part. Your dog's behavior – getting up – makes the good thing – the treat – go away. When he sits again, the treat comes back out and he gets it after he stays again, for at least a second at first, then longer as he gets better at stay. This is the positive reinforcement part: his behavior – sitting and staying – makes a good thing – the treat – happen.

As the stays get longer you can also start "fading" the treat so you don't have to hold it in front of his nose to get him to stay. Over a series of stay repetitions, gradually relax your arm until the treat-hand is at your side. During this process you can still whisk it away if he gets up. As he gets more confident about the stay, you can start asking for the behavior without a treat in your hand at all. Click! when he stays for you, and get the treat out of your pocket or off a table or shelf. He will soon stay without the visible treat as the incentive.

The process for Down-Stay is exactly the same, except your dog is in the down position instead of the sit position.

Adding Distractions

When your dog will stay for 10-20 seconds you are ready to add small distractions. Ask him to "Stay" and take one small step to the side, then step in front of him again. Click! reward, and release. Do another "Stay" and take a hop on one foot. Click! reward and release. Gradually build the distractions until your dog will stay as you hop up and down without stopping, do jumping jacks, clap your hands, sit or lie down on the ground in front of him, spin in circles, bounce a ball, have someone go by on a skateboard – or whatever other creative distractions you can invent.

If Blue gets distracted, her owner should decrease the distance and the duration of the "Stay" in order to help him stay focused. If he remains in place, she can increase the distance again.

Gradually is the key here. You want your dog to succeed. If you go directly from one hop to the skateboard you're probably going to lose him. Gradually is also subjective, depending on your dog. Bailey the Bloodhound may progress to a 20-second stay in the first session, while excellence for Chili Pepper the Chihuahua may be three seconds. Some dogs will achieve a solid stay at a distance, with distractions, within a few weeks; others will take longer.

Adding Distance

When your dog is doing 20 to 30-second stays *with distractions* you are ready to

start working on distance. Now you must lower your expectations for the other two elements: shorten the time and remove the distractions.

Ask your dog to "Stay" and take one step away. Click! return, reward, and release. Gradually increase the distance, remembering that you want to add distance slowly so your dog will succeed. It is important to *always return to your dog to reward and release him.* You want the stay to be rock solid. If you start calling your dog to you from the stay, he may start breaking the stay in anticipation of the joy of running to you – and the reward that ends the stay. If he thinks the stay is *never* over until you return to him, the behavior will become solid as granite. Only in higher training levels do you *occasionally* call him from a stay. Even then, you will want to return and release 10 times for every one time you call him to you.

Final Step - Combine The Elements

When your dog will stay at a distance, you can combine all of the elements. Again, lower the bar, by adding distractions when you are one step, then three steps, and then five steps away from your dog, always returning to him to reward and release.

At this point you can even start leaving the room while he is on a stay, *briefly* at first. Take one step out of the room, step back in, return, reward and release. Gradually increase the length of time you stay out of sight. You can set up a mirror in the doorway if you want to keep an eye on your dog, always remembering that you want to return *before* he moves out of his stay position. You want him to succeed. If he makes several mistakes in a row and you return each time to try the stay again he is learning that the "mistake" of breaking the stay makes you return to the room. Any time he starts making mistakes, return to an easier version of the exercise and get several successes in a row before you raise the bar again.

Whether your goal is to get your dog to park himself on a down-stay while you walk the final 20 feet to the end of the drive to fetch your newspaper, or you have visions of you and Buster earning a perfect 200 score together in the Obedience ring, you can get there with a positive stay – no harsh words, no collar corrections, and no damage to the relationship of trust and respect that you and your dog both value so highly.

CHAPTER 15 ♥
Whether to Tether

I have long been a vigorous and vocal opponent of keeping dogs tied or chained as a primary means of confinement. The hazards of tying a dog are well documented, and include increased aggression, vulnerability to human and non-human intruders, and the risk of hanging or choking.

Supervise your dog and make him comfortable when you tether him.

It may come as a surprise, therefore, to know that I regard the tether as an invaluable piece of training equipment. The difference – and it's a big one – is in the application.

Used as a training tool, the tether is a short (about four feet in length) plastic-coated cable, with snaps at both ends. Its purpose is to temporarily restrain a dog for relatively short periods of time *in your presence*, to allow you to accomplish any one of a number of training and behavior modification goals. It is not used as punishment, or to restrain a dog for long periods in your absence.

Among other things, the tether can be used to implement a time-out to settle unruly behavior, to teach your dog to sit politely to greet people, as an aid in a puppy supervision and housetraining program, and to help your dog learn long-distance downs. There are several different ways to set up your tether, depending on the circumstances. Let's look at how you might use the tether in each of the above situations.

Starting Your Dog on the Tether

You want your dog's time on the tether to be a pleasant experience. Before you actually use it the first time for training purposes, take the time to teach him that it is a *good* place to be, so he doesn't panic when you try to use it.

Start by attaching him to the tether and staying with him. Click! or say "Yes"! and feed him treats, several times. Ask him to sit – if he knows that cue – and Click! and treat him some more. Then take a step back, Click! and return to give him a treat.

Gradually vary the distance and length of time between each set of clicks and treats, until he is calm and comfortable on the tether even if you are across the room. If he seems worried about being on the tether, keep your session brief and try to do several short sessions a day until he accepts the restraint.

Release him from the tether when he is most calm, not when he is fretting. If the tether doesn't worry him, one or two practice sessions should be all you need to start using it in training.

Time-Out on a Tether

Rowdy, your adolescent Lab, is out of control. He's not supposed to get on the furniture, but every time you sit on the sofa he tries to jump in your lap. If you push him off your lap he just comes back for more; in fact he thinks it's a great game. Rowdy needs to learn about "Time-Out."

A time-out is not intended to be a harsh punishment. It is simply an opportunity for Rowdy to calm down, and to learn that his rambunctious behavior makes his house-freedom privileges go away for a while. Believe it or not, with the use of a tether, he *can* learn to control his own behavior in order to maintain his freedom.

Install a tether in the room of the house where you spend the most time – or have several, one in each of your high-use areas. Put a rug or soft dog bed at each tether, so Rowdy will be comfortable. Have a few of his favorite toys handy to give him when you put him on a time out.

Now just sit down on the sofa, and wait. When Rowdy jumps into your lap, say "Oops, Time-Out" in a cheerful tone of voice. Then take hold of his collar and gently lead him to the tether. Be pleasant – no scolding or yelling. Hook the tether to his collar, put his toys on the rug, and walk away. If he fusses, ignore him.

When he settles and is lying calmly on his rug, you can Click! your clicker or say "Yes!" and either toss him a treat or walk over and give him one. After a few Clicks! and treats for calm behavior, release him from the tether and sit on the sofa again. If he jumps in your lap, do another "Oops, Time Out!" and pleasantly put him back on his tether.

The number of repetitions required to get the message across to Rowdy will vary, depending on you and your dog. If he has a long history of reinforcement for jumping on your lap – that is, if he has been lap dancing with you for years – it will take longer to change his behavior than if he's only been doing it for a few days, weeks or months.

Also, if you or other members of your family are not consistent about putting him on a time-out for every lap-jump, the behavior will persist much longer than if everyone reacts in the same way.

Dogs learn through repetition, so if he continues to jump on you after you release him from the tether, just "Oops, Time-Out" him again, put him back on the tether, and consider it a golden opportunity to do lots of training repetitions.

Putting a dog in the back yard when he misbehaves is not as effective as using a tether, because most owners forget to let the dog back inside when he's behaving himself. It is important to reward the behavior you want (being calm), not just manage the behavior you don't want by exiling him from the pack.

Polite Greetings

Jumping up on people is a natural behavior for dogs. It's also a very annoying one. Your dog just wants to greet you and have you greet him back. He quickly learns that people invariably pay attention to him when he jumps up, so he keeps doing it. Remember, dogs do what works.

You can use the tether to teach Rowdy that people only pay attention to him when he sits. If he learns that jumping up doesn't work, he'll stop doing it.

Start by practicing with family members. Put Rowdy on the tether and take several steps back. Now walk toward him. If he jumps up, stop out of his reach and wait for him to sit. If you have been clicker training him, this should happen fairly quickly.

When he sits, move forward again. If he jumps up, stop, and wait for him to sit. Continue until you are standing in front of him and he is sitting in front of you. Click! and feed him a treat. Now do it again, until you can walk right up to him without having him jump up. If he jumps up to get the treat, whisk it away behind your back, wait for him to sit, and offer it again. Several disappearing treats should convince him to sit patiently until you get it to his mouth.

As soon as Rowdy will sit for your approach, add other people to the game – family members, friends, and anyone else you can convince to participate. Set up a tether near your front door for a handy place to attach him when you greet visitors. This will teach him to greet people calmly at the door as well.

You can make use of your leash for the same purpose as the tether when you are walking your dog in public. When anyone wants to pet him, tell them Rowdy is in training and you need their help. Explain that they can pet Rowdy and feed him a treat as soon as he sits. This way, Rowdy will learn that the "Sit" game works for *all* humans, not just the ones in his pack or his den.

Puppy Supervision

The biggest mistake most new puppy owners make is giving baby Rowdy too much freedom, too soon. They spend much of their day two steps behind their darling little dynamo, cleaning up the destruction and doggie-doo. Rowdy gets to practice all kinds of rewarding inappropriate behaviors, such as house soiling, raiding garbage cans, counter-surfing, chewing human possessions, and playing a wonderful game of keep-away when humans tried to get their possessions back.

This is the time in Rowdy's life when it is *most* important to practice behavior management. Along with a crate and a puppy-pen, a wisely used tether can take much of the pain out of puppyhood.

The portable "under-the-door" tether is perfect for this application, because you can take it with you into any room, not just those that are set up for wall tethers. Since puppy teeth tend to find furniture particularly inviting, attaching the tether to the piano or coffee table leg isn't a great idea either. You can slip the portable tether under a door while attached to a 2"x 4"block of wood. Then close it and keep Rowdy nearby instead of worrying about whether he's peeing on or chewing up the Oriental rug.

Long Distance Training

Tethers are not just for basic good manners training. Once Rowdy has learned house manners, you can also use your tether to teach him to respond to your cues from a distance.

In basic training you probably taught Rowdy to sit and lie down right next to your side, or directly in front, facing you. Rowdy now thinks that "Down" means "lie down next to my human." If he's on the other side of the room and you ask him to lie down, he comes to you and *then* drops to the ground. Darn. You wanted him to lie down on his rug on the *other* side of the room. How hard is *that* for Rowdy to figure out?! Remember that your dog is only doing what he thinks he's *supposed* to do. Don't get mad, get training. Using a tether, it's simple to show Rowdy that "Down" means "down wherever you are."

First, you need a good response from Rowdy to a verbal "Down" cue. If you don't have it yet, go back to his basic training. You want him to lie down for you on just the word, without having to point toward the ground or lure him down. When he will do that, attach him to the tether, face him, and ask him to "Down." Click! and reward. Then invite him back to a sit and take a step back. Ask him to "Down" again. If he steps toward you, let the tether restrain him, and just wait. If he doesn't Down after several seconds, lure him down. Click! and reward. Stay in that same spot until he will down on the verbal cue from one step away. Now take another step back and try it again. Lure if necessary, Click! and reward when he does it. Continue to repeat the exercise at each new distance until he responds to your verbal cue.

Then take another step away, until he will do a distance down on the tether from across the room or the yard. Then try it off the tether, again starting with a short distance, gradually moving farther and farther away as he understands what you are asking him to do.

Some dogs can do this in one training session, others take several. Remember to keep your sessions short, 5-15 minutes, and to stop training while you and your dog are both enjoying the game. If one or both of you are getting frustrated or bored, stop, do something easy and fun, and take a break.

Working on the Relationship

Properly used, the tether is a great training tool. It can allow Rowdy to be part of the family instead of shut in his crate or exiled to the backyard. It can help ease domestic tensions when some family members are less enthused about his presence than others. Most important, it can teach Rowdy to control his own behavior, without his humans feeling compelled to constantly punish him for his inappropriate actions. This improves the relationship between dog and owner, and *that* makes it an extremely valuable tool indeed.

CHAPTER 16 ❤
Loosen Up! Teach Your Dog to Heel

My husband and I acquired two temporary canine foundlings recently. Julie is a five-month-old purebred Akita puppy that we rescued from our local shelter, where her cage card identified her as a Shepherd/Husky mix. Her prospects for adoption were dismal, given that the shelter euthanizes 85-90% of incoming animals.

Our second castaway, Princess, is a three-year-old Beagle mix. Paul and I were driving down a busy highway when we spotted her, hunched in the middle of the road, defecating while cars swerved around her on both sides. Princess was wearing a collar and tag, but her owners had moved, and she ended up staying at our house for several days while we tracked down their new telephone number and location.

While Princess was with us, I took her out on several occasions, cruising the neighborhood where she was found, to look for her home and to tack up "Found Dog" signs. Each time we went for a walk I was amazed by the determination with which this little 30-pound dog could pull on a leash. I work with dogs who pull all the time in my dog training business, and believe me, Princess is an Olympic-class puller.

In contrast, Julie (the shelter rescue) heels beautifully. From the moment I took her out of the shelter on a leash, she has shown no desire to pull. Her natural inclination is to stay close to me when we walk, and it was a simple matter, in one short week, to teach her to heel nicely by my side and sit every time I halt, whether she's on or off leash.

The stark contrast between the walking styles of these two wayward woofers prompted me to ponder the whys and wherefores of leash-pulling behavior.

The Gene Pull

Dogs pull on their leashes for lots of reasons. Some leash pulling is attributable, at least in part, to genetics. Scent Hounds, the category into which Beagles fall, and from which at least some of Princess's ancestors claim heritage tend toward pulling. They are bred to put their noses to the ground and go, ignoring the discomfort of brambles, briars, icy creeks or the minor bother of a leash. Indeed, I once had a Bloodhound, Otis, who was an invaluable hiking companion in California's rugged coastal hills. When I felt my strength waning, I could put a hand on his collar and let him pull me up the steep paths. The Arctic breeds – Huskies, Malamutes, Samoyeds and the like – were bred to haul sleds and are also natural candidates for pulling.

It's a pain and a strain for dog and handler alike when the dog pulls hard on the leash.

Akitas, on the other hand, were Japanese hunting and guarding dogs. They tend to be dignified and docile, albeit protective. Hence, Julie's genes make her less likely to pull.

Genes aren't the whole story, however. Genetics are responsible only for our dogs' *predisposition* toward certain behaviors. The way we interact with them can influence them toward, or away from, their preprogrammed tendencies, at least to some degree. I personally know Malamutes and Samoyeds who heel beautifully, and I've seen Akitas flying their owners behind them like kites.

Like most behaviors, it's easiest to teach our dogs good leash manners if we start with blank slates – young puppies who have not yet learned to pull. All of the

basic principles we use in positive dog training apply to the leash challenge. Let's do a quick review of some of the key ones that apply to pulling:

- Dogs repeat behaviors that are rewarding to them. Behaviors that are consistently rewarded increase in frequency therefore you may be inadvertently rewarding your dog for pulling.

- Behaviors that are not rewarded will diminish and eventually extinguish, thus the key is to not reward your dog for pulling.

- It's easier and more effective to manage or prevent behaviors you don't want than it is to correct them after they have become established. This is why it's easier to start with puppies, before they have already learned undesirable behaviors like pulling.

The Taffy Pull

Most dogs who pull do so, whatever their genetics, because we humans are relatively slow and boring. Dogs want to explore their environment, and they want to do it a lot faster than we can move. Think about it. If you take your dog for a hike off-leash, does he trudge along next to you, or does he range ahead, run circles around you, dash up hills and down vales, leaving you to eat his dust? Chances are good that unless he's in his twilight years or physically impaired he's still doing donuts around you even when you're dragging your tired body back to the car at the tail end of the hike.

He also finds the environment to be infinitely rewarding. All the while he's charging about, he's being rewarded with great smells to sniff, deer poop to roll in and eat, squirrels to chase, ball and sticks to fetch, other dogs to romp with, ponds to swim in and puddles to splash in. We can only imagine all the spectacular sensory stimuli that thrill our dog during a good romp. It's no wonder that a sedate walk on leash around the block is dull for him!

Dogs pull because we let them pull. More accurately, we *teach* them to pull. When Jane Q. Dog Owner brings eight-week-old Taffy home, she puts on the collar and six-foot leash and takes her out for her very-first-ever walk. A neighbor stops to admire the pup, and stands chatting with Jane for a few minutes. Taffy gets bored, and spots a beetle ten feet away that catches her interest. She wanders to the end of the leash and leans into her collar. Jane eventually notices the pressure, and, still talking to her neighbor, moves in the direction of the Taffy pull. Taffy gets to play with her beetle, and files away a critically important bit of information in her puppy brain: "Pulling gets you where you want to go." She'll test this hypothesis several times, and each time it works – when she pulls on the leash

to investigate something, Jane follows. Taffy is soon convinced that pulling on leash is very rewarding – it gets you what you want!

To make things worse, Jane subconsciously develops a comfort level with a tight lead. Tension on the leash lets her know where Taffy is. So even on those occasions when she is *not* pulling, Jane lifts her arm or pulls it back to keep tension in the leash. Taffy eventually accepts that a tight leash is the norm. Not a good foundation for polite leash walking!

Pulling Your Own Weight

Whenever you and your dog are together, one of you is training the other. The ideal arrangement is that you are the trainer and Taffy is the trainee, at least the majority of the time. From Day One, you need to make sure that Taffy gets rewarded for desirable behaviors, and that you prevent her from being rewarded by undesirable ones.

In terms of leash-walking, this means that you need to make yourself infinitely more rewarding than the environment, at least at first, in order to program "loose-leash walking is the norm" into Taffy's puppy brain. You need to make a conscious effort to reward her for staying near you (loose leash) and not let her be rewarded when she goes too far away (tight leash). At the same time you have to avoid falling into the common trap of taking up the slack in order to keep tabs on Taffy. That's what eyeballs are for.

Let's take another look at our friend Jane Q. to see how she can accomplish this.

Jane brings Taffy home, puts on her collar and six-foot leash, and takes her out for her very-first-ever walk. In her pocket she has a large supply of tasty treats and a clicker. She heads out the back door to

Walking down the sidewalk, Taffy smells something irresistible and dives towards it.

Taffy is quite strong and quite sure she can out-wait her owner. She continues to focus on her goal, leaning hard.

practice in the back yard where she won't be distracted by neighbors. As soon as she and Taffy reach the patio, she stops and clicks the clicker in her pocket. The sharp sound catches Taffy's ear and she looks up at her, curious. She feeds her an irresistible treat. "Great game!!" Taffy thinks, and keeps her eyes glued to Jane. She clicks and treats again, several times in a row.

Given this interaction, Taffy has no interest in the surrounding environment. She's enchanted by this living, breathing, treat machine and the funny noise that signals to her that another treat is about to magically appear. She sits so she can watch the woman's face more easily, and the Click! happens again. Cool! She stands up to eat the treat, then sits again to watch Jane. Click!

A light bulb goes off in Taffy's head. "Hey!" she thinks. "Every time I put my bottom on the ground, the Click! happens and a treat appears. This 'bottom-on-the

Taffy's reward for releasing the tension on the leash is a bit of kibble.

As they continue on with their walk, Jane pays attention to Taffy. When Taffy looks her way, Jane marks the behavior with an emphatic "Yes!" and a treat.

ground' thing is a great gig!"

Now Jane starts to walk forward, making sure to keep her hand down by her side and a loose leash. Taffy, eager to keep the treat machine in sight, hustles to keep up with her. Jane clicks the clicker and feeds her a treat. She takes another step, and Taffy is right there with her. Click! and treat.

"Hey!" thinks Taffy. "There's more than one way to get a Click! I'm stickin' close to this gal!"

Just then a leaf falls from a nearby tree, catching Taffy's attention. The pup's ears perk up, and she bounces toward the leaf. The leash tightens, and stops her forward progress. Taffy strains toward the leaf – she really wants it! Jane doesn't budge. Finally, frustrated, Taffy backs up a step and sits. Click! Jane lets her know that a loose leash earns a reward. Taffy spins on

her tail at the beloved sound and bounces back to Jane for the tidbit.

Taffy derives no value from pulling so she decides that walking close to her owner is more rewarding.

As soon as the pup eats the treat Jane moves forward quickly so Taffy can reach the leaf without tightening the leash. She sniffs it briefly, decides it isn't all that wonderful after all, and looks back up at Jane. She then clicks and treats her for turning her attention back to her, then walks forward again, clicking and treating – every one to three steps – to teach Taffy that staying near her with the leash loose is a *very* rewarding behavior.

If the puppy starts to move out in front, Jane sometimes turns around and goes the other direction. Now she's behind Taffy again, and she has lots more opportunities to Click! her for keeping the leash loose. She also talks to her in a happy voice, not a commanding one, so that staying near her is fun. If Taffy does reach the end of the leash and starts to pull, she stops again, waits for Taffy to put slack in the lead, clicks, treats, and starts forward once more.

After five minutes of this Jane stops, unhooks Taffy's leash, and spends another ten minutes playing "chase the squeaky" with her. Every once in a while she walks a few steps, and if Taffy walks next to her, clicks the clicker and feeds her a treat. Taffy starts to realize that it's rewarding to be near Jane when she is free as well as when she is on leash. When she takes a time-out from play to pee in the corner, Jane clicks and rewards her for that as well.

"Wow," Taffy thinks. "There are *lots* of things I can do to make that wonderful Click! sound happen and treats appear – this is very cool!!!!"

Later that day, Jane decides to try Taffy on the front sidewalk, since she did so well in the back yard. As she works with her, the neighbor comes out to chat. Jane stops to talk, but keeps an eye on Taffy at the same time. As long as Taffy is sitting or standing quietly near her, she gives an occasional Click! and treat. She hands the neighbor a couple of treats, and tells her that when Taffy sits she can feed the pup a goodie and pet her. Taffy has no desire to leave. After a short conversation, Jane politely excuses herself from the neighbor so she can return her full attention to Taffy's training session.

Jane has already laid the beginnings for a very solid foundation for Taffy to grow into a well-mannered and well-educated canine companion. If she keeps it up, she will never learn to pull on her leash.

Pulling Your Leg

The same method that Jane Q. used for Taffy also works on adult dogs, but you can expect to take more time and make more of an effort to convince the adult dog that pulling isn't going to pay off any more. The longer a dog like our foundling Beagle, Princess, has been reinforced for pulling, the greater the challenge to persuade her to stop. It can sometimes seem like pulling hen's teeth – difficult to do and not very productive.

It can be done, however, with the right preparation. You may need to find an arsenal of irresistible treats to compete with the known rewards of Princess' environment. Freeze-dried liver, chicken, turkey franks, steak and roast beef generally rank high for most dogs. You will also need to start working with her in a very low-distraction environment, and graduate to the front sidewalk only after Princess seems to be getting the hang of it. You may also need the help of one of the many no-pull products on the market.

There is a long list of products that single-handedly promise to teach your dog not to pull. They're pulling your leg a little with that promise, and if you believe them, I know of a lovely bridge for sale! In truth, no-pull products *can* help you *control* your dog while you reprogram her to offer a more civilized walking style. Head halters (see Chapter 36), stretchy leashes, beepers and no-pull harnesses can all offer you a greater degree of immediate control. Unfortunately, they can also become a crutch. Your dog may walk nicely while wearing the special equipment, but pull with just as much determination as ever when you take off the halter or harness. This doesn't mean that your no-pull equipment of choice is worthless. It *can* help you teach Princess to walk politely on leash – as long as you combine it with a positive reinforcement training program to teach her to walk nicely, with or without the crutch. Princess needs to decide that it is more rewarding to walk with you than to pull. Combine your favorite gentle control tool with clicks and treats, be consistent about *never* rewarding her for pulling by allowing her to get where she wants to go, and your Pulling Princess will, in time, be content to prance by your side instead of trying to drag you down the drive.

Our Princess didn't learn to stop pulling during the short three days she was with us. She returned home to her family, people who love her and don't care if she pulls. She will be an Olympic-class puller for the rest of her life. Julie, the rescued Akita puppy, will be with us for a few more weeks, recovering from kennel cough and spay surgery before we place her in a new, carefully-screened home with an owner who will continue to reinforce her good leash behavior. If you'd rather have a Gentle Julie than a Pulling Princess, get out your clicker and treats, and start your leash training program – the sooner the better.

❤ A WORD ABOUT RETRACTABLES

Retractable leashes are leashes that extend up to a distance of 15-30 feet when the dog pulls away from the handler, and then retract into the plastic handle when the dog returns. They are very popular with dog owners, who see them as a way to provide their canine pals with more exercise and a wider territory in which to range, while still complying with leash laws and preventing Ranger from ranging too far.

However, most training classes and many leash laws specify a maximum six-foot leash length for good reason. There are a number of drawbacks to what appears, on the surface, to be a very cool tool:

- A dog who is regularly walked on a retractable leash may have difficulty learning to walk politely with his owner. He learns that pulling on the leash allows him to keep going farther away which is the exact opposite of what we want him to learn. In order to teach polite leash walking, we need to convince that him pulling gets him **nowhere!**

- Unlike a too-long but regular-width leash, a retractable leash is difficult to shorten when the dog is pulling against it. When the leash is under tension it won't retract, leaving you with too much leash and no way to shorten it quickly in an emergency.

- Retractable leads can be a risk to human safety. The farther away from you Ranger is allowed to range, the less control you have of him. Your dog may be 25 feet in front of you, and suddenly spy a fragile senior citizen 20 feet to the side. Before you have a chance to reel him in, he's knocked the woman over and broken her hip. Not good! Also, there have been reports of dog owners losing fingers when the narrow nylon line got wrapped around a digit just before their large dog dashed off, severing the trapped finger.

- Retractable leads can be a risk to animal safety. Unless you are paying **perfect** attention and are **very** skilled at clicking the button to stop the leash from pulling out, the retractable leash gives Ranger the ability to dart in front of a moving car, get tangled around another dog's leash, or charge hot on the heels of a wayward cat. He can work up a pretty good head of steam in 20 to 30 feet, and even if he doesn't catch the cat, he's going to get a pretty good jolt when he does finally hit the end of the leash. A jolt that hard can cause damage to Ranger's trachea, even if he's wearing a flat buckle collar.

- The buttons that stop these leashes from playing out to their maximum length sometimes jam or "pop" out of the locked position, especially when a dog makes a quick bolt. With a strong, unpredictable dog, they simply cannot be relied upon to provide secure restraint 100 percent of the time.

- These leashes are not appropriate for walking on sidewalks, where Ranger should rightfully be restricted to no more than a six-foot radius around you (and often times even less). Other pedestrians have the right to walk without dogs getting in their way and wrapping around their legs. And Ranger should **not** have the freedom to use front yards as toilets, even if he **is** on leash.

I'm not saying don't ever use retractable leashes. Just use them **after** your dog is fully trained not to pull on his leash, and after you have good enough voice control to stop Ranger in mid-charge if he spontaneously charges after something – or someone. Then, by all means, snap the retractable leash on him to give him a little more freedom on the beach or in the park where a little more freedom is appropriate. Other than that, be a responsible dog owner and use a leash that really does what leashes are supposed to do: prevent Ranger from ranging.

CHAPTER 17 ❤
The Retrieve: Does Your Dog Get It?

Who has not watched in awe as a Border Collie at the local park sails through the air, snatches the Frisbee™ in mid-flight and dashes back to her owner, dropping the disc and waiting in eager anticipation for the next throw? Playing fetch with your dog is fun. It's also a great way to strengthen the dog/human bond, satisfy your dog's prey/chase instincts, and provide enough exercise to work off that excess energy that can make him a challenge to live with. A formal retrieve is also required for upper levels of obedience competition, and is an important skill for service dogs.

Some dogs are natural retrievers. Teaching them to fetch is a matter of

Fetching provides great exercise for dogs, but the game gets tedious if the dog doesn't know how to "play" properly.

directing the behavior into the right channels. Other dogs are not, and while teaching them to retrieve may look like an insurmountable challenge, it's not as difficult as it seems. There are limitations, of course. Your 150-pound Newfoundland may never sail through the air like a Border Collie, but he can certainly learn how to fetch.

The Old Way

At one time in the not too distant past, the dog training world almost universally agreed that dogs had to be taught a "forced retrieve." If you wanted a reliable retrieve, dogs had to know that they would be punished if they refused to pick up the designated object and bring it back. Years ago, my terrier mix, Josie, was the unfortunate victim of this training philosophy.

Against my better judgment but convinced that my trainer knew best, I taught Josie to retrieve using the traditional coercive "ear pinch." We were preparing for the Open Class obedience ring exercises, Retrieve On The Flat and Retrieve Over High Jump. My instructor was a top ranked, nationally known obedience trainer and competitor. I admired and respected her. I was just a lowly dog owner – what did I know?

Ignoring my uneasiness, I dutifully folded Josie's ear flap over the choke chain, said "Take It!" and pinched. When she opened her mouth to yelp in protest, I popped the dumbbell into her mouth. Voila! She was learning to retrieve.

It worked. We flew through the Open Class with ease and earned our CDX (Companion Dog Excellent) title in three shows, with a high score of 197.5 out of a possible 200 points.

Meanwhile, we started training for Utility, where we would have to do the Scent Discrimination exercise. In Scent Discrimination, the dog doesn't just retrieve a dumb bell; he must distinguish the one that has his owner's scent on it from several lying together on the ground, and retrieve only that one. The exercise is done twice, once with leather articles, once with metal. The leather dumbbells were no problem for Josie, but she hated the metal ones.

Lots of dogs don't like to hold metal in their mouths. Teeth scraping on metal must give them a "fingernails-on-the-blackboard" sensation. There are tricks that trainers use, such as spraying the dumbbell with a clear plastic coating. We tried all the tricks. Josie still wasn't buying.

"Pinch harder," my trainer encouraged. "You have to *make* her do it."

Josie and I practiced hard. The Directed Jumping and Directed Retrieve were easy for her. The Signal Exercise was a snap. But when I brought out the Scent Discrimination articles the light faded from her eyes and she gave me pleading looks, begging me not to make her do them. I persisted – until one day when I brought out the articles and Josie hid under the deck and wouldn't come out.

Finally, I realized how wrong the ear pinch was. I put away the articles and never brought them out again. If training meant destroying the relationship I had built with my dog then I was no longer interested.

Negative Reinforcement

Many trainers still subscribe to coercive methods for teaching the retrieve. The ear pinch is a widely used, force-based method of training that utilizes a concept known as "negative reinforcement."

Remember that negative reinforcement means that the dog's behavior makes a bad thing go away. That is, you start by applying the bad thing so the dog can do the "right" behavior to make it stop. In the case of the ear pinch, you pinch the ear (bad thing), the dog takes the dumbbell, and the ear pinch goes away. The dog learns that if he retrieves, he can stop the pain. He chooses to retrieve. As with many force-based training methods, it works with a lot of dogs, a lot of the time. It worked with Josie until we encountered the metal scent articles.

Unfortunately, there is a very real potential for negative side effects when we use physical force to train; side-effects that can permanently damage the relationship. The dog learns to associate your hands with pain. He may lose his enthusiasm for training. Worse, he may lose his trust in you. Although traditional trainers like to believe that a forced retrieve teaches the dog that he *has* to fetch even if he doesn't want to, in reality the dog can always choose not to retrieve and risk the consequences, like Josie did when she hid under the deck. The dog always has a choice.

The ear pinch is not the only coercive method used to train the retrieve. Blanche Saunders (now deceased), a highly respected obedience trainer in the 1950's and 60's, taught a forced retrieve in her book, *The Complete Book of Dog Obedience* (now out of print). Her method of teaching the dog to hold the dumbbell is inarguably harsh:

"Every time your dog drops the article, hold him tight while you cuff him across the nose. Say 'Phooey!' in a displeased tone of voice... Each time he drops it, the correction becomes more severe."

I'm happy to say I never cuffed Josie across the nose.

Positive Reinforcement: A New Approach To The Retrieve

Whether you just want your dog to bring back the tennis ball you throw for him in the back yard or you have your eye on advanced obedience titles and Frisbee championships, there is a more effective way to train your dog to fetch, using the concept of positive reinforcement in which the dog's behavior makes a *good* thing happen. As discussed in earlier chapters, with positive reinforcement training, you get the dog to offer the behavior you want *without* using force, and then reward him for it. All living beings repeat behaviors that they find rewarding.

The retrieve is a complex behavior. Not all dogs are natural retrievers who pick things up easily and willingly; some have to be encouraged to take things in their mouths. Even natural retrievers may learn behaviors like "keep-away," that interfere with a good game of fetch. How much effort you need to put into training the retrieve depends on your dog's natural inclinations as well as your training goals. A formal obedience ring retrieve is considerably more complex than simply asking your Lab to drop his tennis ball at your feet so you can throw it again.

Breaking Tasks Into Steps

Whenever you want to train a complex behavior you need to visualize the final product (in this case the retrieve), and break it down into small steps. For the back yard fetch you want to throw the ball, Frisbee or toy and have your dog run after it, pick it up, bring it to you and give it back. Broken into small steps, it would look like this:

1. Wait politely until I throw the ball.

2. Run after it when I throw it.

3. Pick it up.

4. Hold it in your mouth.

5. Bring it back to me.

6. Drop it when you get here.

Let's look at how you would train the simple "back yard fetch". Although we are going to examine the steps of the retrieve in order, *you don't have to train them in order.* Once your dog knows each of the steps you can put them together in the right order to make "Fetch" happen.

Wait For Me To Throw

Dogs who are excited about retrieving are often obsessed with their Frisbee or tennis ball, sometimes to the point of being dangerous. You can lose a finger if Skippy tries to grab the ball from your hand as you get ready to throw. You can use negative punishment to teach Skippy to stop jumping. Although we associate the word "punishment" with harsh corrections, negative punishment is not harsh or physical at all. It simply means, "the dog's behavior makes a good thing go away." Positive trainers frequently use negative punishment because it doesn't involve the use of physical force.

STEP 1: Wait politely for the fetch item to be thrown.

STEP 2: Run after the thrown item

Ask your dog to sit, and hold the ball up to throw. If he leaps for it, whisk it behind your back and wait for him to sit again. Every time he sits, the ball appears. Every time he leaps at you, the ball vanishes.

The first time he stays sitting when you bring out the ball, say "Yes!" and quickly throw it. This will happen much sooner than you think – it often takes less than five minutes. This part is positive reinforcement: Skippy's behavior (sitting) makes a good thing happen (you throw the ball). In this case you don't need a food treat. Skippy gets a "life reward" i.e., he gets to chase the ball, which is even *better* than food! From this moment on, Skippy *never* gets to chase the ball if he jumps up; only if he sits. Once he figures this out, he'll sit his little heart out to try to get you to throw!

Run After It When I Throw

Lots of dogs will chase something that is moving but won't pick it up. That's okay – the pick-up is a separate behavior. Choose a toy that your dog really likes, play with it with your dog until he gets excited, and then toss it a short distance. If he runs after it say "Go!" and when he gets to it Click! or say "Yes!" and feed him a treat. He may even pick it up. If he does, be *sure* to Click! and reward. At first he may only go part way toward it. That's OK too. Just be sure you Click! while he is headed toward it, not after he turns around. Remember, the Click! marks the behavior you want him to repeat. If you Click! too late, you reinforce him for coming back to you, rather than for going toward the toy.

As he gets the idea, you can Click! only for increasingly closer runs to the object. If he does a short run, don't do anything at all. Don't say "No," don't Click! and

don't say "Go!" again. Just wait. When he realizes he's not going to get clicked he may head for the object again. This is a *very* good time to Click! and reward. If he doesn't, calmly try again, tossing it a shorter distance this time. This may be a sign that you have raised the criteria too quickly and you need to take a step back. It is a common training mistake to try to move ahead too quickly. It seems logical that if Skippy will run after the object when you toss it five feet, he will do the same at 10 feet. But he might not. You might need to increase the distance by increments of one foot rather than five feet.

The Pick-Up

This can be either the easiest or the hardest part of a retrieve. A natural retriever will do the pick-up in his sleep. In fact, most puppies naturally pick things up. If you constantly punish your baby dog for puppy pick-ups, you can squelch a budding natural retriever. Instead, if you put away all inappropriate items and consistently reward him with a Click! and a treat for picking up his toys, you will encourage his retrieving tendencies.

If your dog is *not* a natural retriever, don't despair. Designate his favorite toy as his fetch object. He only gets to play with it when you do the fetch game. Now *set* it on the ground. (Don't throw it!) If he picks it up, Click! and reward.

If he only sniffs it, Click! and reward. If he just glances in the object's direction, Click! and reward.

In the beginning, reinforce the dog just for paying attention to the object. In any series of "attention" responses with the fetch toy, sometimes he will sniff or touch it, sometimes he'll just look at it, and sometimes he will put his mouth on it – maybe even pick it up.

Once he understands the game, you can up the ante (this is called "raising the criteria"); you only Click! and treat if he touches it. Later, you only Click! if he actually puts his mouth on it, and finally only if he picks it up. Once he is routinely picking up the toy, add your verbal cue of "Fetch!" or "Take It!" or "Get It," or whatever you plan to use.

If at any time your dog "quits," that is, he stops playing the game, you may have raised the criteria too quickly, or you may have trained for too long. Training sessions should generally be five to 15 minutes in length, several times a day. If you get two or three really good responses in a row, stop the session with lots of praise and a "Jackpot!" – a whole handful of treats. It's always better to stop when you and your dog are having fun and winning, rather than when one or both of you are bored or frustrated.

Hold It

The pick-up is only half the battle. Skippy has to *hold it* in his mouth if he's going to bring it back to you. In any series of pick-ups, sometimes he will hold it longer than others. Once he is picking the toy up easily, gradually raise the criteria by clicking and rewarding for longer and longer holds.

STEP 3 and STEP 4: Pick up the item and hold it in your mouth.

"Gradually" is the key here. Your increments will be in fractions of seconds at first, and it is critically important that you Click! *while the toy is still in your dog's mouth!* If you consistently Click! too late, after he has dropped the toy, you are rewarding him for dropping, not holding.

Bring It Back To Me

Now it gets easier. As soon as Skippy is holding the toy for three to five seconds, back away from him when he is looking at you. (You can try calling him to you, but sometimes saying his name will make him drop the toy.) He should start moving toward you, hopefully with the toy still in his mouth. Click! and reward.

He will probably drop the toy when you Click! but that's OK, as long as the Click! happens while the toy is still in his mouth.

STEP 5: Bring it back to me. In a park full of distractions, you may have to convince your indecisive dog that it is worth returning to you.

Gradually raise the criteria so he comes closer to you before you Click! and in short order he will be bringing it all the way.

Drop It

You can practice this piece of the "Fetch!" any time your dog has something in his mouth. Offer him a treat. When he opens his mouth to take the treat, say "Drop It!" or "Give!" in a happy tone of voice. If you use an angry or intimidating tone he may hold tighter rather than drop. Eventually he will "Drop!" on the verbal cue without the treat. Then you can Click! and treat *after* he drops, and by using random reinforcement, over time you can fade the use of the treat. This is also a useful exercise for teaching him not to be protective or aggressive to you when he is playing with his toys.

If he doesn't want to trade the object for the treat, try dropping one or several treats on the floor, or use a tastier treat. Do this a lot with his own toys. You can then give the toy back (or toss it for him) as a reward also. He will learn that giving you the object keeps the game going. If you only do this with things he is not supposed to have, he will learn that when he drops an object he loses it forever, and he will become less and less willing to give things to you when you ask.

STEP 6: Drop It. This step is often difficult to achieve until the dog has learned to offer to trade the object in exchange for another reward.

You can decide if having Skippy drop the object at your feet is acceptable, or if you want the object placed in your hand. Dropping at your feet is easier. Just let it fall when you offer him the treat. If you think he will try to grab it when you reach for it, keep him occupied nibbling the treat in your hand while you reach down and pick it up. Then let him have the treat. If you want him to place it in your hand, you will need to slip your hand under the object at first so it falls into your hand when he drops it. Later, you can insist he place it in your hand by ignoring it if it falls on the floor, until he picks it up and tries again.

Putting The Pieces Together

Now that Skippy knows all of the pieces, we can put them together. He sits and waits politely until you throw his ball. He runs after it when you throw, picks it up, holds it, brings it back to you and drops it when you ask. His tail is wagging, his eyes are bright, and he is eager for you to throw again. Yes, he has a choice to retrieve or not. He always has a choice. If you've trained well, he's having fun and enjoying the game. What do you think his choice will be?

The dog has learned to drop the fetch item for a treat. Now the game is fun for both parties!

Today, Josie fetches a wide variety of objects with a wagging tail and a happy gleam in her eye. In recent years, when I reintroduced her to the retrieve using positive methods, I realized that she had never really been very happy about retrieving, despite her 197.5 scores. She used to dutifully retrieve the dumbbell under stress, in fear and anticipation of a correction. Now she joyfully chooses to fetch when asked, confident that she won't be punished. We never went back to the metal scent articles; I'm not anxious to resume a show career. But I'm confident that we could, if we wanted to.

> ### ❤ THE OBEDIENCE RING RETRIEVE
>
> The obedience ring retrieve is much more complex than backyard fetching. Broken into steps, it looks like this:
>
> 1. Sit and stay until...
>
> 2. Directed to get the dumbbell.
>
> 3. Go to the dumbbell when directed.
>
> 4. Pick up the dumbbell.
>
> 5. Bring it back without mouthing it.
>
> 6. Return to handler, still holding dumbbell.
>
> 7. Sit in front of handler, close enough to be touched.
>
> 8. Remain sitting and continue to hold dumbbell until told to give it to handler.
>
> 9. Put dumbbell in handler's hands when requested.
>
> 10. Go back to heel position on cue.
>
> I recommend Morgan Spector's book, **Clicker Training for Obedience** for those interested in teaching the obedience ring retrieve.

CHAPTER 18 ❤
Right on Target

Each month, I stand in the middle of my training center during the second session of my newest Level One class and introduce my students to the "Targeting" exercise. "Targeting," I say, "is teaching your dog to touch his nose to a target, on cue." Each month, I am invariably met with a half-dozen blank stares. I can read my students' unanimous thoughts. "Why on earth," they are obviously thinking, "would I want to teach my dog to do *that*?"

Their initial lack of enthusiasm for this exercise is understandable. Targeting is not presented in many dog training books on the market, and only in recent years have modern dog trainers started to include it in their class curriculums. Once they get past their skepticism, however, most of my students are as hooked on targeting as I am. Even my dogs love it!

There are dozens of reasons to teach your dog to target. It's fun and it's easy. It's the perfect exercise for helping you to see the learning "light bulb" go on in your dog's brain. Most dogs love targeting, which makes it a handy tool for getting your dog's attention in a distracting environment, as well as making it a great parlor trick to show off to family and friends.

Targeting is also a wonderfully useful tool for helping timid dogs gain confidence. It is the foundation behavior for teaching your dog a multitude of more complex behaviors, such as ringing a bell on a string at the door to tell you he has to go outside; turning light switches on and off; closing doors; teaching a suspicious dog to come when called; retrieving; learning object discrimination; pausing in the required contact zones in Agility competition; and doing "Go-Outs" – used in advanced levels of obedience competition and in good manners exercises such as "Go To Your Place," where the dog goes and lies down on his bed or rug – to name just a few.

In fact, targeting is one of my all-time favorite exercises. It may be hard to fathom how one exercise can accomplish all of the incredible things listed above, but as I say to my blankly staring students: Trust me. Targeting is fun and useful. You and your dog will love it.

Target Practice

It's ridiculously easy to teach your dog to target. Hold out your open hand at your dog's nose level, palm facing him, fingers pointed toward the ground. When he sniffs or licks your hand, Click! your clicker (or say "Yes!") and give him a treat from your *other* hand. Make sure his nose actually touches your skin – "close" only counts in horseshoes. You must endeavor to Click! the *instant* his nose makes contact with your skin. If you consistently Click! too soon, you will teach him to stop *before* he touches you. If you consistently Click! too late, you will teach him that moving his nose *away* from you is the way to earn a reward.

Targeting – having your dog touch her nose to the object of your choice – is a wonderfully useful tool. Once she learns this technique, you can easily teach her to ring a bell when she has to go outside, turn light switches on and off, close doors, and more.

When you have clicked and rewarded your dog's first touch, remove your target hand, then offer it again, in the same position. When he sniffs, Click! and treat. Do it again. And again. *Notice, we have not used a verbal cue yet.*

Most dogs will do the initial sniff easily. If your dog doesn't sniff your offered palm, rub some hot dog or other tasty, moist treat on your skin to make your hand more enticing. Most dogs will sniff your newly offered hand a few times and then ignore it, looking directly at your treat hand. You can almost hear them think, "Why am I looking at *this* hand? The GOOD STUFF comes from over *there!*" When this happens, hide your treat hand behind your back, offer him the target hand, and wait. He should soon sniff the offered hand. If he doesn't, rub a treat on it and offer it again. If that doesn't do it for him, take a step or two backwards and offer him the target as he moves toward you. Click! and treat for the nose touch.

Repeat this step over and over, until he deliberately bumps your hand with his nose. This is the heart-stopping "Aha!" moment that positive trainers love because you can see that your dog *knows* that the way to make the Click! happen is to touch your hand. Some dogs "get it" very quickly. Louis, a Border Collie client of mine in Santa Cruz, California, got it in a record three repetitions. Others take longer for the light bulb to go on, depending on variables such as the owner's skill and timing, the dog's interest in the training game, the desirability of the treat reward, and the level of distractions in the surrounding environment. You can enhance your dog's learning speed by working in a quiet location, using very delicious treats and paying close attention to your Click! timing.

Most of the behaviors that utilize the "Touch" are somewhat complex to train. Remember to keep your training sessions short, and if either you or your dog are getting frustrated, do something easy and fun to end the session, then take a break and try it again later.

Moving Targets

Once your dog is deliberately bumping your hand with his nose you can add the verbal cue. Start saying "Touch!" *just before* nose touches skin. Click! and reward. Gradually offer the verbal cue earlier and earlier, until he has had the opportunity to associate the verbal cue with the targeting behavior, and is responding to the cue.

Now we raise the bar. So far, your dog understands that he is supposed to touch his nose to your hand when he is sitting in front of you and the target is presented to him, directly in front of him, at nose level. It's time to change the criteria.

You want him to touch the target *wherever* it is, even if it's moving. Back away from him, offer the target and say "Touch." As he gets up to follow you, keep moving slowly backwards. When he catches up to you and touches the moving target, Click! and treat. Move your hand off to one side and ask him to touch it. Click! and treat. Move it to the other side. Move it lower, toward the floor. Move it higher, so he has to jump up to touch it. Put it above a chair seat, so

he has to place his front feet on the chair to reach up and touch it.

When he's really confident about touching the target, put the behavior on a schedule of random reinforcement – ask him to touch two times before you Click! and treat. Then three times. Then once. Then once. Then four times. Then two times. Vary the number of times you ask him to touch before he gets clicked; don't always make it harder and harder or he may get frustrated and give up.

New Targets

If you want your dog's targeting behavior to be really versatile, you now need to teach him to touch other targets. I teach the target stick next. Some trainers start by using the stick as the training target. I prefer starting with the target hand, because most dogs naturally want to sniff our hands, and because some dogs are initially intimidated by a stick in their owner's hands. Plus, you don't need an extra piece of equipment – your target hand is always hand-y.

A target stick can be a small branch off a tree, a dowel from the hardware store, a pencil or Tinkertoy (for small dogs), or an "official" target stick purchased from a pet supply source or a dog training web site. If you are using a homemade stick, wrap a piece of colored tape around one end to designate the actual target. You will accept touches *near* the tape at first, but you ultimately want to shape the touches to the actual target by clicking only those touches that get closer and closer to the tape.

Mark and reward the dog for close approximations of the desired behavior, then gradually "shape" toward your goal.

Sandy rewards Tater for her first several touches, then begins rewarding her only for touches closer toward the tip.

Hold your target stick at a 45-degree angle, with the target end near your dog's nose. Some dogs will sniff the end of the target stick the first time you offer it. Click! and treat. Others may need a bit of hotdog rubbed on the end to motivate them to touch this new object. Still others will be afraid of the stick. If your dog is leery of the stick, hold it so most of it is hidden behind you and only an inch of the tip protrudes from your hand.

Extending Your Reach

When your dog will touch the tip, extend the stick a little at a time, until he is touching it at its full-length. "A little at a time" will vary from one dog to the next. Some dogs will accept a six-inch increase at a time; others will tolerate only half-inch increments. Start small to avoid frightening your dog, and work up to larger increases if he seems to be tolerating them well. As soon as he is readily touching the tip of the stick, at whatever length, start using the verbal "Touch" cue again to elicit the targeting behavior. When he is proficient at touching the target stick, you can use it to extend your reach. With three feet of arm length and three feet of target stick you can get him to touch things a full six feet away from you. If you place the tip of the target stick against a door, wall or other object, you can start teaching him to touch other things, including people.

This is a useful tool for encouraging a timid dog to be brave. When he is very confident about touching his target stick you can place the target closer and closer to a scary object and he will become braver about approaching it.

Useful Tricks

You can also teach your dog to touch other things by holding the intended target object in your hand. I like to teach a dog to ring a bell hanging on a string from a doorknob as a signal that he has to go outside. It's easy – if you take it one step at a time.

First teach him to ring the bell hanging from a string in your hand. Then have him touch the bell when it's hanging on the door, with your hand held near. Gradually withdraw your hand, and then start moving your entire self away from the door until you can send him across the room to ring the bell on your verbal cue.

As soon as he is proficient at ringing the bell on the doorknob, start asking him to ring the bell every time you take him outside. Although we usually use a treat as the reward for the Click! if your dog is thrilled about a trip to the yard, letting him out is an even *better* reward at that moment than a food treat. If you start making the bell a consistent part of his "going out" routine, and keep asking him to ring the bell from greater and greater distances, you should be able to fade (gradually eliminate) the "Ring the Bell" cue, and he will learn to run to the bell and ring it to tell you that he has to go outside.

There is no limit to the ways that you can utilize targeting to accomplish behaviors you like. You can move your dog into heel position (and keep him there) by using your hand as a target next to your leg. You can teach him to close cupboard doors by having him target to a spot on the door. You can teach him to turn lights on and off by pushing up on a stick attached to a light switch or by touching a "Touch Lamp" with his nose.

You can also teach your dog object discrimination by having him learn to identify and touch various objects (or people) by name. The opportunities for application of the touch behavior are virtually endless – limited only by your creativity.

Now, if you'll excuse me, I'm going to go teach my Pomeranian to target-bowl.

PART FOUR

Preventing and Resolving Problem Behaviors

❤ A QUICK OVERVIEW

Even the most accomplished dog trainers and devoted dog owners will face behavior problems from time to time. This section provides information on how to manage and prevent undesirable behaviors – with an emphasis on prevention – and techniques to solve the most common behavior problems.

CHAPTER 19 ❤
The Social Scene: Preventing and Overcoming Shyness

Honey looks as sweet as her name. A one-year-old Border Collie cross, she has fluffy, caramel-colored fur and a flashy white ruff, a broad white blaze, and four white stockings. She doesn't run, she dances, and when she chases a tennis ball she flies – her feet barely touch the ground. She looks soft and huggable, but don't be fooled, looks can be deceiving. Underneath her strong curb appeal, Honey has a serious behavior problem. She is fear aggressive. The circle of friends that she accepts is small, consisting only of her immediate human family: Wayne and Vivian Crocker and their two adult daughters, Kimberly and Marjorie.

The Best of Intentions

A dog couldn't ask for a better home than the Crocker family. They adopted her from the Chattanooga Humane Society when she was just a pup, and provided her with everything they thought a baby dog could need. Following the advice that many well-intentioned veterinarians give their clients, they kept her safely at home until her vaccinations were completed at the age of six months. They enrolled her in an old-style compulsion training class at a pet store, but dropped out of the class because they didn't like the methods used, and because Honey was barking at the other canine students. They went back to keeping Honey at home, other than weekly outings to nearby Nickajack Lake for swimming and tennis ball games.

By the time Honey was a year old the Crockers realized they had a problem. Honey was becoming extremely aroused during her car rides, barking ferociously at anyone she saw through the car window. The extent of the problem became fully evident when they took her back to the vet for her booster shots. Honey was totally out of control, and had to be muzzled and physically restrained for her exam and vaccinations. This experience did nothing to improve her opinion of humans.

Shy Dogs are Often Aggressive Dogs

Honey is aggressive because she is afraid. She suffers from a lack of socialization. During a critical period of her development she did not have the opportunity to have good experiences with many of the things that a dog is likely to encounter in life. Honey also probably has a genetic predisposition to fearful behavior. Some breeds, of which Border Collies are one, are more prone to shyness, sensitivity or fear than others, such as the outgoing Golden or Labrador Retriever. But even within the more confident breeds fearful individuals can be found. Each litter tends to produce a continuum of personalities from least bold to boldest. The more genetically fearful a puppy is, the more critically important it is to provide him with plenty of socialization at an early age, so that his positive experiences can override his genetic programming.

The Social Scene

Responsible breeders begin socializing their pups at an early age – as young as four weeks. Mother Nature gives puppies a relatively small socialization window, from four weeks to about four or five months, during which time a puppy learns what's good in the world. Anything he doesn't encounter during this time is naturally viewed with suspicion in adulthood. The less bold the dog is, the more naturally suspicious he is of new things.

Caution is an important survival mechanism in the wild. Of course, if a pup is too fearful to even venture out of his den he'll eventually starve to death, but if he's too incautious he'll become lunch for a lion. A domesticated dog who demonstrates the degree of caution

that his canine cousin needs in order to survive in the wild is poorly adapted to human society. He lives in a constant state of fear from his exposure to all of the stimuli of the modern world. Fear is stressful, and stress causes aggression. Dog aggression in the human world is often a capital crime. The dog who bites people is likely to end up on the euthanasia room floor. Those who survive generally lead a difficult existence at best, as do their owners, who live in a constant state of fear that someone is going to be bitten. Again.

This dog may look harmless, but dogs raised outside without proper socialization may be anxious and fearful with people.

The good news is that early socialization can prevent fear and fear-induced bites,

Teach Your Puppy Well

With luck, your puppy's breeder knew about the importance of socialization and already introduced him to many different kinds of people before you took him home. Good breeders invite a wide variety of people to come over to play with pups: big people, little people, young, old, light-skinned, dark-skinned people, people wearing big hats and backpacks, people sitting in wheelchairs, and people walking on crutches. The breeder supervises the interactions between people and pups to be sure they are positive. Your pup should know that people come in all shapes and sizes, that they wear and do strange things, and that all people come bearing irresistibly tasty puppy treat-gifts.

Once the pup is in *your* hands, you need to continue the socialization process by taking him out in public and teaching him that loud trucks (at a distance at first), motorcycles, car rides, trips to the vet, mail carriers, busy sidewalks, strangers, and whatever else you can think of are all reliable predictors of *Good Stuff!* (yummy puppy treats). You must also allow him to meet other dogs, so he completes his early lessons in how to "talk" dog and will be able to interact properly with them as an adult. Puppies who do not grow up playing with other puppies and gentle adult dogs frequently

end up being dog aggressive because of their own fear of the unknown. They may also trigger aggressive responses in other dogs when they fail to respond properly to the other dogs' signals. They are socially inept.

Look for people of every description to help you socialize your dog.

Of course, there is a slight risk in taking a young puppy out in public. A puppy's immune system is immature, and there is a period of time when the immunities he received from his mother's milk are fading and his own system is not yet working at full strength. That period differs for each puppy, depending on how strong his mother's immunities were, and how quickly his own system develops. If he is exposed to distemper or parvovirus at this time, he is vulnerable. This is why some veterinarians recommend wrapping a puppy in cotton wool and keeping him home until he is fully vaccinated.

There is a much greater risk, however, in failing to socialize, and ending up with serious behavioral problems. Members of the Association of Pet Dog Trainers report that the incidence of puppy-to-puppy disease transmission in their puppy classes over the last ten years is negligible – a case or two, maybe, of kennel cough. In contrast, just about every trainer can tell tales of poorly socialized dogs who met untimely ends because their behavior was unacceptable in human society. Puppy socialization and training can help avoid the vast majority of these problems. Just be smart about it. Don't take your pup to the public dog park where you have no control over who he plays with. Go to a good puppy training class. Arrange play dates with other responsible puppy owners. Protect your puppy from unhappy encounters with unpleasant dogs or unpredictable people. Teach your puppy well, and you won't have to deal with fear-related behaviors when he's an adult dog.

A Day Late

So you've already missed your dog's socialization window, and he's showing some signs of fearfulness? The second piece of good news is that many dogs *can*

overcome their fears through a process known as desensitization and counter-conditioning.

Fear is a classically conditioned response. That means that it is an involuntary reaction. The fearful dog does not stop and think about being afraid of the approaching male stranger with sunglasses, or make a conscious decision to attack. In the dog's brain, the presence of the "male stranger with sunglasses" stimulus package automatically triggers the fear response. The brain has been conditioned to respond to that set of stimuli with a "BAD STUFF!!!!!" reaction. The trainer's job is to *change* (counter) the dog's conditioned response to that stimulus package to "GOOD STUFF!!!!!" In a desensitization pro-gram, we start with a low enough level of the stimulus so it doesn't provoke the response, and associate that stimulus with "really good stuff" (absolutely wonderful treats). As the dog begins to not just accept but actually look forward to the stimulus as a predictor of absolutely wonderful treats we increase the level of intensity of the stimulus, and work at that level until the dog is comfortable. Then we move it up another small notch.

When there are several fear-causing stimuli in the package, we break them up and desensitize the dog to each one until he is comfortable with each, then combine two and start over again at a low level of intensity. It's important to be very observant about which stimuli trigger a dog's fear. The more stimuli we can identify and separate out, the more likely our success. The more specific the fear-causing stimuli, and the shorter the period of time the dog has had to practice the undesirable behavior, the better the prognosis. Here's how it would work with our "male stranger with sunglasses" package. We have:

1. Male

2. Stranger

3. Sunglasses

We might start with the "Male" part of the equation. If the dog is comfortable with males that he knows, we start with one male stranger at a distance, just beyond the point where the stranger's presence makes him uncomfortable. If he seems stressed by *all* men, then we start with men he knows, who stress him the least. We feed the dog treats until he is relaxed and happy, then gradually move the male stranger closer, feeding treats all the while. *Lots of treats.* We want the dog to think that the presence of male strangers *causes* treats to rain from the heavens.

Note: The sequence is important here. We want to first introduce the stimulus (male stranger), have the dog notice it, and then start dropping treats, so it appears to be cause-and-effect.

Then we could do the same thing with the sunglasses. First we might want to check the dog out with *female* strangers with sunglasses to make sure the "Male" part of the equation is valid. Perhaps it's really only the sunglasses that are the problem! Then we put sunglasses on men the dog *knows,* and go through the desensitization process. When he is perfectly comfortable with *known* males wearing sunglasses, we try it with male strangers wearing sunglasses, once again retreating to a distance the dog is comfortable with, and causing treats to rain when he notices the man in sunglasses.

The stressors for a fearful dog could be anything, and are usually many things. Kids, cars, loud noises, other animals, stairs, the vacuum cleaner, hand movements. The more stressors you can identify and desensitize him to, the less stress there is for all concerned, the less likely he'll be to bite someone, and the better his life (and yours) will be.

Slow and Steady

Just don't expect overnight results. Successful fear modification programs take time and patience. You cannot rush a dog into accepting something he is afraid of. In fact, the more you try to push him, the worse you make it. It is *never* a good idea to allow a fearful dog to be restrained or cornered and forced to accept the attention of someone or the presence of something that is frightening to him. An ideal desensitization program *never* triggers an obvious fear reaction from the dog. If this does happen, it's a signal that you have tried to progress too quickly and that you need to back up and slow down.

The goal: Happy, friendly, confident dogs that you can take anywhere, anytime.

Honey's progress has been painfully slow in some areas, more promising in others. Seven months after we started working with her, she appears to be much more relaxed and happy in her own home environment, and only rarely shows fear-aggression when riding in the car. Changes to her routine include more exercise, and a switch to a low-protein diet. Her thyroid test was within normal ranges (low thyroid can contribute to aggression problems). She is more tolerant of strangers passing by her, but still turns ferocious if a stranger makes eye contact or approaches her head on. We're working on that. We recently decided to add 5-IITP (a naturally-occurring brain chemical) to her protocol, to see if additional serotonin might help regulate her mood. (See "With a Little Help From Pharmaceuticals" next page). Her owners are committed to continuing her behavior modification program as long as it seems to be helping, and are resigned to managing her behavior if we don't ever fully succeed in convincing her to accept the presence of strangers. Honey is a very lucky dog. A lot of owners would have given up long before this.

❤ WITH A LITTLE HELP FROM PHARMACEUTICALS

While it's often advisable and effective to implement a desensitization and counter conditioning program to modify a dog's fear behavior **without** the use of drugs, there are times when a little pharmaceutical help may be necessary, either because the program isn't progressing well, or because a dog's fear is initially so extreme that a drug may be needed to crack open a window of opportunity to enable us to work with the dog. Dr. Nicholas Dodman, head of the Animal Behavior Department of Clinical Sciences for Tufts University School of Veterinary Medicine, agrees.

"Sometimes," says Dr. Dodman, "anxiety reducing drugs or anti-depressants can be helpful to get a foothold on the management of this problem. There are no "miracle pills," but we do find that pharmacological intervention helps some dogs relax, which facilitates the implementation of the behavior modification program."

continued on next page...

❤ WITH A LITTLE HELP FROM PHARMACEUTICALS (cont.)

The Tufts Petfax Behavior Consultation Clinic receives numerous queries about using drugs for modifying fearful behavior. They are always careful to point out that since they have not examined the particular dog in question they cannot prescribe medication – they can only provide information for the dog owner to review with her own veterinarian and trainer, to determine if drug therapy is appropriate.

For fear aggressive dogs, Dr. Dodman's first choice of drugs is fluoxetine (Prozac), administered at 1.0 mg/kg once a day. One of the benefits of fluoxetine is the unlikelihood of increased aggression (paradoxical increases in aggression) as a side effect. The major drawback of fluoxetine is the cost. Prozac can be prohibitively expensive, even for a medium-sized dog. Side effects are uncommon, but can include lethargy, decreased appetite, constipation or digestive upset. Dogs who exhibit these or other side effects should be seen by a veterinarian. If side effects become problematic, the owner should recontact the veterinarian, who will adjust the dose or discontinue the medication.

Clomipramine (Clomicalm), administered at 2.0 – 3.0 mg/kg **twice** a day, is Dr. Dodman's second choice of drugs for treating fear aggression. Clomipramine is considerably less expensive than fluoxetine. The drug's packet insert cautions that a small percentage of dogs show **increased** aggression on the medication, but this is rare. While Tufts veterinarians have not experienced this side effect with their clients, it is a factor to be considered. Other side effects may include lethargy, decreased appetite, increased thirst, constipation or digestive upset. Again, dogs experiencing these or other side effects should be seen promptly by the prescribing veterinarian.

Prozac is an SSRI – a **selective serotonin reuptake inhibitor.** Serotonin is a body chemical that regulates mood, sleep, and other brain-related functions. Antidepressant drugs like Prozac work by blocking the breakdown of serotonin back into nerve terminals, leaving the body chemical in place to continue regulating mood. Some clinical studies have shown that supplements of another naturally-occurring amino acid, 5-HTP (**5-hydroxy-L-tryptophan**), can actually boost levels of serotonin, and thus improve the brain's ability to regulate anxiety.

Many behavioral medications have not been licensed by the FDA (Federal Drug Administration) for use with animals. Clomicalm has, but Prozac and 5-HTP have not. They can, however, be prescribed by your veterinarian if s/he determines that the drugs are likely to be of benefit.

Dr. Dodman reminds us that the purpose of drug therapy is to **assist** in behavioral modification and training, not to replace it. The goal is to have the proper behavior remain after a gradual withdrawal of the drug. Fluoxetine, for example, should be tapered off over a two to three week period before it is discontinued.

Behavior cases which require medication need good follow-up care. Stay in close contact with your veterinarian and behavior consultant!

CHAPTER 20 ❤
Bite Me! Avoiding and Overcoming Aggression

There are few things quite as disconcerting as having your own dog bite you. I can recall with crystal clarity the time our Scottie, Dubhy, nailed me with a Level 3 bite in a classic case of redirected aggression (see "Classifications of Bites" below). Dubhy had taken an intense dislike to a Labrador Retriever who had entered the room, and when I touched the feisty Terrier on his back to try to distract him, he whirled around and redirected his aroused state, and his substantial Scottish Terrier teeth, at my hand.

Despite the horror stories of free-roaming Pit Bulls mauling children on the school playground, the majority of dog bites occur in the owner's home, and the majority of dog bite victims are friends or members of the owner's family. According to statistics posted at www.dogbitelaw.com, a non-profit educational website run by attorney Kenneth Phillips who specializes in dog bite cases, 61% of dog bites occur in the home or a familiar place, and 77% of dog bite victims are family members or friends. A relatively small percentage of bites are inflicted by the errant stray dog who lurks behind bushes waiting for the opportunity to chomp on unsuspecting school children. This means that most

bites leave a shocked owner feeling betrayed by his loyal canine, and wondering whether he can ever trust his four-footed friend again.

Why Dogs Bite

Dogs bite because they are dogs. All dogs can bite, and given the right (or wrong!) set of circumstances, all dogs will. Biting is a natural and normal means of canine communication and defense. As such, it's actually surprising that our dogs don't bite us more often than they do!

Aggression is generally caused by stress, which can come from a variety of sources. Some dogs have high bite thresholds – it takes a lot of stress to push them into biting the hand that feeds them. Some have low thresholds. That is, it doesn't take much to get them to bite. A dog with a high bite threshold may seem like the best choice to have around kids. This is often true, but if noisy, active children are very stressful to the dog, even a high-threshold dog might bite them. Conversely, a dog who has a low bite threshold may be a fine child's companion and confidante if children are not one of his stressors, and if he is kept in an environment that is relatively free of the things that are.

Pain, fear, anxiety, and arousal – any kind of threat to the dog's well-being can be considered stressors. A timid dog whose space is trespassed upon will try to retreat, but if prevented from retreating, will bite out of fear. An assertive dog or mother with pups whose space is trespassed upon may feel threatened by the intrusion, and bite. A resource-guarder bites because he is offended (stressed) by a human's attempt to take his valuable possession. In many cases, the bite resolves the situation – for the dog – and relieves the stress, which is why a dog can bite in one instant and seem fine the next. The resource-guarder bites, the human withdraws and since the threat to his food bowl has gone away he is perfectly calm and happy again.

In many cases, wounds to the human victim's skin heal far more quickly than the breach in the relationship between dog and human. This is unfortunate, because the majority of bites are perfectly justified, at least from the dog's point of view, although very often misunderstood by the human. It's interesting to note that some misguided humans believe they have the right to hit, jerk, kick or shock their dogs into obedience without damaging the relationship, but one bite from the dog can damage the trust permanently, and is often the first tragic step on the path to euthanasia.

Sadly, if humans understood dogs better, we would realize it's about behavior, not trust. Many biting dogs could

A dog who signals his intent to bite is actually a far safer companion than a dog who has been punished for this behavior and has learned to suppress it.

easily remain in their homes and lead long and happy lives, with a low risk for a second bite, if their owners only understood how to identify and minimize their dogs' stressors. The old-fashioned method for dealing with a biting dog, still employed far too frequently today, was to physically punish the dog into submission, sometimes severely. These methods were supposed to be employed at the dog's first sign of aggression. A warning growl or snarl was met with a harsh verbal correction and a leash jerk, followed by more serious measures such as hanging or helicoptering on her leash if the dog continued to resist. While this did manage to "whip" some dogs "into shape," others continued to escalate their resistance, fighting back until dog, human, or both, were seriously injured or even dead.

Even worse, what this method often did was to teach the dog not to give a warning prior to the bite. It certainly didn't do anything to minimize the dog's stressors. If anything, it increased the stress, since the dog now associated a severe beating along with whatever other bad feelings he had about the stressor. Let's say, for example, our dog, Snappy, is not fond of children. A child approaches and he growls – his attempt to let us (and the child) know that her presence is stressful to him and she should go away. We jerk on his leash and tell him to knock it off. He snaps at us in response to the jerk on the collar, so we punish him harder, until he stops fighting back and submits. The end result is a dog who isn't any happier about being around small children, and who has learned that it isn't safe to growl. Snappy is now more likely to *bite* a child next time he sees one, rather than growling to warn her away, since he has learned that his growling makes *us* unreasonably aggressive. We may have succeeded in making the growl go away, but we haven't helped him feel any better about being around children!

A growl is a good thing. It tells us that our dog is being pushed near his bite threshold, and gives us the opportunity to identify and remove the stressor. Snarls and air-snaps are two steps closer to the threshold. They are our dog's last ditch attempts to warn off the stressor before he is forced to commit the ultimate offense – the actual bite. If Snappy

growls or snaps frequently, you need to sit up and take notice. He is telling you that there are lots of stressors that are pushing him toward his bite threshold. If you don't take action, chances are good that he will eventually bite. Dogs who bite tend to have short life spans.

Without knowing this dog and his individual risk factors, it is impossible to say whether he is using a hard stare to intimidate the photographer in an attempt to make her back way, or merely concentrating. The safest course would be to interpret this look as a warning.

If Your Dog Bites

If Snappy bites, you have four options. You can:

1. Manage Snappy's behavior to prevent him from ever having the opportunity to bite again.

2. Manage Snappy's behavior to prevent him from biting while you implement a comprehensive behavior modification program to minimize the bite risk.

3. Rehome Snappy with a new owner who is willing and able to do one of the first two (new owners like this are not easy to find!).

4. Have Snappy euthanized.

What you cannot do is close your eyes and hope and pray that he doesn't bite again. You are responsible for protecting your family as well as other members of your community. Denial will only result in more bites.

Now let's take a closer look at each of your options.

1. **Manage Snappy's behavior.** While difficult, this is possible. It means greatly restricting his movements so he has no access to humans, other than adult family members. If company comes over, Snappy is crated in a closed room. If the grandkids are visiting, Snappy is crated or sent to a kennel that is fully appraised of his bite history and equipped to safely handle a biting dog. Even if he *adores* the grandkids, the fact that he has bitten puts them at unacceptable risk. Unless you are 100 percent confident that you know what his stressors are and can prevent them from occurring during the kids' visit, you cannot take the chance. Of course, selecting this option means a greatly reduced quality of life for Snappy – no more walks in the park, on *or* off leash; no more rides in the car; and no more spending hours on

his own in the fresh air and sunshine in the fenced back yard.

2. **Manage while you modify his behavior.** This requires a serious commitment to a behavior modification program. If Snappy's behavior is relatively new and mild, you may be able to accomplish this on your own (See "Modifying Aggressive Behavior" below). Most owners, however, need the help of an experienced, positive behavior counselor or behaviorist to help them succeed – and those services can be costly. The behavior professional will help you identify Snappy's stressors, and set up a program with you to use desensitization and counter conditioning to convince him that the things he now perceives as "bad" (stressors) are really "good." If he changes his perception of them, they will no longer cause him stress, and they will no longer push him over his bite threshold. This won't happen overnight. The longer Snappy has been practicing his unacceptable aggression responses, the longer it will take to modify them. The more committed you are to working with him on a daily basis/several times a day, the more opportunities he will have to reprogram his responses and the faster it will happen. Meanwhile, he must be crated or kenneled while visitors or grandkids are at the house, and not taken for walks, car rides,

nor left to his own devices in the back yard.

3. **Rehome.** This is a long shot at best. Depending on the circumstances of the bite and the dog's general nature, some dogs who have bitten may be accepted into training programs for government drug or bomb-sniffing dogs, or in police K9 programs. Your average pet dog home, however, is no better equipped than you are to make the commitment necessary to keep the community safe from or modify the behavior of a biting dog. Most rescue groups will not accept dogs who have a history of biting, and shelters that do accept them will usually euthanize, rather than take the risk (and the liability) of placing them in a new home. If you rehome him yourself, you risk having Snappy fall into the hands of someone who will punish him severely for biting, or otherwise not treat him well. You may even continue to bear some liability, moral if not also legal, should Snappy do serious damage to his next victim at his new home. Besides, there are millions of dogs looking for homes who *haven't* bitten anyone. You *love* Snappy and are trying to rehome him. What are the chances of finding a good home for Snappy with someone who doesn't have that emotional connection and is willing to take the risk of bringing home a biting dog?

4. **Euthanasia.** This is never a happy outcome. Still, you need to think long and hard about Snappy's quality of life. If you can only manage his behavior, will he be happy, or miserable, being shut out of the activities he loves? Can you guarantee that the home you find for him will treat him well? What if he bites again? If you can manage and modify, and still maintain your own quality of life as well as Snappy's, by all means, that is the best choice. But if not, remember that aggression is caused by stress, and stress is not an enjoyable state of being. If Snappy is so stressed that you can't succeed in managing and modifying his behavior and he is a high risk for biting someone else, he can't be living a very enjoyable life. Nor can you! As difficult as the decision may be, it is sometimes the right and responsible one for the protection of all of your loved ones, including Snappy.

The Good News

The good news is that relatively few dogs are beyond help and hope. If you make a commitment to helping Snappy feel more comfortable with the world around him, there's a good chance you will succeed. You will understand why he has bitten in the past, and be able to avoid his stressors while you work to convince him that what are now stressors for him are actually good things, not bad. Like my own encounter with Dubhy's capable canines, you will realize that the bite wasn't personal, but simply the end result of a chain of events that were beyond Snappy's control. What a great accomplishment, and what a proud day for you both, when you can take him out in public with confidence, knowing that he is as safe as any dog can be in the face of the unknown elements of the real world.

❤ MODIFYING AGGRESSIVE BEHAVIOR WITH CHILDREN

Aggression is a classically conditioned response. Your biting dog does not generally take a seat and ponder whether he is going to bite the next child that tries to pet him. When a stressor appears, it triggers an involuntary reaction – the brain screams "CHILD – BAD!!!!" and the dog bites. If you want the dog to stop biting children, you have to change the brain's reaction to "CHILD – GOOD!!!" in which case the child is no longer a stressor and the dog is not pushed toward or over his bite threshold in the presence of children. Since food is a very powerful positive reinforcer, you will use food to change the way the brain responds when the dog sees a child. This process is called counter conditioning and desensitization (CC&D). Here is one possible CC&D program for a dog who is aggressive with children:

NOTE: Because the risks associated with a failed program for aggression are high, I strongly recommend that you work with a competent positive behavior professional to implement a CC&D program. The following program is not intended to take the place of professional guidance.

1. Observe dog to determine distance threshold. Dog is calm with one child at 50 feet, becomes tense with child at 40 feet.

2. Owner sits in chair with dog on leash, 45 feet from entrance. Child enters at 45 feet.

3. Dog alerts to child's presence. Owner begins feeding high value treats to dog (something wonderful that the dog only gets in the presence of children).

4. Child walks across room and back at distance of 45 feet. Owner feeds treats the entire time, dropping them on floor.

5. Child leaves room. Owner stops feeding treats. Dog only gets treats when child is in the room.

6. Repeat this exercise a number of times, watching the dog's behavior. You are looking for a change in the dog's response when the child enters the room. When he sees the child and looks happily at you in anticipation of the next treat rather than watching the child warily, you know he is beginning to understand that the child's presence is linked to the yummy treats. In effect, the **child** is making the treats happen. Now you can move a little closer to the entrance, or have the child move a little closer to you and the dog. How much closer depends on the dog. You want to avoid triggering an overt aggressive response. You may be able to move in five-foot increments, or six-inch ones. It is better to err on the side of caution than risk a setback in the program. If the dog barks aggressively or lunges at the child, you have moved too far too fast.

7. When the dog is doing well with one child at increasingly closer distances, you can start to vary the stressor. Retreat to your original distance and introduce a different child. (You want the dog to think that **all** children make the yummy treat happen, not just the first child.) Then try two children. Then one child skipping, or bouncing a ball. Gradually move closer to each of these new stimuli as the dog's reaction tells you he is ready. Remember that every time you introduce a new stressor you move back to the original safe distance, or farther, if necessary.

8. At some point in the program, when he is quite comfortable with several children moving around the room, return to one child walking past at a comfortable distance of five or six feet, and have that child toss treats toward the dog **without making direct eye contact**. Children who feel threatened

by dogs tend to stare at them, which makes dogs feel threatened and doesn't encourage them to like children.

9. As the dog's behavior dictates, have more children toss treats, until he is quite comfortable receiving treats from them.

10. Have one child at first, then several, sit in chairs and toss treats at a distance of about six feet. Allow the dog, on leash, to approach the child, then children, and clean up the treats. Gradually have the children toss treats a shorter and shorter distance, until the dog is eating them from the floor near the children's feet. If you proceed with any closer contact between dog and children beyond this step, you must be very certain that your dog is relaxed and comfortable with them, and continue to progress very slowly. Any sign of stress or tension on the dog's part should cause you to back up at least one or two steps in the program. Only when the dog is very relaxed and happy around the children should he be allowed to eat treats from their hands or they be allowed to pet him.

To minimize as many stressors as possible for your dog, make a complete list of all the stressors you can identify, and then create and implement a program such as the one above to counter condition and desensitize him to each stressor. There may be some stressors for which this is impossible, but remember that the more stressors you desensitize him to, the less likely it is that he will be pushed past his bite threshold and bite someone.

When your dog is very comfortable with children at a distance, recruit a reliable child to approach within a few yards and toss him some treats.

If the dog remains relaxed, the child can approach even closer. Over time such a training session can lessen a dog's stress level around children.

Praise your dog as the child moves closer to the dog continuing to offer treats.

❤ CLASSIFICATIONS OF BITES

Well-known veterinarian, dog trainer and behaviorist Ian Dunbar has developed a six-level system of classifying bites, in order to make discussions of biting behavior more consistent and understandable. Those levels are:

- **LEVEL 1 BITE** – Harassment but no skin contact. This is the so-called **snap**. Don't kid yourself. A snap is an intended "air bite" from a dog who did not intend to connect. He didn't just "miss." It is a lovely warning signal, telling us that we need to identify his stressors and either desensitize him or manage his behavior to avoid exposing him to the things that cause him undue stress.

- **LEVEL 2 BITE** – Tooth contact on skin but no puncture. Again, this is a bite from a dog who didn't intend to break skin, and a warning that this dog is **serious**. It's a very good idea to remove the dog's stressors at this point, before he graduates to the next level.

- **LEVEL 3 BITE** – Skin punctures, one to four holes from a single bite (all punctures shallower than the length of the canine tooth).

- **LEVEL 4 BITE** – One to four holes, deep black bruising with punctures deeper than the length of the canine (which means the dog bit and clamped down) or slashes in both directions from the puncture (the dog bit and shook his head).

- **LEVEL 5 BITE** – Multiple-bite attack with deep punctures, or multiple attack incident

- **LEVEL 6 BITE** – Killed victim and/or consumed flesh

At one time, more than a dozen labels such as "dominance aggression," "submission aggression," "protection aggression," and "territorial aggression" were commonly used to classify various manifestations of aggression. Today, behaviorists are increasingly recognizing aggression as an anxiety disorder, terminology is the subject of much debate, and most definitions are in flux.

© Dr. Ian Dunbar. Used with permission.

CHAPTER 21 ❤
S.O.S.! Save Our Shoes: Appropriate Chewing

One California winter evening our four dogs were suffering from a serious bout of cabin fever. It had been raining for several days, our normal vigorous daily walks had been sharply curtailed, and the canine energy level in the house was reaching dangerous levels. Rather than escalating our disciplinary efforts to maintain peace, I resorted to a simple behavior management tool. Reaching into our doggie provisions, I pulled out a pack of knuckle bones and distributed them – one to each dog and two extra for the floor. Calm settled over the house in seconds, and soon the only audible sound was the grinding of teeth against gristle and bone. Canine boredom and stress, conquered by the simple instinct to chew.

The wolf, ancestor and cousin to our dogs, chewed to survive. His meals weren't served to him as measured rations of kibble in a stainless steel bowl. Using his strong teeth and jaws, he brought down his prey, chewed through tough moose hide to consume the life-sustaining flesh beneath, and crushed elk leg bones with powerful jaws and teeth to slurp up the rich, tasty marrow inside. He chewed to eat, to live. Wolves today do exactly the same.

More than 15,000 years of domestication and a steady diet of packaged foods haven't extinguished the dog's need and desire to chew. Dogs chew for a variety of reasons, from the pain-relieving and exploratory teething of a young pup to the destructive behavior of a dog who cannot tolerate being left alone. They chew by instinct, they chew in play, they chew to relieve boredom and stress, they chew because it feels good, and they chew because, after all, that's what a dog's teeth are for.

When dogs chew items that you prefer they didn't, they aren't being revengeful, bad, spiteful, stubborn or contrary. They're just being dogs, acting on their basic instincts, not out of malice. When you understand this you can look at the behavior for what it is – natural – and work *with* their instincts instead of against them to achieve the desired behavioral results. With the proper combination of management and training, your dog *can* learn to ply his teeth only where they belong, and join the ranks of model, trustworthy canine citizens.

Chewing And Puppies

Teething is an important part of growing up for a young dog. To a puppy, everything is new and chewable. A pup tastes and tests new objects with his mouth in order to learn about the world. What is this? Does it taste good? Is it edible? Can I play with it? Is it soft or hard? Does it bite back? Chewing also aids the growth and development of puppy teeth and helps ease the pain as adult teeth erupt through gums, until they are fully in place by the age of 12-14 months.

As the allegedly more intelligent species in our canine-human relationships, it's up to us to figure out how to direct a puppy's natural desire to chew into acceptable channels. Leaving it up to the pup to figure it out is a recipe for disaster, yet many new dog and puppy owners do just that.

Recipe For Disaster

The Smith family arrives home with 10-week-old Buddy in arms, walks in the door and sets him on the floor. Buddy, overwhelmed by a flood of new scents and objects, starts checking things out – with his mouth, of course, because he doesn't have hands.

"Hmmm...great pair of Birkenstock sandals here under the coffee table, the leather has terrific flavor and gives nicely against my gums. Oh boy, look over there – a stuffed bunny! It's just like the squeaky toy they gave me at the animal shelter. It'll shred nicely... And I don't know what this square thing is but it's fun, hard on the outside, soft on the inside with hundreds of papers I

can rip out one by one... Maybe next I'll concentrate on the antique table leg or the Oriental rug!"

Buddy doesn't understand why the humans are yelling at him. He charges around the coffee table with a sandal in his mouth, the entire Smith family in hot pursuit. "What a great game!" he thinks, and grins at Mr. Smith as he darts between his legs. "We'll have to play this one again!"

A puppy running off with a shoe to chew is an all-too frequent occurrence if the owner doesn't supervise the pup's activities well.

The next day, the Smiths head off to work and school. Like a two-year-old child, Buddy spends every waking moment of his free time exploring his environment. Anything he can reach is fair game for his needle-sharp teeth. Not only does he wreak havoc on his new family's possessions, he risks serious injury to himself as well. Electrical cords are prime targets. As are poisonous houseplants and toxic household cleaners. In just three days Buddy does several thousand dollars worth of damage to household possessions, spends one night at the veterinary emergency clinic after eating a half-pound of chocolate covered peanuts, and is banished to the back yard. The Smiths are planning to return him to the shelter Saturday.

Boy, this is sure fun!

The Right Stuff

The Wilson family, on the other hand, prepares for their new pup's arrival. Before bringing Annie home from the shelter they clean the house, pick everything up off the floor and put baby gates across the doorways of the kids' rooms (where they know that keeping the floors clutter-free is not realistic). They've purchased a portable puppy pen and set it up in the den on a thick pad of unfolded newspapers to function as a playpen to keep Annie out of trouble when she's not under direct supervision. An airline kennel, or crate, where Annie will sleep at night, sits in the corner of the master bedroom. A large basket in the living room holds a generous supply of dog toys suitable for Annie to punish with her puppy teeth.

When the Wilsons arrive home they place Annie in the puppy pen, give her two chew toys, and engage in quiet activities in the room. The family's calm presence gives the puppy time to settle in, relax, and focus her attention on an appropriate chew object without feeling alone or abandoned. She's not overwhelmed with stimuli and doesn't have the opportunity to chew on things she shouldn't. She sleeps in her kennel in the Wilson's room that night, and when the Wilsons head off to work and school the next day, Annie is safe in her pen with a bowl of water and two toys. Mrs. Wilson comes home at lunch to feed her, clean her pen and give her the chance to relieve herself outdoors. In the beginning she is only allowed out of her playpen when someone is directly paying attention to her. If she does start to chew the wrong thing, one of the Wilsons gently substitutes one of her chew toys instead.

In three days Annie sleeps through the night, is almost housetrained, and hasn't destroyed a single thing. The Wilson's will keep her until she dies of natural causes at the ripe old age of 16.

Adult Chewing

Puppies aren't the only ones who chew. Adult dogs chew to relieve boredom and stress, for grooming purposes, as a play activity, and to satisfy the instinct to gnaw, crush and tear at the flesh and bones of prey. A side benefit of chewing is dental hygiene – many commercial chew objects are designed to help promote clean teeth – although the dogs don't know this, nor do they care. When a properly raised puppy learns to focus chewing attention on appropriate objects, inappropriate chewing will not be a problem as an adult. But many adult dogs that are rehomed through shelters or rescue groups come with a package of behavior challenges that frequently includes out-of-control chewing.

Whether you are starting with a puppy or an adult dog, dealing with chewing behavior is a three-step process. You must:

1. Prevent
2. Manage
3. Train

Applying any one of the three steps can improve an out-of-control chewing problem, but to achieve the ultimate goal of a well behaved, trustworthy adult dog who chews only when and where appropriate, you must do all three.

Prevention

It is always easier to prevent inappropriate behavior than it is to correct it. A puppy who never has the opportunity to learn the joys of chewing table legs and Oriental carpets will be trustworthy at a much earlier age than one who must be convinced to give up a favorite inappropriate chewing target. Prevention involves restricting the dog or puppy's access to forbidden chewables through the use of kennels, crates, pens, baby gates, leashes and supervision. Covered trash cans will correct a garbage-dumper. Aversive substances (deterrents such as Bitter Apple™) that can be applied to surfaces to prevent chewing are useful but not 100% effective. They should only be used in conjunction with a complete controlled chewing program.

Caution: Dogs who chew as part of a separation anxiety syndrome often do not tolerate confinement well. Separation anxiety is a complex problem that requires extensive behavior modification to correct (see Chapter 23). Crating and kenneling is generally not recommended for dogs with separation anxiety.

Management

Because dogs have a natural instinct to chew, it is unreasonable to think you can eliminate all chewing behavior. While preventing your dog from chewing what he shouldn't, you want to direct his teeth to things he can and should chew. By providing appropriate chew objects you can relieve his boredom and stress and prevent damage to your own cherished possessions. Catalogs and pet supply store shelves are filled with tempting chewables – from rawhide, pig ears and cow hooves to squeaky toys, plush teddy bears and nylon bones. Each has advantages and disadvantages. Criteria that help you decide which chew items to provide include safety, durability and attractiveness to the dog.

It is of paramount importance that you not overwhelm the dog or pup with toys. It's easy to make the mistake of offering several dozen toys in the hope that if you give him enough he'll leave your possessions alone. When a dog has a few toys, he can keep track of what is his. If the floor is littered with toys, he may think that anything on the floor is fair game – and there go your $100 tennis shoes. Instead, offer one or two items at a time. When he tires of a chew toy put it away and get out a fresh one. In a few days, the first one will have regained its attraction and you can swap again. Be sure to stick to "official" chew toys. When you substitute household items you can confuse your dog. A knotted up old knee sock or worn-out sneaker is still a sock or a shoe, and can teach him shoes and socks are fun to chew.

Providing a dog an "official" chew toy allows you to direct and limit his chewing to those items you choose for him.

Training

While you are preventing inappropriate chewing and managing chewing be-havior with acceptable chew toys, you must also train your dog to respond to requests to give up an item on request, or to leave it alone (see Chapter 13). Verbal cues commonly used for these behaviors include: Give, Drop It, Leave It, and Off. It is best to teach these behaviors using a positive, non-punishment approach. Positive training methods work with a dog's natural behaviors and instincts, by rewarding the behaviors you want, and to the extent possible, ignoring the behaviors you don't want.

You would never think to correct a dog's house soiling problem by forbidding him to go to the bathroom at all. You teach him to eliminate in the appropriate place and manage his behavior so he doesn't have the opportunity to poop or pee indoors. It's just as absurd to think of correcting a dog's chewing problem by forbidding him to chew. Rather, teach him to chew appropriate items, and manage his behavior so he doesn't have the opportunity to chew things that he shouldn't. Like most dog training basics, this is simple – just not always easy. It takes a real commitment to keeping inappropriate chew objects out of the dog's reach, and keeping him under close supervision until he has demonstrated his clear preference for chewing on his own toys. It's well worth the effort to help your dog become a well-behaved canine citizen who can be given house freedom without fear for your personal possessions.

CHAPTER 22 ❤
Barking Up the Right Tree

While scooping horse manure in my barnyard recently, I heard a cacophony of dog noise over a nearby hill. My "dog radar" alerted immediately as I listened for canine distress sounds. Upon concluding that it was a pack of hounds that some hunter had let loose, joyfully giving voice to their pursuit of quarry, I returned to my rural exercise program.

My manure meditation was next interrupted by Tucker, our 75-pound Cattle Dog mix, whose guttural barks warned off the Australian Shepherd who routinely strays over from three houses away and fence fights with our dogs. The ugly sounds ceased before I could intervene, and I made yet another mental note to go plead with the Aussie's owners again to keep him at home where he belongs.

Barn chores completed, I walked back to the house, and was welcomed by the staccato greeting barks of Katie, my Australian Kelpie. Her cheerful greeting always ends in a most endearing series of "woo-woo" sounds that brings a smile to my face. Entering the house, I could hear the irritating and persistent, high-pitched demand barking of Dusty, my Pomeranian, who knew that his breakfast was next on the morning agenda. As I let him in to stop his chatter, Dubhy,

the Scottie, issued several gruff "alert" barks, announcing the arrival of the neighbor cat who provides gratis rodent patrol in our barn.

Who says dogs can't talk? In less than 30 minutes, I had been treated to five audible canine communications, each with a clear and distinct meaning and purpose. While dogs are exquisite body language communicators, they are no slouch in the vocal communication department either. It behooves us to pay attention to what they have to say, and to use their vocalizations to our advantage to enhance our relationships with them.

Dogs bark for many reasons.

When we discuss barking in a dog-training context we tend to focus on canine vocalization as a *problem*. However, like so many other dog behaviors that may be considered unacceptable or inappropriate in *our* society, barking serves a useful purpose to the dog. To him, it's all appropriate barking! Only when human and canine cultures clash does it become a problem.

Let's look at some of the reasons dogs bark – and make other sounds – and what we should do about them.

Territorial/Protective Barking

These utterances may start as low growls or barks that become sharper and more rapid as the intruder approaches. The dog's posture is usually threatening – tail high, ears up and forward. While territorial barking may be diminished to some degree by spaying or neutering, surgery won't stop it completely. Tucker and Dubhy, both neutered, were exhibiting territorial barking; one at a canine intruder, one at a feline trespasser. They also do protective barking at cars or delivery trucks that venture up our long driveway, and when visitors knock at the door.

A limited amount of protective barking *may* be a good thing. Backyard protective/territorial barking can be reduced by minimizing the visual stimuli such as by making the fence a solid privacy fence rather than chain-link see-through variety (or worse, electronic, non-visible). Living in the country, I like to have a little audible deterrent for any

trespassers who may have evil intentions. I suspect those living in the city do too. However, whether city or country, indoors or out, it's nice to be able to turn off the deterrent after two or three barks.

Don't make the mistake of yelling at your dog for barking. He may well think you're joining his attempts to ward off the intruder, and redouble his efforts. There's no point in getting angry – it just gets your adrenalin pumping as well as his! Besides, he has no way of knowing who he should bark at and who he shouldn't. It's simply his job to alert you to the presence of a non-family member. The best way to turn off his bark is by teaching him a "quiet" cue. It's easier than you might think.

I start by teaching a "positive interrupt" independent of the barking behavior. When your dog is calm and relaxed, say "Over here!" in a cheerful tone of voice, make a kissy noise if necessary to get his attention, and feed him a tasty treat when he looks at you, or comes to you. Repeat this exercise until your "Over here!" elicits a prompt and happy response every time. Now you are ready to try it out with the barking.

Ask a friend to help you. Have her come to your house, walk up and knock on the door to elicit the barking. When your dog starts to bark, let him bark three times, then tell him "Over here!" (remember to keep it cheerful). If he doesn't respond, put a bit of delectably high-value treat

– such as canned chicken – under his nose to turn his attention to you. When he stops barking, tell him he's a good boy, and feed him a few more chicken tidbits. Then have your friend knock again. Repeat the exercise several times, until he will respond to your "Over here!" cue as soon as you give it. Then take a break and invite your friend in for coffee and cookies. Remember to let your dog bark three times each time before you give the cue, or he may learn to not bark at all!

You might need to invite your friend back for a few more visits to get your dog reliably responding on the first knock each time. When he seems to have the idea, you can start calmly adding the word "Quiet!" or "Quiet, please" before the "Over here!" cue. Eventually you will be able to just say, "Quiet, please," without the "Over here!" to stop the barking. I personally love the "Quiet, please" cue, and always follow it with a "Thank you!" You can easily generalize this to other protective barking situations, and over time, you can gradually randomize the treat reward, replacing it with praise and petting (if those are rewarding to your dog), with only an occasional treat.

Attention-Seeking/Demand Barking

This is the kind of barking that dear little Dusty does when he wants his breakfast. While we generally consider demand barking to be "bad," it is also what our Scottie Dubhy does when he

makes a sweet, soft grumbling noise in his throat to tell me he has to go outside. Many of our dogs use attention-seeking sounds and behaviors to let us know they have a need that they would like taken care of. Whining is another common manifestation of demand behavior, often with an anxiety component. If we are in the habit of meeting our dogs every demand, then yes, it can become oppressive. If we handle it well, it becomes a charming communication tool to help us understand our canine companions.

Dusty's breakfast barking is the epitome of annoying little dog yapping. If I wanted to fix it, I would need to very consistently ignore the behavior I don't want (breakfast barking) and reward the behavior I do want (waiting calmly outside for me to open the door to let him in for breakfast). I know this, and I will confess that I have deliberately chosen to simply let him in to eat to stop his barking. It is the *only* time he does it, and the time and effort it would take to change the behavior just isn't worth it to me.

Making a behavior go away by removing the reward that the dog enjoys for it is called "extinction." It is often a very effective behavior modification technique, and I use it often with clients whose dogs liberally engage in demand barking. We see it most often in class, when the dog knows his human is in training mode and has treats at hand.

Since I almost always have treats at hand, my dogs don't see this as a reliable predictor that they will necessarily *get* a steady flow of treats, hence, no demand barking.

In class, I tell my students that they must consistently turn their backs on their dogs *as soon as* the demand barking starts, and then, when the dog is silent, say "Yes, quiet!" and turn around to give the dog attention and/or a treat. The dog must learn that it is "Quiet" that earns attention and treats, not barking or whining.

When the human is consistent, the method works beautifully – especially if the person is savvy enough to recognize the behavior in its early stages, before it is deeply ingrained. However, dog owners have varying degrees of success with this, for several reasons:

- **Lack of Promptness and Consistency.** The quicker and more consistent you are in ignoring the dog, the faster the dog gets the message. A lack of consistency greatly decreases the effectiveness of this method. Behaviors that are *occasionally* rewarded become very durable, so if you *sometimes* give in to the dog's demand barking, even inadvertently, the dog will keep trying, and it becomes even harder to extinguish. Eye contact is attention, so if you just *look* at the dog before turning away, you have rewarded the barking behavior.

- **The Extinction Burst.** When you are trying to extinguish a behavior

that has been very successful for your dog in the past, he is likely to engage in an *extinction burst,* which is akin to the temper tantrum of a spoiled child, and another cause for varying degrees of success. Your dog may bark louder, longer, and more insistently in order to try to get the behavior to work that has worked so well in the past. If you give in during the extinction burst, you have taught him to offer a much more intense level of behavior, and your life becomes even harder.

- **Failure to Reward Quiet.** The degree to which you reward your dog's quiet behavior will also affect your rate of training success. If your dog is demand-barking for your attention, it is important to remember to frequently give him attention *before* he barks. Otherwise he will learn a behavior chain of: bark, get ignored, be quiet, *then* get attention.

I put up with Dusty's demand barking because I don't want to go through the headache of his extinction burst. I treasure Dubhy's "potty grumbles," however I make sure to reward them not because he *wants* to go out, but only when I think he really *has* to go out. He gets to communicate, but not control.

Play/Chase/Excitement/ Greeting Barks

This can be a fun kind of barking, as long as it doesn't get carried away. It's sort of nice to have someone who is "woo-woo" happy to see you even if you've only been out of the room for a minute or two. It can, however, get out of hand, and it's nice to have a turn-off switch. You can use the same "Quiet, please" cue that we discussed under the "Protective Barking" section.

This is also an ideal place to use the "Ask for an Incompatible Behavior" technique. Simply teach your dog to greet you (or others) with a toy in her mouth. Have a basket of toys next to the door, and when someone comes in, pick up a toy and toss it for your dog to chase and bring back. With her mouth full of toy, the best she can do is a muffled bark. She's more likely to be focused on "toy" than "bark" anyway! Before long, she'll be seeking out the toy to greet people with, and you won't even have to throw one.

Play barking can be a tad more difficult. Some dogs, especially the herding breeds, seem to have a genetic predisposition to bark when playing with other dogs, and with rowdy humans. Actually, I suspect they aren't really playing – with their workaholic personalities I am sure they are actually hard at work, trying to round up their uncooperative playmates. Your best recourse with these barkers might be to come to an understanding with neighbors about appropriate barky play-times, and perhaps passing out earplugs to the entire neighborhood. Seriously though, when excited play leads to over-aroused barking, time-outs are an appropriate remedy. I suggest using an

"Oops" as a "punishment marker" when removing the vocal offender from the playgroup in order to mark the behavior that earned the time-out. In time, the barker may learn to control her own voice in order to enjoy uninterrupted play privileges.

For the hunter whose dogs I heard baying over the hill, the "chase" barking of his hounds is beautiful music, and he wouldn't dream of trying to modify that behavior!

Fear/Startle Barking

Dogs who bark out of fear can generally be identified by their body language. Unlike the protective barker who leans forward with ears pricked and tail high, the fear-barker is likely to hold her tail low, flatten her ears, and back away from the fearful object. The best approach to modifying fear-barking behavior is to counter condition and desensitize the dog to the things that frighten her. A puppy who is well socialized during the first four weeks to four months of her life is unlikely to become a fear barker if her humans continue to provide her with positive social experiences throughout her lifetime (see Chapter 19).

Counter conditioning and desensitization are modification techniques that help a dog learn to have positive associations with things that she previously viewed as negative and scary. The process involves presenting a scary stimulus at a safe distance, and associating its presence with something wonderful, such as canned chicken. As the dog learns to tolerate the scary thing – even looks forward to it because it means something "wonderful," the intensity of the stimulus is gradually increased. You may need professional help with this process in order to successfully desensitize your dog. Meanwhile, you want to try very hard to avoid putting your dog in situations that cause her to bark out of fear.

Health/Age-Related Barking

As our faithful friends age, they sometimes succumb to a condition only recently identified as Canine Cognitive Disorder (CCD), where they become disoriented easily and can get lost in their own back yards, trapped behind furniture, forget that they are housetrained, pace, stare into space and not always recognize friends or family members.

According to Pfizer Pharmaceutical, 62% of dogs age 10 years and older experience at least some of the symptoms related to CCD. Along with this syndrome, or unrelated but also linked to age and its accompanying impaired hearing and vision, may come an increase in barking, whining or howling, as the dog expresses frustration with the mysterious changes in her ability to function.

In either case, it can help to keep your dog's world as simple as possible, and avoid making major changes in her environment. Understanding why

the barking has increased can help you be sympathetic rather than angry with her, and give you the patience to simply extricate her when she barks because she's stuck in the corner again. If you think your dog may be suffering from CCD, you can consult with your veterinarian about a new drug, Anipryl, which has been shown to alleviate some of the symptoms of aging.

Perhaps also related to some environmental frustration, or their own inability to hear themselves, deaf dogs are sometimes reported to be barkier than normal hearing dogs. A positive interrupt, using a light beam or vibrating collar as the interrupt signal, can also be effective in teaching deaf dogs a non-verbal "Quiet, please" cue.

Social Isolation/Boredom/ Frustration Barking

This is by far the saddest category of barking behavior, and probably the least normal. It is the incessant barking of the dog who is removed from the normal social interaction of the rest of his family, be it canine or human. It's the dog who barks all day and all night in the backyard, bored and lonely. It's the puppy who is crated in the basement, miserable, crying to be back with her littermates. It's the dog who suffers from separation anxiety, who screams for hours, voicing his panic at being left alone.

In his normal, natural world, a canine lives with other members of his pack virtually 24 hours a day. It speaks volumes for the adaptability of the domestic dog that he *can* learn to tolerate being left alone. But if you have a dog whose barking falls into this category, then it's time to examine your lifestyle and make some changes to better meet *his* needs for social interaction and stimulation.

If he's a backyard dog, bring him in. If he's a neighbor's backyard dog, talk to them about bringing the dog indoors, or at least enriching the dog's environment with interactive toys and other activities that will improve the quality of his life and reduce the need for barking. You can use crates, tethers and pens to prevent chaos while the backyard dog learns house manners.

If the barking dog must be left alone all day, search out a daycare situation, perhaps a commercial doggie daycare, or a friend or neighbor who would like company, or whose home-alone dog might also like a pal. Take him to a training class – or several. Have him go jogging or hiking with you. Discover a dog sport that can showcase his natural talents. Join a dog club. Find a dog park in your community. Or better yet, start one!

If your dog has separation anxiety, seek the help of a qualified trainer/behaviorist who can help you overcome his panic attacks (see Chapter 23). Make him a full-fledged member of your family, and

he will no longer be bored, lonely and frustrated.

Next time you hear a dog bark, rather than being angry or irritated, stop and try to figure out what the dog is saying. Enjoy the fact that dogs can communicate with us vocally as well as with body language, and decide if it's a communication that merits reflection, a response, or just a smile.

❤ JUST SAY "NO" TO NO-BARK COLLARS

There are several different electronic devices that purport to convince your dog to stop barking through the use of an aversive. One type uses electric shock as the aversive, another uses citronella spray, and a third relies on the emission of a high-pitched sound that dogs supposedly find unpleasant. Another method sometimes used to literally cut off the dog noise is debarking, where a dog is silenced by a surgeon's knife.

My own personal philosophies about the use of aversives aside, I don't recommend any of these short-cut tools to resolving a barking problem. Dogs bark for a reason. Aversives and debarking are most commonly used to silence dogs who are barking because of social isolation, without sufficient effort being made to improve the quality of the dog's life. They all punish the dog for appropriate barking as well as what the human decides is inappropriate.

How arrogant of some humans to simply punish or mutilate a dog for expressing his loneliness! The appropriate way to deal with inappropriate barking behavior is to determine the cause of the barking and work in partnership with your dog to resolve the problem behavior, either through training, changes in the environment, medication if appropriate, or perhaps through a re-evaluation of the human's perception of the behavior, not by cutting, shocking, spraying, or otherwise punishing your best friend for his attempts to communicate with you.

CHAPTER 23 ❤
Don't Leave Me! Dealing with Separation Anxiety

I have never owned a dog with separation anxiety. Thank goodness. This complex behavior challenge can be one of the most difficult to live with, and one of the toughest to resolve. The dog who panics when left alone may manifest a range of behaviors that the average owner finds intolerable, including serious household destruction to the point of self-injury, hysterical vocalization (non-stop whining, crying, barking, howling and screaming), and inappropriate defecation and urination – on floors, carpets, beds, and owners' possessions.

Separation anxiety (SA) stems from a dog's natural survival instinct to stay in close proximity to the pack. In the wild, a dog who is left alone is more likely to die – either from starvation, since he has no pack to hunt with, or from predation, since he has no pack mates for mutual protection. Given the vital importance of a dog's canine companions, it speaks volumes about the dog's adaptability as a species that we can condition them to accept being left alone at all! We're lucky we don't have far more SA problems than we do, especially in today's world, where few households have someone at home regularly during the day to keep the dog company.

Recipe For Failure

It's not enough that our dogs are naturally inclined to become anxious when left alone. Many well-intentioned new-dog owners inadvertently set the stage for their new four-legged family members to develop SA by misguidedly doing all the wrong things when little Maxx first comes home. Lots of families adopt their new dog or puppy at the beginning of the summer, when the kids will be home to spend a lot of time with him. Others take several days off from work, or at least arrange to bring Maxx home on a Friday afternoon so they have the entire weekend to help the new kid settle in. At the end of the summer – or the long weekend – Maxx is suddenly left alone for 8 to 10 hours and may panic, thinking he's been abandoned. You can avoid triggering a case of separation anxiety by acclimating your dog to being left alone for short periods at first, gradually working up to an eight-hour day. If it's too late – Maxx already has Separation Anxiety, you will need to work hard to fix it.

A Typical Case of Separation Anxiety

You are at your wit's end. You were only gone for one hour, and when you returned home, your dog Maxx had already destroyed your new sofa, defecated on your antique Oriental rug and inflicted deep gouges in the just-repainted front door frame.

Researchers have learned that dogs with separation anxiety are the most upset and destructive in the first 30 minutes after their owners have left home. Teach your new dog to be comfortable by himself for short periods of time at first, then gradually increase the length of time you leave him home alone.

You have tried leaving him in the back yard, but he chewed through the fence and got picked up by animal control. You tried crating him, but he scraped his toenails bloody and broke a canine tooth trying to dig and chew through the crate door. When you left him in the garage he tore everything within reach to shreds. When you left him in a covered chain-link dog pen on the back patio, you got complaints from three different neighbors about his non-stop barking and howling. You've even tried showing him the damage and punishing him for it, but it hasn't helped. No matter what you do, Maxx gets in trouble. Each time you come home and find something else destroyed Maxx looks guilty, so you *know* he knows he's been bad, but it doesn't seem to stop him the next time. You love him dearly – he is such a sweetheart, and when you are home he is a perfect angel, following you around the house and lying quietly at your feet wherever you go. You hate to think of giving him up, but you don't know what to do with him. If he would only behave himself when you are away from home.

Maxx has separation anxiety – a behavior problem that results from a dog's natural instincts to want to be near other members of his pack. It is a normal survival instinct, but one that can usually be derailed early in a pup's life through proper conditioning. For you and your dog, however, it's too late for the proper early stuff. Mad Maxx already has a full-blown case of separation anxiety, and now you need to try to fix it.

It won't be easy. Separation anxiety is a panic attack, your dog's classically conditioned response to the terror of being left alone. When you walk out the door, Maxx doesn't sit around and muse about whether or not to eat the sofa. Separation anxiety behavior is not a conscious choice – it just happens.

In fact, his anxiety begins before you even leave the house. Your dog can tell from your morning routine whether this is a get-up-and-go-to-work day (which leaves Maxx home alone) or a relax-and-stay-at-home day. As soon as Maxx determines that it's a workday, he starts to worry. Every step in the routine increases his anxiety. The 5:00 a.m. alarm clock. The hurried rush to put Maxx out to potty and then toss him his food dish. The shower and shave. The suit and the shiny shoes instead of blue jeans and sneakers. Coffee and a banana instead of bacon and eggs. The grab for the briefcase and car keys; the pause at the front door for dramatic hugs and kisses to Maxx; promises of undying love; and the fervent admonitions to behave himself while you're gone.

Phew! By the time the door slams in his face and you rush down the sidewalk to the car, Maxx is already worked up into a high state of arousal. He makes no conscious decision to go on a destruction binge, he is simply stressed to the max. Effective ways for him to relieve his stress include chewing, digging, urinating, defecating, and vocalizing.

Anxiety or Hijinks?

Most separation anxiety behavior happens within 30 minutes of the owner's departure, and within a similar period before the owner's anticipated return. The behavior rarely occurs when the owner is home with the dog. This is one of the keys to determining whether Maxx's behavior is truly an anxiety reaction or simply a bout of puppy hijinks.

If you can leave and come back in an hour to an unscathed home, but four hours puts Maxx over the top, chances are you're dealing with boredom, excessive energy, or a housetraining issue rather than true separation anxiety. Some dogs will become destructive in their efforts to go outside to relieve themselves if they are very committed to not soiling the house.

If, on the other hand, your dog displays immediate signs of anxiety upon your exit, he's a candidate for SA retraining. If you can just get the anxious dog through the first half-hour or so, and avoid raising his anxiety level at homecoming time, you are usually home free. Simple – but not easy.

This task is best accomplished through a program of counter conditioning and desensitization (CC&D), fancy terms to describe getting Maxx to like something he now intensely dislikes or fears. In this case, the "something" is being left alone.

The challenge with using CC&D for separation anxiety is that ideally you start with a very low level stimulus that the dog can tolerate, associate it with something wonderful (like the dog's favorite treats) and gradually work up to a level of normal stimulus, *while taking care not to trigger the unwanted response during the process.*

If you are desensitizing a dog to kids, it is relatively easy to avoid his exposure to children between training sessions. It's considerably more difficult for the average pet owner to design a schedule that leaves Maxx alone for no more than a few seconds at first, then minutes, then hours, during the weeks or months that it takes to build his tolerance to being alone. If you are truly committed to working through the problem, and have the time and energy, you can get through this.

No Malice Aforethought, No Post-Destruction Guilt

Because Maxx's behavior isn't malicious or premeditated, it's a misinterpretation of his body language to think that he is acting guilty if he cringes and grovels at your feet when you walk in the door to find the latest episode of destruction. He is more likely responding to your body language as you react in horror and anger to the mess on the floor.

In normal dog society, a display of submission is intended to appease the attacker and turn off the aggression. Maxx's submissive behavior is simply his attempt to divert your visible wrath.

Alternately, perhaps you have gotten angry with him so many times that he is anticipating your inexplicable transformation into a raging lunatic as you walk in the front door, and he is making a proactive effort to forestall your unpredictable behavior.

Since punishment is only effective if it occurs within a few seconds of the transgression, anything you do to punish him when you get home hours after the destruction has occurred only serves to make him anxious about your homecoming, which – you guessed it – makes his separation anxiety even *worse*!

Managing Maxx

You can't confine him, you can't trust him loose in the house or yard, and you can't punish him. What *are* you supposed to do with a Mad Maxx who is rapidly wrecking everything you possess? You need to do two things:

- Manage his environment while his behavior is being modified so he can't hurt himself or destroy things around him

- Use counter conditioning and desensitization to teach Maxx that it is safe for him to be alone.

Let's start with the easy one: managing the environment. This means not leaving Maxx alone until he has decided that being alone is okay. You might be able to find a friend, neighbor or relative who is home during the day, where Maxx can stay and be safe. Perhaps you are fortunate enough to work in a place where your dog could come to the office with you. It never hurts to ask!

Doggie daycare is another excellent option (see Chapter 38). Commercial daycare centers are thriving in an increasing number of communities around the country; there might be a good one near you. Be sure the daycare operator knows that Maxx has separation anxiety and understands how to deal with it – that he can't be left alone and must not be punished for anxiety-related behavior.

Sometimes, although only very rarely, getting another dog can help. If you are considering this, you should only get a second dog because you want one, and are committed to keeping the newcomer whether it helps Maxx's problem or not. *Be careful – you could end up with two dogs with separation anxiety/destructive behavior!*

Finally, there are pharmaceuticals that have appeared on the market relatively recently that purport to help with resolving a multitude of canine behavior problems. Clomicalm(TM) (clomipramine hydrochloride) is the one most commonly prescribed for separation anxiety, but it must be used in conjunction with a good behavior modification program in order to be truly effective – the drug alone will not solve the problem.

Maximized Training

A behavior modification program will help your dog understand that he can survive being left alone. Depending on the severity of the problem, this may happen relatively quickly, or it may take a long time and never be completely resolved. If you have a Velcro dog who can't even tolerate you being in the next room, you will need to start with very small steps. Here's one program for working with separation anxiety:

1. Teach your dog to accept a tether with you standing right next to him (see Chapter 15). When he is comfortable on the tether, take one step away, say "Yes!" before he has a chance to get upset (or Click! your clicker, if he

Your dog can benefit from being in a room with you but separate, not interacting, as well as being left in a room by himself. It is important for him to be able to feel secure entertaining himself.

is clicker-trained), then step back to him and feed him a treat. Repeat this step until he shows no sign of anxiety when you are one step away. Be sure that you remain very matter-of-fact about stepping away. If you get excited or emotional, so will he.

2. Now, gradually increase the length of time that you remain one step away before you "Yes!" (or Click!) and return, until he will tolerate your one-step distance for a full minute or longer. Vary the longer times with shorter ones, so he doesn't start to get anxious about the exercise getting harder and harder each time. You want him to never know how long you will be gone, and at the same time you are teaching him that you always return.

3. Now take two steps away, say "Yes!" and immediately return to feed him a treat. Repeat at this distance until he is comfortable with you being two steps away; then again gradually increase the time at this distance.

4. Very gradually increase the distance, repeating the exercise at each new step until he is calm, then increasing the time at each new distance. If he panics at any point, you have moved too quickly. Go back to the previous distance and work there again until he is calm. Then work in half-step increments, if necessary, to avoid triggering his panic.

5. When he will remain calm while you walk to the other side of the room, sit down and read a magazine, you are ready for the next phase. Start the exercise as before, but this time walk to the doorway to another room, step outside briefly, say "Yes!" and step back into the room before he has a chance to get upset that you are out of sight. Return and reward. Repeat this until he is calm about you stepping out of the room, and then gradually increase the length of time that you remain out of sight.

6. Now, sometimes close the door as you step out of the room, briefly at first, then for longer periods.

7. Do the same exercise with each of the doors leading from the room, including the door that leads to the outside. Sometimes leave the door open, sometimes close it. Be sure to return and reward each time *before* your dog goes into panic mode. If he starts acting anxious at any time, slow down, and go back to a part of the exercise that he can tolerate. Then, when he is calm, proceed more slowly to the step that upset him.

8. Now take him off the tether and repeat Step 6, closing the door each time to prevent him from following you out of the room. Start with very brief departures, so he doesn't have time to start digging at the door. Gradually increase the length of time

you are out of the room, but remember to intersperse the longer absences with short ones so he never knows how long you will be gone. Remember, too, to remain calm yourself. If you start getting anxious or excited about the process, so will he.

9. When he is comfortable with you stepping outside for several minutes, start adding bits of your departure routine to the exercise. Pick up your keys, step outside briefly, return, say "Yes!" and reward. Then put the keys down. Go outside, open and close the car door, then come back inside. Say "Yes!" and reward. As he gets better with pieces of the routine, add more pieces.

10. Assuming that you drive a car to work or school, the next step is to actually start the car engine, then come back inside and reward. Start the car engine, and then vary the amount of time you wait before coming back in to reward. Drive down the driveway, then drive back to the house, come back in and reward. Your goal is to gradually increase the length of time you can be outside to 30 minutes or more. If you can hit the magic 30-minute mark, you are well on your way to success.

Pacing Is Key

Be sure to proceed through these 10 steps at a pace that your dog can tolerate. Short, successful sessions at first (five to ten minutes), are better than long, frustrating sessions that end in failure. You may be able to proceed through the eight steps in a week or two if your dog's separation anxiety is mild, but it is more likely that it may take you several weeks, or months, to work up to 30 minutes. If you aren't making any progress at all, talk to your veterinarian about adding Clomicalm to the equation.

Companion Exercises

There are a number of other steps you can take to help reduce your dog's separation anxiety behavior. These are things that can help *prevent* the problem as well as help modify the already existing anxiety behavior:

1. Exercise your dog well before you leave. A tired dog has less energy with which to be anxious and destructive. Be sure to end your exercise session 20 to 30 minutes before you go, so he has time to settle down.

2. Five minutes before you leave, give him a well-stuffed Kong to take his mind off your imminent departure (see Chapter 37).

3. Make your departures and returns completely calm and emotionless. No huggy/kissy "Mummy loves you" scenes. If he gets excited and jumps all over you when you return, ignore him. Turn your back and walk away. When he finally settles down, say hello and greet him very calmly.

4. Defuse the pieces of your departure routine by also doing them when you are *not* leaving. Pick up your car keys and sit down on the sofa to watch TV. Dress in your business suit and then cook dinner. Set your alarm for 5:00 a.m. on a Saturday, then roll over and go back to sleep.

5. Mix up the pieces of your departure routine when you *are* leaving, so his anxiety doesn't build to a fever pitch. We are creatures of habit too, so this is hard to do, but can pay off in big dividends. Eat breakfast before you shower instead of after. Pick up your keys and put them in your pocket before you take your dog out for his final potty break. Put your briefcase in the car while you are still in your bathrobe. Make the morning ritual as unpredictable as possible.

Fixing separation anxiety is hard work, and it's easy to get frustrated with Maxx's destructive behavior. Remember that he's not choosing to do it out of spite or malice. He is panicked about his own survival without you, his pack, there to protect him. It's not fun for him – he lives in the moment, and the moments that you are gone are long and terrifying. If you make the commitment to modifying his behavior and succeed in making him brave about being alone, you will not only have saved your home from destruction, you will have enhanced the quality of Maxx's life immensely, and perhaps saved him from destruction too.

Dusty, my diminutive eight-pound Pomeranian, grabs a chew-hoof and darts under the coffee table with his prize. Tucker, the 75-pound cattle dog mix approaches, eying the hoof covetously. Dusty curls his lip and emits a surprisingly convincing growl for such a tiny canine. Despite the fact that he could easily take the hoof away from the smaller dog, Tucker backs off, leaving Dusty to chew in peace. I watch, and chuckle at the mini-drama playing out in my living room.

It's most common for dogs to defend their food, but edible items are not the only things that dogs will keep from all potential rivals. Some dogs will defend their "ownership" of toys, a favored sleeping spot, or even the water bowl. Behaviorists and dog trainers call these protective behaviors "resource guarding."

A dog who defends his food from other dogs is exhibiting a perfectly normal and appropriate canine behavior. In the wild, where food supply equals life, the dog who gives up his resources easily has a poor chance for survival. Because survival of individuals is important for survival of the pack, higher ranking pack members often, although not always, subscribe to a "possession is nine-tenths of the law" philosophy. It's generally not worth the risk of injury to a pack member to argue over a bit of food or bone.

Guarding From Humans

Resource guarding is far less acceptable, however, when it's directed toward *us*. For our own safety, we want our dogs to be willing to share. But dogs are probably somewhat confused by our species' apparent ignorance of the "nine-tenths" rule. Accommodating creatures that they are, most dogs learn to give up coveted possessions to their owners without much of a fuss, but from time to time one of our canine pals decides to aggressively assert his ownership rights to a precious toy, a tasty rawhide chew, or a bowl of food. If this describes your dog, you have a serious problem.

The Warning Signs

The more specific the guarding, the easier the behavior is to manage. If your dog only guards truffles, you're pretty safe – at $3,000 per pound, your dog won't often stumble across a forgotten pile of the costly fungus. If anything remotely edible falls into his definition of "guardable," however, you have a much bigger problem.

If this dog was a serious "resource guarder," this would be quite dangerous for the person. As it is, this dog is showing a low – but detectable – level of anxiety about having someone so close to his food.

Generalized food guarding is the most common manifestation of resource guarding, and often the most dangerous, since it is virtually impossible to control the presence of food in the dog's environment. No matter how diligent you are, he will inevitably find the cookie that fell between the cracks of the sofa, the bag of fast food remnants in the gutter, or the deposit of kitty-poo in the garden. While we may not consider cat poop to be edible, to a dog, anything consumable is food.

Determine Extent of Guarding

Resource guarding describes a continuum of behaviors, all of which indicate that a dog is not comfortable with the presence of you or some other human in his "space" while he is in possession of a valuable article. Let's look at a description of various food-guarding behaviors, from those that pose no risk to the dog's human companions to those that pose a grave risk:

Level 1: The ideal and safest response when you approach Fido at his food bowl is that he stops eating, wags his tail, and comes over to greet you. He is telling you that he doesn't perceive you as a threat to his food, or if he does, he doesn't care, the food's not all that important to him; he'd be happy to share it with you.

Level 2: A slightly less perfect but still very safe reaction is that Fido looks at you, wags his tail and continues eating, but is still very relaxed about your presence in the food zone.

Level 3: The first sign of discomfort on Fido's part is usually a slight tensing of his body as you approach. He may also wag his tail. However, if the speed of the wag and the amount of tension in his body increases as you get closer to him, he is communicating that your presence near his resources makes him uncomfortable.

Level 4: As the dog's discomfort escalates, so does his behavior. At the next level you are likely to see a glare in his eye when he looks at you, perhaps a lifting of the lip in a snarl, and an obvious increase in eating speed. One very effective way to prevent you from getting any of his food is for him to eat it all himself, quickly.

Level 5: If the resource is portable, such as a chew-hoof or pig ear, at this level of guarding the dog may carry the item under a chair, a bed, or into his crate, then growl at you when you come too near. If he can't pick it up, he may try to push the item, such as a food bowl, farther away from when you continue to trespass.

Level 6: A serious food-guarder is more than willing to put some teeth into his warnings. A snarl or snap is the next step on the continuum. No contact with your flesh, but a no-uncertain-terms statement that Fido is not prepared to share his food with you.

Level 7: As Fido's protectiveness increases, so does the threat to your safety (or the safety of the child passing by). More serious than a snap is the actual bite. Rarely does a food-guarding bite *not* break skin. The contact is usually very quick and hard, and may consist of several puncturing bites that move up the transgressor's arm or face.

Level 8: Severe food guarding can be triggered even at a distance. At the strongest level, even a person on the far side of the room can be perceived as a threat to the highly valued food or item, and the dog's behavior can escalate very quickly and alarmingly.

Paws rushes to take a toy. Don't use your dog's favorite toy at first. He should want it, but not be obsessed with it.

After just a couple of treats, Paws readily drops the ball for a treat. He doesn't mind her owner's reach for the ball.

After more repetitions, Paws doesn't want the toy at all. That's fine! He should anticipate rewards for sharing.

Behavior Modification

The key to winning the resource guarding battle lies in:

1. Excellent management of guardable resources in the dog's presence.

2. Convincing the dog that your presence is not a threat to his food supply.

Rather, he needs to see you as the welcome harbinger of all delicious consumables. Your presence near the dog should be a reliable predictor of the advent of *more* good stuff, not less. Your role as benevolent distributor of valuable resources is the foundation of your behavior management and modification program.

The good news is that a dog who displays low-level guarding behavior does not automatically advance to higher levels. The behavior you see may be the worst that he ever offers, especially if you institute a behavior modification program *before* the response escalates. The prognosis for successful behavior modification improves greatly if you begin a program as soon as possible.

The bad news is that the higher level dogs do not necessarily give you lower level warnings before they launch an attack. Higher levels of resource guarding can be very challenging to modify. Meanwhile, the behavior presents a very high risk of injury to those around the dog, especially children.

A skilled and knowledgeable owner *may* be able to effectively modify food-guarding behavior up to Level 4 or 5. Anything beyond that definitely begs the assistance of a qualified trainer or behaviorist. An owner who is not confident about working with the dog's behavior at lower levels or who tries and is not making progress should also seek professional help with the dog.

It can be a serious challenge to manage and modify the behavior of a resource-guarder. You will have to:

- **Manage** the behavior through resource control unless and until the behavior has been completely and successfully modified. You must identify and remove all potential guarding triggers. Food bowls, even empty ones, should not be left lying on the floor. Stuffed Kongs, favorite toys, balls, and pillows – anything that triggers even a mild possession response needs to be put away, and given to the dog only in very controlled circumstances.

- **Relocate** the dog's feeding area from a high traffic area to a low one to minimize risk. A dog regularly fed in the kitchen may guard the entire room. A dog fed on the back porch may guard the entire yard. Choose a little-used room that visitors are not likely to stumble into, such as the basement office, or the pantry.

- **Spend** two to four weeks preparing your dog for the program. Feed two to three times a day. Confine him away from the feeding area while you place the food bowl in the feeding room. Then bring the dog to the room, leave the room and close the door until the dog has finished eating, or until 30 minutes has passed.

- **Attend** a positive dog training class using a variety of desirable food treats as rewards. (Do *not* do this if your dog lunges aggressively for food in your hand). Be sure to let the trainer know that your dog is a resource guarder.

- **Implement** a "Say Please" program, where the dog has to earn all good things. Have him "Say Please" by sitting or lying down in order to get anything he wants, including food, toys, and going outside to play.

- **Exercise** him more. A tired dog is a well-behaved dog. Weather permitting, three to four 15-20 minute tongue-dragging sessions of fetch can work wonders in reducing inappropriate behaviors. Watch out for heat stroke – do not overdo exercise in hot weather. Spend more time with the dog in general, doing things that both of you enjoy.

- **Identify** and avoid situations that trigger aggression.

- **Teach** the dog to "Give" on cue.

- **Avoid** punishing the dog should a food guarding or other aggressive incident occur.

- **Implement** a Food Bowl Desensitization program (next page) after 2–4 weeks doing all of the above. This complete program can take four to eight months or longer.

The Final Outcome

Some dogs are successfully and completely rehabilitated through resource guarding modification programs, especially those who exhibit only the lower level behaviors. Many are not. There is a strong likelihood that you will always need to reinforce your resource guarder's new non-guarding behavior, and be cautious about situations that could retrigger the guarding.

Because small children almost always come with food – cookies, crackers, etc. – and they are naturally closer to the dog's own level, many prior resource guarders are *never* trustworthy around children. Of course, dogs and small children should *never* be left together unsupervised, but this goes far beyond that. Many families understandably choose to rehome their resource guarding dogs rather than risk a serious bite to a small child. Finding a good home for a dog with a history of aggression is yet another big challenge.

Rehabilitating a resource guarder can take a huge commitment of time, resources and emotion. Throughout the program, you, other family members, and visitors to your home are at risk of being bitten if there are inadvertent slips in the program.

I applaud responsible dog owners who are willing to make the commitment required to change their dogs' behavior.

I also urge them to think long and hard about their commitment and liability, and to be realistic about whether they are able to do what it takes to ensure the safety of others during the process of reprogramming a resource guarder. And I cheer when I receive reports from those who have been successful in getting their dogs to "share."

❤ FOOD BOWL DESENSITIZATION

This program can take four to eight months (or longer) to rehabilitate a serious food-guarder – and even then, your dog may, never become completely trustworthy. If at any point you are fearful or feel inadequate to deal with the dog, call a qualified positive professional trainer or behaviorist. Only adults or very responsible older teens should implement this program. Do not move to the next phase before the minimum time indicated, or before the dog's demeanor is perfectly calm at the previous phase. Also, keep in mind that following the program outlined below does not guarantee your safety.

PHASE 1: No bowl (one to two weeks)

Place the dog's daily meal in a bowl on a counter or shelf in his feeding room. Include some high-value treats as part of the meal. Schedule several feeding sessions throughout the day. Feed him one-quarter to one-tenth of his day's ration in each session, a piece at a time, by hand. If he lunges aggressively at your hand while feeding, tether him and feed him his meals, a piece at a time, by tossing them from just out of lunging reach. Wait until he is sitting quietly each time to toss him another piece.

PHASE 2: Empty bowl, single pieces (two to four weeks)

Schedule several feeding sessions throughout the day. Place the dog's daily meal in a bowl on a counter or shelf in his feeding room. Place his empty bowl on the ground at your feet. Alternate between feeding him several pieces from our hand **a piece at a time**, and dropping several pieces of food, **a piece at a time**, into his food bowl from waist height. Wait until he has finished each piece before dropping the next.

PHASE 3: Empty bowl, multiple pieces (two to four weeks)

During several feeding sessions throughout the day, place the dog's daily meal in a bowl on a counter or shelf in his feeding room. Place his empty bowl on the ground at your feet. Drop **several** pieces of food into his food bowl and wait until he has finished them. Then feed him **several** pieces, one at a time, from your hand. Now drop several more pieces into his bowl. While he is eating those, drop more treats, one at a time, into his bowl from waist height.

PHASE 4: Two partial bowls (two to four weeks)

Again, schedule several feedings throughout the day, and place the dog's meal in a bowl on a counter or shelf in his feeding room. Put a handful of food in each of two bowls and place one bowl on the floor. Put lower-value food into the bowls; save the higher-value food for treat dropping. If you cannot safely put down the bowl in your dog's presence, tether him, put him on a sit-stay, or shut him out of the room while you put the food bowl down.

PHASE 4: Two partial bowls (two to four weeks) CONT.

While he is eating from the first bowl, place the second bowl on the floor a safe distance away "Safe" will depend on your dog and could be as much as 10 to15 feet or more. Err on the side of caution. Return to the first bowl and drop into it as he continues to eat.

When he has finished the first bowl, stop dropping treats and direct him to the second bowl. While he is eating from the second bowl, return to the first bowl and pick it up. Continue to drop treats into the bowl from which he is eating.

Over the two to four weeks of this phase, very gradually – a few inches at a time – place the bowls closer and closer together. Watch for signs of tension or aggression. If you see any, you have closed the distance too quickly; go back to the distance between bowls where he was relaxed and work at that distance for several days before moving the bowls closer together again.

PHASE 5: Several partial bowls (two to four weeks)

Repeat the previous phase, using several bowls (up to six). You can prepare all the bowls at the same time and set them on the counter, but place them on the floor one at a time, while he is eating from the first bowl. Continue to drop treats into the bowl he is eating from, and occasionally pick up an empty one that is a safe distance from the dog. During this phase, reduce the number of meals to two or three. Also look for opportunities outside of feeding time to drop treats near the dog when he is in possession of other reasonably valuable items.

PHASE 6: Calling the dog (two to four weeks)

Repeat Phase 5, except try to call the dog to you from a distance of six to eight feet just as he finishes the food in a bowl. Have the other bowls set out so he must pass you to go to another bowl. Be sure to give him a very high value treat when he comes to you.

Gradually start asking him to come to **you before** he finishes the food in the bowl – first when he is almost done, then when there is more and more left. As long as he stays relaxed, gradually move closer to the food bowl he is eating from before you call him.

Practice this phase for at least one full week before moving closer to him. Also, look for opportunities outside of feeding time to call him to you to feed him high value treats when he is in possession of other reasonably valuable items.

PHASE 7: Adding people (two to six weeks)

Starting back at Phase 1, have a second person repeat the exercises. This should be another person who is close to the dog, not a child, and not a stranger. Have the person move through the phases, spending up to a week at each phase or longer if necessary. If he is doing well with a second person, add a third, then a fourth. Be sure to use people who are well educated as to their training duties, and able to follow directions.

PHASE 8: Coming out of the closet (two to six weeks, for the rest of the dog's life)

Again, starting back at Phase 1, move the food bowl exercises out of the dog's feeding room into other areas of the house: the kitchen, the dining room, the den, etc. Assuming the training has been progressing well, you should be able to move through the phases relatively quickly. Continue to look for other real-life resource-relevant opportunities to reinforce the message that your presence means more good stuff. Remember that, depending on the success of your desensitization program, your resource guarding dog may never be totally reliable in the presence of valuable items. For the rest of your dog's life, always be aware of the environment and be prepared to intervene if there is a potential risk.

CHAPTER 25 ♥
Plays Well With Others

If you are ever in California, you might want to make it a point to visit Carmel Beach, at the end of Ocean Avenue in Carmel Village, Monterey County. Carmel Beach is a canine utopia. Dogs are allowed, even encouraged, to run off-leash along a breathtaking Pacific Ocean backdrop. On any given day, at any given time, you'll see Golden Retrievers racing along the sand after tennis balls, Labradors fetching sticks from the surf, Border Collies herding shorebirds, and any and all varieties of mixed-breeds and purebreds romping together in happy groups. Rarely, if ever, does a fight happen. Oh, an occasional brief scuffle maybe, as two-ball obsessed Aussies squabble over possession rights. But it's hardly ever serious.

Thus the community of Carmel was shocked two years ago when a Pit Bull terrier attacked and killed a small Poodle. What happened? Why was there bloodshed on the normally peaceful Carmel Beach?

Dogs are pack animals. Their wild ancestors necessarily had to get along for the very important purpose of survival. Even after thousands of generations of domestication, most dogs still play well with others of their species. When they don't, it's usually for one of three reasons: genetics, learned behavior, or poor socialization.

It's In The Genes

Sadly, humans have bred some dogs for dog aggression, most notably the Pit Bull. Dogfighters deliberately selected for dogs who were willing and eager to fight with their own kind until, over time and generations, the quality that they call "gameness" was deeply instilled in the gene pool. A litter of puppies from fighting lines must often be separated by the age of seven weeks or they will fight with each other and cause serious harm. Chances are the tragedy on Carmel Beach was a result, at least in large part, of those genetics.

Other types of dogs were bred for the exact opposite quality. Because they hunt in packs, scent hounds such as the Beagle, Bloodhound and Foxhound, were bred to be exceptionally amenable to pack life. This is one of the reasons Beagles are so often the breed of choice for research colonies. Other breeds fall on a continuum, from the relatively gregarious sporting breeds like Labrador and Golden Retrievers who are generally good with other dogs, to the guard-type dogs like Rottweilers and Chows, who have a greater tendency to be dog aggressive.

Learned Behavior

To some extent, the natural tendencies derived from a dog's genetic package can be countered by learning. Beagles can be made to be dog aggressive under the right (wrong!) circumstances. Some Pit Bulls can be raised peacefully with other dogs, providing care is taken to avoid exposing the dog to incidents that might turn on his fighting "lightbulb." This is why it is critical to raise your dog in an environment that doesn't allow him to be teased, tormented or attacked by other dogs. Tying a dog up or fencing him in a location where other dogs can agitate the confined one, is a classic recipe for dog aggression.

Poor Social Skills

By far the most common cause of inadvertently induced dog aggression is lack of proper socialization. While some veterinarians still urge their clients to keep their young puppies cloistered until they have completed their vaccination series at age four to six months, more and more animal care professionals are recognizing the importance of early socialization with other puppies and dogs in a controlled environment.

Playtime with other puppies and non-aggressive adult dogs gives a puppy the opportunity to learn how to talk and read "dog-ese" through appropriate interactions with and responses to other dogs' body language. If this doesn't happen during the pup's critical learning period, well before the age of six months, you may end up with a canine social nerd whose inept use of canine body language consistently gets him into trouble. This happens either because he sends inappropriate messages or fails to respond appropriately to other dogs' messages.

As with virtually *all* dog behavior problems, prevention is a far better approach than rehabilitation. If you have the luxury of working with your puppy's critical learning window you are light years ahead of the game. The more your pup's breed characteristics and individual personality predispose him to dog aggression, the more critical it is that he be well socialized during the learning period. The following steps can maximize his opportunities for socialization while minimizing his exposure to disease:

DO keep him current on his vaccination schedule. Be especially careful with those breeds who are known to have weaker immune systems (see Chapter 33).

DO invite friends over with their healthy, vaccinated puppies and gentle adult dogs to play with your puppy.

DO enroll your puppy as soon as possible in a well-run puppy class where classmates are allowed to play together. Most trainers require proof of vaccinations for all participants. You may need to convince a trainer that a reduced vaccination schedule is acceptable.

DO talk to the trainer and watch a class first. Puppy play should be closely monitored to avoid bullying of small or timid puppies by bigger, older ones. The facility should be clean indoors and out, and training techniques involving the use of choke chains, prong collars or physical force should not be permitted.

DO intervene – or ask the trainer to intervene – if another puppy starts to bully yours. A pup can learn to be defensively aggressive if he is frightened by the intensity of another pup's play.

DO intervene if your puppy starts to bully another. A gentle interruption of the behavior every time it occurs combined with brief time outs if necessary, offset by praise and treat rewards when he is playing well with others, can keep him on the right track. A time out is what behaviorists call "negative punishment." The puppy's behavior (being too rough or aggressive) makes a good thing (playing with other puppies) go away. If you are consistent he will learn that he has to be nice if he wants to keep playing.

DON'T intervene if two pups are engaged in mutually agreeable rough play. Rough play is perfectly acceptable if both pups are enjoying it. Do keep an eye on the participants to make sure they are both having fun, and gently intervene if the tone of play starts to change.

DON'T take your puppy to dog parks or public areas where lots of dogs congregate. You face a much greater risk of exposure to disease in those environments.

DON'T allow your puppy to sniff piles of feces from unknown dogs when you take him for walks around the block.

DON'T allow your puppy to interact with any dogs or puppies who appear unhealthy, and don't allow the owners of sick dogs or puppies to play with yours.

If you follow these simple guidelines your chances of having a well-socialized dog are high, and your disease risk is very low. Remember: far more dogs face tragic ends to their lives due to poor socialization than to illnesses encountered in well-monitored puppy play groups.

Predictors of Success

What if you're not so lucky? Maybe you already missed your puppy's learning period, either because you weren't aware of the importance of socialization, or because you adopted a pre-owned older dog. If this just meant that the other dogs wouldn't play with yours on the playground, it wouldn't be a big deal.

But the most common behavior problems manifested by a dog who is poorly socialized with other dogs are fear and aggression.

Is she doomed to a life of isolation from other dogs because she responds intensely and negatively when she sees other dogs, or because there have been incidents of aggression when you have allowed her to play off-leash with others? Not necessarily. The following factors will be key to the success of a rehabilitation program for your dog:

1. **How old is she?** The younger she is, the better the prospects for rehabilitation. The older she is the more likely that the behavior has been happening for a long time and is a deeply ingrained habit.

2. **How intense are the fights?** The more serious the intent to do harm, the more difficult the behavior may be to change, and the more at risk you are (and other dogs are) when a fight does occur.

3. **How capable are you of preventing fights?** If you cannot control the environment to prevent her from getting into fights while you work to correct the behavior, chances of successful rehabilitation are low. If the kids leave the gate open and she gets out, or if you aren't willing to curtail your off-leash walks and she continues to get into fights, she is

reinforcing the undesirable behavior far more effectively than you are working to change it.

4. **What are her breed and temperament predispositions?** A submissive young Beagle whose occasional bouts with other dogs are triggered by fear and defensiveness is much easier to rehabilitate than a poorly socialized but dominant Pit Bull, Rottweiler or Akita with a long history of violent encounters.

5. **How much time are you willing to dedicate to changing your dog's behavior?** This is not an easy fix. Successful aggression behavior modification through counter conditioning and desensitization takes time and patience. Beware of any trainers who offer to fix an aggression problem overnight. Chances are they are likely to use coercive techniques that may drive the aggression underground temporarily but not truly change the dog's mind-set about other dogs. You must be willing to invest a significant amount of time and effort, maybe even money, if you want to succeed.

The Rehabilitation Process

The more positive answers you had to the above five questions, the better your chances are of ending up with a dog who "plays well with others." If the problem is still in its embryonic stages you might be able to accomplish the desensitization and counter conditioning on your own. If the problem is more serious, you might want to make use of the services of a competent professional who uses positive methods to work with aggression problems. You will need to be realistic about your goal. Most dogs can be taught to walk calmly on leash around other dogs. Some will eventually be safe off-leash around other dogs, but not all.

Caveat: If at any time you don't feel confident in implementing the next step of the following training program, it's time to seek professional help. Similarly, if you feel you are not making progress, or if your dog's aggression or fear reaction is constantly being triggered, look for a trainer to help you. Some trainers offer group classes specifically for dogs with aggression and socialization problems.

STEP 1:

Counter conditioning: You want your dog to think that being around other dogs is a *wonderful* thing, not something to be feared. Start by finding a location where you can control the distance between you and your on-leash dog and other dogs in the vicinity. A training class in a park is perfect. You know the dogs will stay in their class location and you can position yourself as far away as necessary. Another potential location is a large parking lot outside a pet supply store.

Find the distance that is far enough from the other dogs that yours doesn't feel threatened. Setup a lightweight lawn chair (or sit on a park bench) and hang out there for at least 20 minutes. If there is likely to be canine foot traffic passing by, set up signs politely asking people to keep at a distance with their dogs because you are training yours. Do not do this in a location where loose dogs are likely to run up to you.

While you are sitting in your chair, toss your dog a steady stream of the most irresistible treats you can find. Take a *huge* supply with you so you don't risk running out. Right now, she is conditioned to think that dogs are dangerous, and something to be feared. By pairing the presence of other dogs with extra-yummy food, you can counter condition her to think that the presence of other dogs is a *good* thing.

At this point you do not need to wait for "good" behavior or pair the food with a reward marker such as a Click! or a "Yes!" You are not trying to train a behavior, you are just trying to change the way her brain involuntarily reacts to the presence of other dogs.

Note: Many dog-aggressive dogs will get so tense and wound up over the sight of other dogs that they will ignore your usual treats. This generally means two things: First, you might have to work a little harder of be a little more creative in your search for irresistible treats. Then, if especially yummy treats such as pieces of hot dog, meatballs, roast beef, cheese or canned chicken aren't working, it's an indication that the situation you have created is still too stressful. Increase the distance between your dog and the other dogs until he will take the treats, or consider finding an entirely different, even less stressful environment in which to work.

Also, some dogs will become so stressed by the mere sight of distant dogs that they will forget their usual treat-eating manners and snap at the treats, endangering the treat-feeder's fingers! Rather than putting yourself in a position where you feel compelled to verbally "snap" back, toss the treats on the ground in front of the dog. Or, if he's too preoccupied with the other dogs and doesn't notice the treats on the ground, wear gloves when you hold the treats near his muzzle. Remember: You want this to be a pleasant experience for the dog. Don't "correct" his lapses at this point; it will only confirm his negative feelings about other dogs.

STEP 2 :

Desensitization: Desensitization is the process of gradually increasing the intensity of the stimulus that causes a reaction. It often goes hand in hand with counter conditioning. When your dog is eagerly looking forward to her trips to the park, you will *very gradually* start moving your chair closer to the training class – or other controlled source of

dog presence – until you can sit next to the class and watch without a negative reaction from your dog.

The speed with which you do this will vary, depending on your dog's response. If she starts acting uneasy when you move five feet closer, you may need to move in one-foot increments. If she is totally sold on the concept of "treats + other dogs = great stuff," then you can move more quickly. You will still shower her with treats to continue the counter conditioning. You can also, at this point, Click! and reward specific good behaviors, such as a tail wag or happy glance at you when she sees another dog. The reaction we are looking for is, "Cool!! There's another dog!!! Where's my treat?"

STEP 3:

Interacting with other dogs: If and when you get to this point, find a friend with a very calm, easygoing dog, and introduce the two dogs off-leash, in an enclosed, controlled, neutral environment. Many dogs will fight on-leash and be perfectly fine off-leash. This is due in part to something called restraint frustration (when the frustration of being restrained by the leash raises the dog's level of arousal, making a fight more likely) and in part to the fact that the owner's control of the leash inhibits a dog from displaying normal body language signals.

Your dog should now be relaxed and happy when other dogs are around. Start by letting her see the other dog with both dogs on leash, and if her reaction is positive, drop both leashes and let them greet.

Note: I suggest that you put soft nylon muzzles on both dogs before releasing them for the first time, as an added precaution. Both dogs should be conditioned to wearing the muzzles prior to meeting, so the extra equipment doesn't add stress to the greeting. If there is a scuffle with muzzles on no one will be hurt, and you can give them a bit of time to work through the disagreement. If it doesn't resolve itself after 5-10 seconds then break it up and remove the dogs.

This first meeting should be relatively short. You want to end on a high note so your dog goes away with a positive experience. It is important that *you* remain calm during this interaction and that any verbal communications with your dog are done in a relaxed tone of voice. This is not easy to do when you are wound tight in anticipation of a possible fight, but any tension in your body or voice will be transmitted to your dog, and increase *her* level of tension.

Assuming positive results from the first interaction, schedule several more of gradually increasing length. Meanwhile, seek out other people with dog-friendly dogs who are willing to participate in your training program. When you find yourself relaxing while your dog plays with her first canine friend, it is time to introduce her, one-at-a-time, to other play partners. Once she has several congenial friends you can try a threesome, then gradually increase the size of the playgroup.

Your dog's reaction to the increased levels of arousal in larger groups will help you decide if she will ever be ready for off-leash play at Carmel Beach, or if discretion dictates that she restrict her recreational activities to pre-screened pals. Whichever you decide, she will have come a long way from where she started, and be able to reap the physical and mental benefits of interactions with others of her own kind.

CHAPTER 26 ❤
Break It Up! Dog Fights

Hang around with dogs long enough, and sooner or later you're likely to encounter a dogfight. It might be a battle over resources – food, toys, territory, or your attention, or one dog taking offense at another's non-verbal communication style. It could be a struggle for position within the social status hierarchy, or simply a matter of a dog being in the wrong place at the wrong time. Perhaps it's a case of redirected aggression. Fido *really* wanted to attack the stray dog on the other side of the fence but couldn't get to him, so he turned on Snoopy instead. Or you may have the misfortune of experiencing one of the most frightening dogfight scenarios such as when an aggressive stray dog attacks yours for no apparent reason (although you can be sure *he had one*) while the two of you are taking a simple walk-on-leash around the block

Dogs fight. Despite the genetic programming that generally allows dogs to live harmoniously in groups, from time to time the harmony is shattered and a real fight occurs. When it does, it can be terrifying and dangerous both to the humans as well as the canines who get involved in the fracas.

Your first instinctive response may be to yell at the top of your lungs to try to break up the battle. Your second is often to reach in and attempt to bodily rescue your canine pal – especially if it appears he is getting the worst of it. Neither of these actions is likely to be effective. Yelling often adds to the stress and arousal that led to the fight in the first place, and only intensifies the battle. Reaching into the fray more often than not results in multiple lacerations to human skin – sometimes inflicted by your own dog, who is too engaged in the battle to recognize or respect his own person's hand, arm or face.

Of course, you can't just stand back and watch when a ferocious dogfight is in progress, especially if a 150-pound bully is mauling your tiny teacup of a pup. So, what *should* you do?

Management Is Key

I've lost track of how many times I've said this, but as always, preventive management beats cure all to pieces. It is imperative that you manage and train your own canine family to minimize the risk of serious dogfights. Identify situations that are likely to light the dogfight fuse, such as fence fighting or resource guarding, and figure out how to avoid them and/or modify the behavior that is causing them. In addition, establish a calm home atmosphere. Dogs who live in a structured environment where it is clear which behaviors are allowed and which are not, are much more likely to live in harmony than those who live in homes where chaos reigns. Something as simple as requiring all dogs to sit politely before the door is opened to the backyard can help instill order in the pack and respect for you as the benevolent leader of the family.

It's fine to allow your dog to play in groups at places like dog parks, daycare and neighborhood dog romps, as long as you make sure that members of the social groups are appropriate playmates in terms of size, personality and play style. Play group opportunities help to keep dogs well socialized, which helps prevent dogfights. Most dog parks have rules that require their canine park users to "be nice." Politely ask human guardians of inappropriate members to remove their dogs from the group. If they refuse, remove your own dog(s), and report the offender to the users' group or other authority responsible for monitoring dog park use. If your dog has trouble being "nice" around other dogs, then you will need to take a pass on these social outlets.

If you live in an area where aggressive stray dogs are common, request that your local animal services agency step up their patrol efforts so that you can safely walk your dog. If Animal Services is reluctant to step in, speak with your elected officials about what needs to be done to make the agency more responsive to community needs. If you can identify owners of the errant dogs and feel comfortable approaching them, explain that their dogs are causing problems, and politely ask them to keep the dogs safely at home where they belong!

Protection

You can't always predict and prevent incidents of serious dog-dog aggression. You can, however, be prepared to intervene safely to protect your dog and yourself should the necessity arise. Familiarize yourself with various tools and techniques that have the greatest chance of successfully quelling doggie disputes with the least injury to all parties. Then determine which are most appealing to you, and be sure to have them on hand (and in your head) should the time come when you need them.

These tools and techniques range from small and simple to big and bold. It is important to remember that none of them are foolproof; they all involve some inherent risk to the dogs who are fighting and to the humans who are trying to intervene, and they can all be applied with varying degrees of success. You will need to weigh the odds and decide, in each case, if the risk outweighs the potential for injury from the fight itself.

Some Protection Tips

The topic of breaking up dogfights came up recently during a discussion between Association of Pet Dog Trainers (APDT) members, and generated an interesting list of suggestions. Let's look at some of them and see how useful they might be (or not!) for the average dog-on-the-street:

PREVENTION

Prevention means making wise decisions about dog husbandry that will keep you in the best position to avoid dangerous conflict.

Beverly Hebert, of Sugar Land Texas, no longer walks both of her German Shepherds at the same time, so she can better manage a situation if it does arise. She realized that having more than one dog on leash puts her at an impossible disadvantage if an unfriendly dog or pack of dogs approaches her and her canine friends. She feels much more confident about her ability to use appropriate tools and techniques to protect one dog than two.

She also tries to use good sense about when and where to walk her dogs. She says, "When we were on vacation with our dogs in Taos, New Mexico, my husband wanted to go for walks with the dogs down a mountainside road in an area filled with dogs. He thought I was a 'Nervous Nellie' because I wouldn't do that, but every time we passed a home with no fence and a loose dog I heaved a sigh of relief that our dogs weren't with us."

AVERSIVES

Aversives are tools that a dog finds offensive to the senses including smells, sounds, and other stimuli that are strong enough to stop a behavior. In general, aversives can be most effective if used to interrupt fighting dogs prior to full arousal in an altercation; their effectiveness decreases as arousal levels increase – although they may still succeed in stopping many full-scale fights. Aversives should also be considered primarily a tool for crisis intervention. I don't recommend using them as basic training tools.

Marni Fowler, of Gainesville, Florida, reminds us that blasting dogs with water from a nearby hose is a tried and true method of separating fighting dogs. She's right that it often works, assuming a hose happens to be nearby with a powerful enough spray to do the job. A good tool to keep in your arsenal for the right time and place – like your own yard. Not particularly useful, however, when there's no hose handy!

One of the easily portable aversive sprays, such as Direct Stop™ (citronella) or Halt!™ (pepper spray) might be an effective alternative to the hose. Of the two, Direct Stop, available from Premier, is the safer choice, since pepper spray products are more corrosive, and the spray can drift and affect innocent bystanders – humans as well as dogs. There are laws in some jurisdictions requiring that users of pepper spray products complete a training course and carry a permit. In a pinch, even a fire extinguisher, while not easily portable, might just happen to be a handy and effective aversive tool.

Debi Davis, of Tucson, Arizona, trains service dogs from her wheelchair, and is always accompanied by one or more of her own service-trained Papillons. The dogfight topic is of great interest to her, both because her dogs are small and more vulnerable than many others, and because her own mobility and ability to protect them is limited.

Davis has an air horn attached to her chair that makes 10 different sounds – sirens, horns, barnyard animals, etc., and she can crank the sound up to a deafening level. Air horns, available at boating supply stores, can be effective at warding off attacking dogs – but your own dog has to be desensitized to the cacophony, or you are likely to lose him as well! You can also risk damage to eardrums, both canine and human, and you do take a chance of frightening your own dog beyond repair.

Nicole Wilde, of Gentle Guidance in Santa Clarita, California, says that she had good success most of the time with air horns when she worked at a doggie daycare center several years ago. They were quite effective in breaking up fights in a majority of the cases.

Physical Intervention With Objects

A number of trainers suggested intervention with a physical object of some kind. If fights are a regular problem in your household you might attach a couple of handles to a sheet of plywood so you can lower it between two sparring dogs and force them apart.

Dogfighters and some Pit Bull owners who don't fight their dogs but know the breed's potential, carry a "parting stick" or "break stick" with them wherever they go with their dogs. This is usually a carved or whittled hammer handle, tapered to a rounded point at one end. When two dogs are locked in combat, the parting stick can be forced between a dog's teeth and turned sideways, to pry open the jaws. Parting sticks can break a dog's teeth, and a dog whose jaws have just been "parted" may turn on the person doing the parting. Like many other techniques offered here, this method should only be considered for dire emergencies.

A blanket can also be a useful tool. Tossed over the fighters (one over each works best), it muffles outside stimuli, thereby reducing arousal. This also allows the humans to reach in and physically separate the combatants by picking up the wrapped pooches with less risk of a serious bite. The blanket will also cushion the effect of teeth on skin if the dog does whirl and chomp.

Laura Van Dyne of The Canine Consultant, LLC in Carbondale, Colorado, suggests a defensive technique she saw demonstrated at a conference by Trish King, Director of the Behavior and Training Department at the Marin Humane Society in Novato, California. King paints *big* eyes and teeth in bright paint on an umbrella – the kind that explodes open at the touch of a button – then carries it, folded up, when walking in places where stray dogs are a threat. When an aggressive dog approaches, *whoosh!* the "Defend-A-Brella" leaps into action and wards off the threat. You would, of course, need to desensitize your *own* dogs to the umbrella action prior to using it in real-life. This is not as likely to stop a fight in progress, but may well forestall an attack from an approaching dog.

Janet Smith, Behavior Program Manager for the Capital Area Humane Society in Lansing, Michigan, offers a somewhat drastic technique, reminding us that when a dog's life and limb are at stake, drastic measures may be called for. Smith says, "You can wrap a leash round the aggressor's neck or get hold of a collar and twist to cut off the dog's airflow,

until he lets go to try to get a breath of air, then pull the dogs apart."

Of course, this could be more difficult than it sounds. It might be a challenge to get a leash around the neck of a dog who is "attached" by the mouth to another dog without getting your hands in harm's way, and grabbing a collar to twist also puts hands in close proximity to teeth.

Physical Intervention By Humans

Jackie McGowan, of Click Start Dog Training in Calgary, Alberta, Canada, attended a seminar given by Turid Rugaas, author of *On Talking Terms With Dogs*, and reports that the highly respected Norwegian trainer had a few suggestions for magic techniques for breaking up fights. According to McGowan, Rugaas said that she usually gives dogs a chance to work it out, but if it is apparent that this is not going to happen, she will try and walk between and/or gently pull one dog away by their collar. Rugaas also cautioned seminar attendees that she would *not* recommend this to others handling a fight because the risk of injury to the human is high.

Carla Baker of A to Z Training in Olympia, Washington, recalls a technique she observed in action at a dog show some 20 years ago. "Two dogs got into it and were going to cause some major damage," Baker says. "The elderly judge was a very tiny woman, and she had the handlers both grab their dogs and hold on *tight*. Then she went up and took the dog on top by the tail and jammed her thumb up his rectum. He let go in an instant and whirled around to see what the heck was happening. The judge excused the two dogs, calmly washed her hands, and then continued her classes without a hitch – just as if it happened every day."

"Don't know that I'd try this myself," Baker concluded, "but it sure did work!"

Valerie Poulton, of Omaha, Nebraska, offers one more approach to physical intervention; one that could be a little difficult if the clearly identified aggressor is a 150-pounder, but sounds worth trying with a smaller dog. This method was demonstrated at Poulton's training club last year by author and trainer, Suzanne Clothier. Poulton has since tried it herself and reports that it worked for her on two separate occasions with her own dog, but only in a one-on-one dog brawl; she would not recommend it in a multi-dog fight situation.

"Lift the rear of the clearly-identified aggressor so that he is suspended with his fore-feet barely touching the ground," Poulton explains. "The dog lets go, and the target can scoot free."

Poulton cautions that her dog is dog aggressive only, and will *not* turn on a human. "Supposedly, in this position the dog is not able to turn on the human suspending him, although I cannot say I have used it with a dog who might try."

Armed and Ready

Now, all you need to do is stuff a canister of Direct Stop in your pocket, hang an umbrella over your arm, attach a parting stick to your belt, carry a blanket over your other arm, balance a sheet of plywood on your head, wear an air horn around your neck, and be sure you have at least two friends with you to hold dogs while you put your thumb in private places, and you are ready for anything.

Seriously, if and when that next fight happens, take a deep breath, resist your instincts to yell or leap in the middle of the fray, quickly review your available options, and choose the one – or ones – that are most likely to work in that place and time. When the fight is over and no one is being rushed to the hospital in an ambulance, remember to take a moment to relax and breathe, and then congratulate yourself for your quick thinking.

CHAPTER 27 ❤
MY Human! Canine Perspectives on Love Triangles

Jeal-ous *adj* **1a:** intolerant of rivalry or unfaithfulness **b:** apprehensive of the loss of another's exclusive devotion **2:** vigilant in guarding a possession

Tucker, our Cattle Dog mix, loves to play active, noisy games with my husband, Paul. Unfortunately, Katie, our Australian Kelpie, doesn't approve. If Paul and Tucker try to engage in a rousing game of Growly Butt-Scratch or an energetic bout of Tug-'O-War, Katie charges into the den and effectively breaks up the game by making ugly faces at Tucker and biting his heels. Once Tucker is squelched, Katie runs to Paul, ears back, eyes squinting adorably, and demands attention for herself with a burst of irrepressible Kelpie energy. (I like to fondly describe Kelpies as Border Collies on uppers!)

You may have a dog at home who uses other methods – perhaps less aggressive, perhaps more – to come between you and another dog with whom you are interacting. Is this jealousy? If not, what is it? And whatever it is, how do we deal with it?

A Working Definition

Trainers have mixed opinions about whether dogs truly display the emotion known as jealousy. Behaviorists don't even use the term. A glance at the definitions may explain why. If we define jealousy as "intolerant of unfaithfulness" or "apprehensive of the loss of another's exclusive devotion," then dogs would not be accurately described as being jealous. This definition implies the ability to analyze and react to past events, or anticipate future ones. Because dogs live pretty much "in-the-moment," they are virtually incapable of anticipating a future loss, or of reacting belatedly to an event that is over and done with. When you walk in the door and your dog sniffs you all over because you have been petting someone else's dog, a more likely explanation than jealousy is that he is reading the other dog's scent with intense interest because it is new and different.

By the second definition, however, "vigilant in guarding a possession," some trainers will argue that dogs certainly may be perceived as being "jealous." Some dogs have mastered the art of resource guarding, and for many dogs, their owners are very valuable resources indeed. So, although we humans are sometimes prone to sitting around feeling jealous and miserable because something diverted our beloved's attentions (or we think something *might* divert it), a dog may experience "jealousy" in the resource guarding sense only when a threat to the coveted resource (the dog's human) is present and immediate.

Deb Jones, Ph. D., psychologist, author and positive trainer and canine behavior specialist for Planet Canine, in Akron, Ohio, agrees that dogs display behaviors that we can categorize as jealousy. "I believe that with both humans and animals there is an unpleasant emotional experience connected with the loss of desired resources," Jones says. "When that resource is a person and the experience is connected with competition for that person, we tend to label it as jealousy. When important resources are threatened, the result can be an increased effort to retain that resource."

Positive trainer Leslie Nelson, Training Director at Tails-U-Win! Canine Center in Manchester, Connecticut, prefers to think more in terms of basic resource guarding. "While many dogs, especially in multi-dog households, appear to be jealous of one another," says Nelson, "I think what we are actually witnessing is a bit more basic. One of the reasons I enjoy my dogs so much is that they live very much in the present and don't waste their lives held captive by destructive emotions." Nelson continues, "Having said that, dogs are very possessive about valuable resources. Your attention, your voice, your touch are all to be prized, and

it is only natural that a possessive dog would want them all for himself."

Identifying the Monster

Whether you prefer to call it jealousy or resource guarding, the behavior is the issue, and it can be problematic. While it may be ego-gratifying to think that our dog wants our undivided attention, it can interfere with our relationships with other loved ones, and can even result in severe injury to other dogs or humans. It's a behavior that we should discourage, but before we can do that we need to be able to identify when it rears its ugly head.

A human resource-guarding dog can be obviously aggressive, as our Katie is with Tucker, or the display may be more covert. Jones describes the behavior of her Labrador Retriever (coincidentally, also named Katie). "My own Lab, Katie, is the queen of passive aggressive methods for gaining attention," Jones explains.

"When I pay attention to another dog she'll sidle up to me and worm her way under my arm. She'll offer her paw or roll over to show her belly (asking for a belly rub). All these are very endearing ways of gaining attention," Jones continues, "but they are still quite demanding and purposeful. They serve to move attention away from the other dog and back to her – where she thinks it belongs!"

A dog's human resource-guarding can

be defined as any behavior displayed by your dog that is intended to draw your attention and or physical presence away from another dog and back to him. Or away from another human! Most trainers' files are liberally salted with case histories of dogs who, with varying degrees of success, try come between husband/wife, boyfriend/girlfriend, parent/child, and any other permutations of human relationships.

This can be manifested by a behavior as apparently benign as your dog worming his way between you and another dog or person, or as serious as full-blown aggression. It might be cute if little Chico the Chihuahua tries to bite your boyfriend when he kisses you, but it could get in the way of a long-term relationship and it certainly won't be cute when you have to drive your boyfriend to the emergency clinic for stitches in his lip! Unfortunately, what may initially be perceived as an adorable attempt on your dog's part to claim your exclusive attention sometimes ends up in a one-way trip for the dog to the euthanasia room, when the behavior escalates to a level that draws blood.

Wherever your dog may be on the human resource-guarding continuum, the sooner you start modifying the behavior the easier it will be to prevent it from escalating to dangerous levels, and to return to healthier relationships between your dog and your other loved ones.

Modifying Resource Guarding

The first step toward changing your dog's behavior is a good, positive training class. Training opens the channels of communication and strengthens the relationship between you and your dog.

The more dogs you have, the more important it is for pack harmony that you train them. Good verbal control of your dogs raises your status in your dogs' eyes as benevolent pack leader, and greatly enhances your ability to intervene peacefully and appropriately when necessary.

Nelson lives in a household with seven dogs (three Afghan Hounds, two Whippets, one Standard Poodle and a Shih Tzu), ranging in age from seven months to eleven years. The pack consists of both sterilized and intact animals. Nelson told us she hasn't had a fight in years in her pack, but she sure used to! Through a combination of training and the judicious use of "negative punishment," she has taught her dogs to coexist in relative peace.

"We have one hard and fast rule," says Nelson. "No fighting in front of us! The second any inappropriate behavior starts I say 'If you are going to do that Go Outside.' I run to the door and send all the offenders out. With my older dogs now I simply say 'Do you need to go out?' and the bad behavior stops! By the way – I also am very generous rewarding appropriate behavior..."

Dogs do what feels good, or, as behaviorists say, "behavior is reward driven." Nelson reminds us that if your dog is doing something that you want to change, at some level it is rewarding to him. "Find out what the reward is," she says. "And you are well on your way to changing the behavior."

Find out how to remove the reward (negatively punish the behavior), make the good thing go away, and there's a good chance the behavior will diminish and eventually stop. With human resource-guarding, the good thing is you, or your attention.

"If your dog has a pattern of aggressive behavior toward your other dogs when you are paying attention to them, you are probably reinforcing the aggressive dog with your response," says Nelson. "Think what it is that you do. Most of us instinctively turn our attention toward the aggressor and yell at him or try to soothe him. Our attention is a huge reinforcer. Even negative attention is better than no attention."

Dr. Jones concurs with Nelson's feelings about the positive reinforcement power of attention, and the effectiveness of negative punishment. She recommends a time-out in mild cases of human resource-guarding.

"We use a two-minute isolation in a crate as soon as the behavior starts," she says. "In many cases both dogs are contributing to the situation, even though one may look like the victim. In these cases, both dogs are isolated and/or ignored for a short time as soon as the unacceptable behavior starts."

By using a time-out, you negatively punish the behavior. You may be able to accomplish the same result just by walking away from both dogs, closing a door if necessary to prevent them from following. The behavior is negatively punished by the removal of the reward that the dogs are seeking - your attention or your very presence.

Time-outs work best when they are short, like Jones's two-minute example, and should be done with a pleasant body language and tone of voice. We are not trying to intimidate the dog into behaving, we are simply showing him that the consequence of his misbehavior is that all the good stuff goes away.

Jones suggests a few other possible approaches for dealing with human resource-guarding:

- Instituting very clear structure in terms of acceptable behavior

- Practicing responsible management by keeping the dogs separated as necessary

- Using counter conditioning to teach the dogs that they are not a threat to each other, but rather a predictor of good things. For example, the dog only gets treats and attention in the presence of the other dog, and is ignored when the other dog is not present.

When to Get Help

When injuries are occurring to dogs or humans, you are in over your head. Nelson and Jones both agree that there are times when you need the help of a professional. This is one of them.

"In severe cases the owner must work with a qualified trainer and/or behaviorist," warns Jones. When there are puncture wounds and stitches, things will probably escalate until there is a very serious injury."

Nelson concurs. "If your dogs have escalated to serious aggression involving blood and stitches, find yourself a good behaviorist who uses positive reinforcement, not punishment, to modify behavior. This is a serious situation beyond the scope of this article."

Back to Katie and Tucker

I use a combination of the training tools suggested by Nelson and Jones to deal with our own dogs' human resource-guarding.

Katie and Tucker are both trained, and can be asked to go lie down on a verbal cue. We use positive reinforcement for good behaviors, and negative punishment for the undesirable ones. We also use management, by crating Katie or putting her outside when Paul wants to play with Tucker without interruption from the Kelpie shark.

I probably will never completely extinguish her guarding behavior – the compulsive herding dog instincts are just too strong. I can, however, keep peace in my pack of four dogs. Katie's behaviors don't prevent me from enjoying our canine companions either individually or as a group, and I have no fear of bloodshed – a reasonable enough goal for me.

CHAPTER 28 ❤
Bouncing Off the Walls: The High-Energy Dog

The elderly man's voice quavered haltingly in my ear. "Whiskey is just too energetic for us. We have to keep him penned up in the kitchen, and when he's outside he just bounces on the door. He already broke the glass once! How do we stop him from bouncing on the door?"

Whiskey was an 18-month-old Labrador Retriever, adopted three weeks prior from the local humane society, to a couple in their mid-70's. His new humans were experienced dog owners and had owned Labradors before, but their last dog died a decade earlier, at the ripe old age of 14 years. It had been almost a quarter of a century since the well-meaning couple had managed an active young dog, and it was clear that they had made an ill-advised adoption choice when they brought home an adolescent Lab with an unknown history, who had clearly missed more than a few of his early good manners lessons. Rather than being the loving companion they had envisioned, Whiskey was making this couple's life miserable.

Unfortunately, their solution – banishing Whiskey for longer and longer periods of time to the back yard – was compounding the problem, making Whiskey lonely and even more over-stimulated when he was finally granted any time in their company. They would, they promised, bring him in the house once he calmed down, but the more time he spent outside, the less calm he got. The relationship was spiraling rapidly downward, with the wife insisting that Whiskey was beyond help, and threatening to take him to their veterinarian for euthanasia.

We hastily scheduled an appointment for a private consultation. I assured the couple that there was no need to rush Whiskey to the euthanasia table. The young dog's behavior sounded pretty normal for an untrained adolescent Lab, and even if he wasn't suitable for their home, there were other options available to him, such as Labrador Retriever Rescue, or one of the many government search dog programs.

Sadly, Whiskey's is not an isolated case. A generation or two ago, Mom stayed in the home and taught the dog good manners while the rest of the family went off to work or to school. Today, many family canines are latchkey dogs, left to their own devices all day, and family members are often too busy or too tired when they get home to spend the time necessary to properly train the dog. So, while it's increasingly the social norm to spay and neuter, and many animal shelters are seeing fewer litters of unwanted puppies as a result, shelter kennels are often filled with out-of-control adolescents like Whiskey.

Clicks For Calm

Whether you have a baby dog with normal puppy energy or an obstreperous teenager who has good manners lessons to catch up on, clicker training (see Chapter 2 for more details) can be a magically effective and gentle way to convince a dog to calm down. No yelling, no physical punishment; just clicks and treats for any pause in the action. The biggest challenge with a "hyper" dog is that any praise or reward may cause her to begin bouncing off the walls again. It is nearly impossible to deliver the treat to the excitable dog while she is still in the act of being calm. By the time you get

It can be a challenge to teach an active dog like this to sit quietly.

the treat to her mouth she is once again doing her Tasmanian devil act. She may well perceive the treat as a reward for her jumping jacks rather than for the sought-after calmness that occurred briefly several seconds before.

Timing and consistency are keys to successful training with the overactive dog. If you give the reward to your dog more than a second or two after she exhibits the desired behavior, she will lose the connection, and will likely believe she was rewarded for whatever she was doing at the moment you gave her the reward. Hence the value of the clicker or other reward marker. An instant of calm elicits a Click! and a treat. If your timing is impeccable then your training will be successful. An added advantage of the clicker is that once dogs understand that Click! = treat, when they hear the Click! they pause in anticipation of the coming morsel, drawing out the relatively calm behavior even longer.

The "All Is Calm" Program

Here's how you can turn your Tasmanian Devil into a Serene Sally. Follow this simple program to help her get rid of excess energy, prevent her from being rewarded for out-of-control behavior, and consistently reward her for being calm.

1 – REST FOR THE WEARY

The first element in an "All Is Calm" program is to provide your dog with lots of exercise. As I have said before, wise dog trainers and owners know that a tired dog is a well-behaved dog. Often, when dogs are behaving badly, they are simply chock-full of energy bursting to find an escape. Tug-o-war on your pants leg, donuts around the dining room table, and record high-jumps over the back of the sofa are just some of their outlets for that pent-up energy.

If this sounds like your dog, schedule at least three tongue-dragging sessions of fetch per day. Climb to the top of a hill or staircase and throw the ball down so she has to keep climbing back up to return it to you. Set up an obstacle course in your living room, basement or back yard, with lots of things to climb and jump over. Be careful not to send her into heat stroke, but definitely play until she is pooped. Keep your exercise breed-appropriate. An athletic Border Collie can handle lots more physical challenges than an English Bulldog.

Don't think that a walk around the block will do it. A walk on leash, even a long one, is nothing but an exercise *hors d'ouerve* for a young dog. You may be tired when you get home from the walk, but your dog is just getting warmed up! If no one in the family has time to give her adequate exercise, arrange for a dog walker to come by a couple of times a day and wear her out, or take her to doggie daycare as often as possible. Eight hours of romping with other dogs

is guaranteed to take the wind out of her sails! See Chapter 38 for more on daycare options.

2 – MANAGE, MANAGE, MANAGE

While wearing out your dog should be part of your regular routine, there are other changes you can make in your dog's routine in order to manage her inappropriate behavior (see Chapter 4). Whiskey, the Labrador mentioned earlier, repeatedly bounced against his family's sliding glass door because it was rewarding to him. It brought him the greatly coveted attentions of his owner when he did so, and when he succeeded in breaking the glass, it actually gave him access to indoors, where he wanted to be.

All living things repeat behaviors that are rewarding to them. Whiskey's owners needed to find ways to reward him for *good* behavior, and prevent him from being rewarded for the unacceptable ones.

The management answer is to physically control your dog's behavior through the judicious use of leashes, pens, crates and tethers (see Chapters 8 and 15).

3 – BE QUICK WITH THE CLICK!

As soon as you have laid the foundation with exercise and management, you can begin an effective clicker-training program. Don't procrastinate – you can accomplish this on Day One of your All is Calm program.

Your dog doesn't have to do anything special to get the Click! and treat, as long as she isn't doing something unacceptable, like jumping on you or chewing the corner of the coffee table. If necessary, use one of your management tools to keep her out of trouble while you Click! and treat. Most dogs catch on pretty quickly that the Click! means a treat is coming. When your dog's ears perk and her eyes brighten at the sound of the Click! you know she's getting it. Now you can use your charged clicker for training.

Remember, the goal of clicker training is to get Taz to understand that *she* can make the Click! happen by offering certain behaviors – in this case, calm.

At first, you can't wait for long, leisurely stretches of calm behavior to click; you probably won't get them. Instead, begin by giving your dog a Click! and treat just because all four feet are on the floor at the same instant. Be quick! You want her to understand that the behavior she got rewarded for was pausing with all four feet on the floor, so your timing needs to be sharp; the Click! needs to happen the instant all four feet are down.

If your timing is good and you catch her with four-on-the-floor several times in a row you will see her start to stand still deliberately, in order to *make* the clicker go off. Light Bulb!! A door has opened in her brain, and you can see her thinking. You now have a very powerful tool for

promoting calm in your little plastic clicker box.

Okay, back to calm. How does "pausing briefly on all four feet" translate into a calm dog? *Very gradually.* You are going to "shape" the pause into longer and longer periods of stillness, by extending the time, in milliseconds at first, that you wait as she is standing still before you Click! and treat. If you err and she starts to jump around again, just wait. Eventually there will be another pause that you can Click! and then start the shaping again.

Reward your dog for staying calm.

As your dog gets better at being calm for longer and longer periods, be sure to reinforce randomly, sometimes for shorter pauses, sometimes longer. If you just keep making it harder and harder and longer and longer, she may get frustrated and quit playing the game.

Each training session should be relatively short, 5-15 minutes, to avoid frustration for both of you, but you can do several in a day. You will have the most success, at least at first, if you practice working on calmness right after one of her exercise sessions when she is tired anyway. As she gets the idea that "calm" is a very rewardable behavior, it will work even when she has more energy.

When your dog can hold still for several seconds at a time, add the verbal cue of your choice – something like "Easy" that you will eventually be able to use to cue her for calmness. Over time, you will be able to phase out the Click! and treat and use petting and praise as a reward instead of food. Keep your voice and body language calm and soothing to reflect and support her own growing calmness. Petting should be done as a massage – slow kneading or stroking, not vigorous patting or thumping.

4 – EVERY DOG NEEDS HER OWN SPOT

You can use a management tether and a clicker to teach your dog a very useful calming exercise, called "Go To Your Spot." Arrange her tether station so it is very comfortable, with a soft bed, really good chew toys and unspillable water. Toss a treat onto the bed and say "Go To Your Spot." When she gets there and is about to snatch up the treat, Click! your clicker.

Repeat several times, clicking and treating each time until she goes to her spot easily, and then attach the tether to her collar. Sit in a chair nearby but out of

her reach, and read a book. If she fusses, ignore her. When she is quiet, Click! and toss her a treat. Keeping calm and quiet is making something good happen – she gets a Click! and treat.

Occasionally when she is being calm, get up, go over to her bed and quietly pet and praise her (also positive reinforcement). If she starts to get excited when you are with her, go back to your chair and sit down again. This is "negative punishment." Her inappropriate behavior makes a good thing – you and your treats – go away. Negative punishment is considered effective and humane by most positive trainers.

When she is calm on her tether for long stretches of time, up to five or ten minutes with occasional treats and visits, you can remove the tether and continue to reward her for lying calmly on her bed. If she revs up again, you can re-tether her and practice more calm.

You can also practice this when guests are visiting. Give your dog an extra tiring play-session before they arrive so she can be on her best behavior. If she still tends to greet them too enthusiastically at the door, have her go to her spot before they arrive, tethered if necessary, and wait until she is calm to allow guests to greet her. When she is relaxed, untether her so she can mingle with the visitors politely. If she gets carried away, she can do another session on her tether.

All is Bright

Dogs don't learn to be calm by being banished to the back yard. Dogs are social creatures, and time spent in isolation causes stress, which causes hyperactivity. Dogs learn to be calm by spending time with their humans and being rewarded for their calm behavior. Rewards can be attention, praise, petting, and yes, Clicks! and treats.

My evaluation of Whiskey confirmed my suspicions. He was a normal adolescent Labrador Retriever with no manners, very trainable for someone with the time, energy and commitment to teach him how to be calm. His owners are still considering whether they are the right people for him, or whether he would be better off in the home of someone more able to deal with his energy level.

Like so many of the things we expect our dogs to learn, "calm" is easier to teach sooner, rather than later, but it is rarely too late. So, whether you have a baby dog doing puppy rushes around the coffee table or an adolescent who is breaking down your doors, it's time to get clicking for calm!

CHAPTER 29 ❤
Obsessive Compulsive Disorders

The dainty, 18-month-old Cavalier King Charles Spaniel appeared perfectly normal and happy when she and her owner greeted me at the door, but I knew better. Her owner had already advised me over the phone that Mindy was a compulsive "fly-snapper" and that the stereotypic behavior had intensified in recent weeks, to the point that it was making life miserable for both Mindy and her owner.

Indeed, it was only a matter of minutes before I saw Mindy's expression change to one of worry, then distress and anxiety, as her eyes began to dart back and forth. Shortly thereafter she started snapping at the air, for all the world as if she

OCD is believed to have a genetic component. Obsessive compulsive fly-snapping is found in a number of Cavalier King Charles Spaniel families.

were trying to catch a bevy of irritating flies that our human eyes could not see. Her efforts grew more frantic and her demeanor more anxious, including stereotypic tail chasing, until she finally ran from the living room into the safety of her crate in the darkened pantry.

Mindy's fly-snapping is one of a number of repetitive behavior syndromes, also known as obsessive compulsive disorders, from which dogs may suffer. Other such behaviors include spinning, tail-chasing, freezing in a particular position or location, self-mutilation (biting or licking) and flank-sucking. Some behaviorists also include pica – the ingestion of inedible objects such as rocks, sticks, socks, and who knows what else, in the obsession compulsion family.

Until recently, many behaviorists argued that the term *canine compulsive disorder* was more appropriate to describe the behaviors in dogs.

In human psychology, *obsessions* are persistent intrusive thoughts that cause extreme anxiety and that the patient tries to suppress or ignore. *Compulsions* are repetitive behaviors that the patient performs in order to prevent or reduce the anxiety. Behaviorists argued that because we don't know whether dogs actually have obsessive thoughts (although Border Collie owners could argue this!), we should omit the word "obsessive" and use the term "canine compulsive disorder" (CCD) to describe the syndrome in dogs. Recently, however, the pendulum has swung back; current studies support the used of the term "obsessive compulsive disorder" in reference to canine repetitive behavior syndromes.

Clinical Signs, Causes and Treatment

Very little research has been done into OCD – much of what we know about the syndrome is based on anecdotal evidence, and even that is relatively rare. The primary cause is believed to be a situation of conflict or frustration to which the dog must try to adapt. The disorder often begins as a normal, adaptive response to the conflict or frustration. Eventually the response becomes removed from the original stimulus and occurs whenever the dog's stress or arousal level exceeds a critical threshold.

Strong evidence exists that genetics play a role in at least some obsessive compulsive behaviors. There is a higher-than-average incidence of tail-chasing in Bull Terriers and German Shepherds, fly-snapping in Cavalier King Charles Spaniels, and excessive licking (*acral lick dermatitis*) to the point of causing a lesion (*lick granuloma*) in many large breeds, including the Doberman Pinscher, Golden Retriever, Labrador Retriever

Given the opportunity, this Jack Russell Terrier would spend hours each day compulsively licking his favorite toys. His eyes glaze over, he drools, and he loses interest in all other activities.

and German Shepherd. Flank-sucking is an often-seen obsessive compulsive behavior in Dobermans as well.

Trainers and behaviorists suspect that OCD is probably underdiagnosed, as very few veterinary schools give their students thorough training in animal behavior, and many owners don't recognize or don't report obsessive compulsive behaviors. A behavior falls into the OCD category when it becomes a *stereotypy* – a repetitive and unvarying pattern of behavior that serves no obvious purpose in the context in which it is performed. Obsessive compulsive behaviors often evoke a response from the owner, and thus may be unwittingly reinforced as a result.

This was certainly the case with Dodger, an 8-month-old Golden Retriever in Carmel, California, whose owner was battling the challenge of pica. Perhaps because they are bred for a genetic predisposition to hold things in their mouths (i.e. retrieve), Goldens and Labrador Retrievers seem to suffer from a higher incidence of pica than many other breeds of dogs. Dodger was allowed outside only under strict supervision, as he would compulsively eat sticks and rocks, and had already had one emergency life-saving surgery to unblock his digestive tract.

Now Dodger was beginning to chase his tail. Since the pup already was engaging in one compulsive behavior, his owner was rightfully concerned that that tail-chasing was another manifestation of OCD. Physical restraint – chaining, kenneling or other close confinement

– is one of the situations of conflict or frustration that can contribute to compulsive behavior. (See Conflict and Frustration below). *Frustration* refers to a situation in which an animal is motivated to perform a behavior but is prevented from doing so.

The obvious solution to Dodger's tail-chasing was to give him more freedom and exercise in his fenced yard, thereby reducing the confinement frustration while also, hopefully, tiring Dodger out to the point that he didn't have enough energy left to chase his tail (from the "a tired dog is a well-behaved dog" school of behavior modification). Because of his pica problem, this wasn't an option for Dodger.

I hypothesized that owner attention was also feeding the tail chasing, so I established a modification protocol that consisted of the owners immediately leaving the room as soon as the behavior started, and making an effort to pay more attention to Dodger when he *wasn't* chasing his tail.

Dodger was fortunate. His owners, despite the considerable responsibility of a newborn baby, adhered faithfully to the modification program while also increasing the length and frequency of Dodger's supervised walks. Inside of a month, the tail chasing had subsided.

Several factors contributed to the unusually quick and complete success in Dodger's case. Dodger was young, and his owner noticed and reported the behavior very early in its development. Early implementation of a behavior modification program provides for a much more positive prognosis than does a situation where the dog has had years to practice the stereotypic behavior. Dodger's tail chasing had a clear attention-seeking component, so removing the reward of the owners' attention for the behavior was an effective approach. Finally, both owners were committed to the training and were consistent about applying the recommended treatment, which was instrumental to success.

Don't Use Drug Therapy Alone

Mindy was not as fortunate as Dodger. Her fly-snapping behavior had started when she was about six months old. Because it was relatively mild at first, her owner didn't seek treatment. When she did report it to her veterinarian, she was told that it was a form of mild seizures and that the only treatment was a lifetime of therapy with Phenobarbital, a drug that has serious side effects and is highly likely to shorten the dog's life expectancy. Mindy's owner was understandably and rightfully reluctant to resort to such an approach, and believing there was no alternative, chose to do nothing. By the time I saw her a year later, the behavior was well established, very strong, and extremely difficult to modify solely through a behavioral approach.

At one time, seizures were believed to play a role in fly-snapping behavior, but that is no longer the case. Behavioral scientists also hypothesized at one time that an endorphin release accompanied the performance of obsessive compulsive behaviors, which was believed to reinforce the behavior, but recent research has also determined this to be untrue. While the cause of OCD is still not well understood, there is some evidence of serotonin involvement, and drugs that inhibit serotonin re-uptake have been used effectively to treat dogs with OCD.

Know your dog. Chasing soap bubbles helps this energetic JRT burn off excess energy, but she calms down afterward and does not persist in running or snapping.

Treatment consists of both environmental and behavioral modification, and, often, pharmacological intervention. Here are 10 steps to a successful treatment program:

1. **Intervene as early as possible.**

2. **Have your veterinarian conduct a complete physical examination** and evaluation to identify and eliminate any medical conditions that may be contributing to or causing the behavior.

3. **Identify and, if possible, remove the cause(s) of the stress,** conflict or frustration.

4. **Avoid rewarding the obsessive compulsive behavior.** Remember, it can be rewarding to the dog simply to have his owner pay attention to him.

5. **Eliminate any punishment** as a response to the obsessive compulsive behavior.

6. **Provide sufficient exercise** on a regular schedule.

7. **Interrupt the behavior** when it occurs and replace it with an alternative behavior using positive reinforcement training methods. For example, teach a dog who licks his paws excessively to lie with his head on the floor between his paws, and then reward him consistently for this behavior. Work with a qualified behavior consultant to implement an appropriate behavior modification program.

8. **Manage the behavior** to the extent possible. For example, you can use an Elizabethan collar on the licking dog when you are not present to supervise his behavior.

9. **Consult with an alternative practitioner** to apply alternative modalities such as massage techniques, herbal therapies, acupressure and acupuncture, to help relieve the dog's stress.

10. **Utilize appropriate drug therapy as needed**, using serotonin-related drugs such as Clomipramine (Anafranil) and Fluoxetene (Prozac) rather than Phenobarbital. Remember that these drugs are not a cure, but rather are intended to be used in conjunction with a behavior modification program. The goal is to eventually wean the dog off the serotonin re-uptake blockers. This must be done very gradually, in consultation with a veterinarian and behavior consultant. If done too suddenly, there may be a rebound affect, and the obsessive compulsive behavior may reappear more strongly than ever.

Good Prognosis

There is hope for dogs with OCD. A study conducted in 1997 at the behavior clinic of the Ontario Veterinary College (now Purdue University) by A. U. Luescher, DVM, PhD, Dipl. ACVB, resulted in successful behavior modification for approximately two-thirds of the dogs participating. The remaining one-third included owners with poor compliance as well as owners who chose not to participate in the treatment program. An analysis of the cases in that study found that the longer the duration of the behavior, the less positive the outcome, thereby confirming the importance of early treatment in cases of OCD.

And what of Mindy, our fly-snapping CKC Spaniel? Conversations with her breeder elicited the information that her sire and at least one of her littermates are also fly-snappers, which supports the genetic predisposition theory. Sadly, both of those dogs are being kept on regular doses of Phenobarbital, and their owners are making no attempts to modify the behavior. The breeder has not contacted the owners of any of the other puppies from the litter to determine if they also are exhibiting signs of OCD, and he has no plans to change his breeding program.

Mindy's condition is slowly responding to a combination of drug therapy and behavior modification. Her owner is very committed to the modification program, which bodes well for Mindy's future, and we have high hopes of eventually being able to wean her off of the re-uptake drugs. Mindy is very fortunate to have a human companion who is committed to providing her with a long and happy life.

❤ CONFLICT AND FRUSTRATION

Certain environmental conditions are known to contribute to the development of stereotypic behaviors in dogs, especially those who are otherwise already predisposed to obsessive compulsive disorders. These include:

- **Physical Restraint** – Dogs who are kept in the very stressful environment of a shelter or kennel for extended periods of time often begin spinning in their kennels, many of them to a very marked degree. This obsessive compulsive behavior may or may not diminish when the dog is removed from the kennel and placed in or returned to a calm home environment. Constant chaining or confinement in the home can also elicit spinning and other OCDs, especially when the dog is constantly stimulated by the environment.

- **Inappropriate Play Stimulation** – Some people find it amusing - at first - when dogs display repetitive behaviors, and encourage the dogs in such activities as spinning in circles or chasing the light from a laser pointer. Unfortunately, some dogs seem to get "hooked" on these activities, with their new passion for the game resulting in an onset of obsessive compulsive behavior. Due to the risk of developing OCD, these sorts of games should be avoided with dogs who have a predisposition for obsessive compulsive behaviors.

- **Unpredictable Environment** – Inconsistency in the environment (inconsistent training methods or application of punishment or rewards; lack of training; ineffective training methods) can frustrate the dog, as can a dog's inability to control or avoid aversives such as thunderstorms or punishment. A poorly socialized dog will also be stressed and frustrated by changes in the environment, even minor, seemingly insignificant ones.

- **Conflicting Motivations** – Two equally strong motivations that are in conflict with each other (approach and withdrawal) can elicit obsessive compulsive syndrome. For example, a dog who is both fearful and territorial may be in conflict when a stranger approaches his territory. A fearful dog who is constantly called upon to defend his territory may develop stereotypic behaviors. A non-visible electronic fence that provides no physical protection or blockage of visual stimuli for the enclosed dog may also be a contributing factor.

- **Lack of Appropriate Outlet for Normal Behaviors** – Dogs are very social animals, highly motivated to interact with others. A dog kept in isolation has no outlet for these important hardwired social behaviors, and may develop obsessive compulsive behaviors to cope and compensate. Puppies deprived of the opportunity to suck may also exhibit stereotypic behaviors such as excessive licking and flank sucking, as well as sucking on other objects such as cushions and toys.

CHAPTER 30 ♥
When Felix Meets Fido

Despite media insistence that there are "cat people" and "dog people," many of us, probably the majority of us, are both. Despite a common misconception that dogs and cats can't get along, most of them can. If the introduction is done with proper precautions, your potential "mortal enemies" can become fast friends, and we can enjoy the rewards that both species have to offer.

When my husband and I first saw our now 18 year-old gray cat, Gewürztraminer, he was a cocky, adolescent, stray tom, walking up to and touching noses with leashed dogs on a Santa Rosa, California, city sidewalk. Recognizing his irresistible personality, we scooped him up and took him home, where he casually sauntered past our three dogs, hopped up on the sofa, and curled up as if he'd lived there all his life. Throughout the ensuing years Gewürz maintained his equanimity as scores of dogs passed through our home, some as permanent residents, others as temporary fosters and rescues.

Jackson is a cat of a different color. I hand-raised him from the age of four weeks, a wee survivor of a feral litter. Now 16, he has always been cautious of strangers, both canine *and* human. He lives comfortably with our dogs, but let a

A dog and cat enjoying a meal together.

new pooch or person enter the house and Jackson makes himself scarce until the intruder leaves.

Survival Strategies

Both Jackson and Gewürztraminer have developed useful survival strategies for dealing with dogs. They know that running elicits the prey/chase response, even in their "own" dogs, so they move slowly when the dogs are in the house, saving their kitty-romps for when the pack is out in the yard. Gewürz trusts that dogs coming into our home won't eat him. We are careful not to breach that trust. Jackson believes that discretion is warranted, and relies on himself rather than us to protect him. Either way, we closely observe and control any new dogs coming into the house until we are confident that they are compatible with the cats.

Risk Factors

The greatest risk factor in the war between the species is the great outdoors. While cats may see themselves as mighty predators, to many dogs, cats are prey. Inside, we can control our cats' doggie encounters. Outside, they are at the mercy of neighborhood predators. If your cats must go outside, building a cattery, keeping them on harness and leash, or installing a Cat-Fence™ will greatly improve their chances of survival. Personally, I prefer to keep mine safely indoors.

If your resident dogs and cats already have established peaceful relations, you don't need to worry. But anytime you add a newcomer to the pride or the pack, you take the chance that the next encounter won't be a positive one. Safeguards are definitely needed to protect your pets from violence.

We should remember that the risk goes both ways. We are all too aware of the potentially lethal threat that the jaws of a Cujo can hold for Felix. But there are risks for Cujo, too. While it's unlikely that your cat would kill a dog, Fluffy's sharp claws can cause mayhem and easily inflict permanent damage to the eyes of a dog, even one whose intentions are innocent. While dogs will be dogs

and cats will be cats, proper introductions and good behavior management tools can greatly reduce the risk of injury to both species.

Know Your Purrsonalities

The more you know about the animals you are about to introduce to each other, the better prepared you can be. Has Fluffy been around dogs before? How has she reacted in the past? Does she hiss and spit when she sees dogs walk past the front picture window? When you are walking Fido on a leash, does he show an unhealthy interest in neighborhood cats? Does he tolerate cats that jump into the back yard, or charge after them with murderous intent?

You probably have answers to some of these questions for your own pets. But the ones you are bringing into the family don't always come with extensive histories, especially if you are adopting from a shelter or rescue group. Here are some tips for making those first encounters positive ones:

Old Cat Meets New Dog

When you are bringing a new dog into the house you must protect your cat until you are sure that the dog "plays well with others." Begin before you bring the dog home by creating safe places for the cat where the dog cannot go. Baby gates and cat doors are a big help, as are catwalks and other cat-friendly perches that are out of dog reach. Be sure your cat knows how to use them. Help Fluffy learn how to use kitty-doors by holding them open and luring her through with a treat. Gradually lower the flap as you lure Fluffy through so she starts pushing it open herself – a little bit at first, and eventually with the flap all the way down.

Make sure she can easily jump over the baby gate, by tossing her favorite treats over it and watching her sail. Baby gates are great for providing exercise for a sedentary cat, even without dogs in the home! And putting the feed bowls and litter boxes in a gated room keeps the dogs from chowing down on cat chow or cleaning litter boxes in search of "kitty rocca" treats.

A mature, well-socialized cat can tolerate the antics of an active dog.

Encourage Fluffy to explore perches and catwalks by baiting them with treats and catnip crumbs. A few years ago a cat magazine published an article on a cat owner who built catwalks throughout her entire house, even cutting holes through walls, just to provide her cats with more exercise, perch space and entertainment!

Preparing Fido

Once your cat is familiar with all her escape routes (this could take days or even weeks, so plan ahead), you're ready to introduce the canine element. Before you bring Fido in the house, spend a little time outside teaching him to sit. Use tasty, meat-based treats, and lure him into a sit by lifting the treat just above his nose and back over his head. Most dogs will sit when you do this so they can keep watching the treat. When he sits, say "Yes!" and feed him the treat. Do this several times, until he sits quickly every time you move the treat. Then start saying "Sit!" as you move the treat over his head. You have begun to teach him to sit on a verbal cue!!

Now bring the Fido into the house on a leash. If he is strong and you doubt your ability to restrain him, use a head halter such as a Snoot Loop™ or Gentle Leader™ (see Chapter 36). Sit down in the living room with Fido on the leash, and invite Fluffy into the room with a happy voice and tempting treats. *She needs to come in under her own power... do not carry her into the room!!!* If you are carrying her and she panics you could be badly scratched or bitten. Let Fluffy take her time, even leave the room if she chooses to. You want her comfortable with the interaction, not stressed. Tossing her favorite tasty treats on the ground near her will help convince her that having a dog around is a good thing.

Meanwhile, keep observing Fido. If he is sitting or lying down, calmly watching Fluffy eat her treats, you have a winner! Tell him "Yes!" and feed him treats for his good behavior. Keep him on a leash for a while, while you, he and the cat walk around. If he continues to stay calm even when the cat is moving you can probably trust him off-leash with the cat. Be sure to keep the pair under close supervision until you are confident that a sudden movement on Fluffy's part won't suddenly awaken Fido's prey drive.

If Fido is showing benevolent but active interest, use treats to distract him from the cat. Wave a tasty treat in front of his nose and lift it over his head to get him to sit. When he does, "Yes!" and reward with the treat. Keep repeating this until he is more focused on you and the treats than on Fluffy. This may take several sessions, over a period of several days. In the meantime, you must keep him on a leash until you are convinced that he will do no harm.

Time Out!

If Fido is so amped about the presence of the cat that he won't pay attention to the treats, quickly, calmly and happily say "Time out!" and walk him into another room. When he settles down in the other room use your treats to get him to sit, then Click! or say "Yes!" and reward him. Now walk back into the room where the cat is. If Fido gets revved up again, step out of the room, and repeat the sit and reward routine. Repeat this until he doesn't go overboard when he sees the cat. When this happens tell him "Yes!" and feed him several treats in the cat's presence. Keep doing this until he stays more focused on you and the treats than on Fluffy. Again, this may take several days or longer. Until you are confident that he will not do harm, you must keep him leashed in Fluffy's presence.

If Fido has obvious malevolent intentions toward Fluffy, you can work with him as in the previous scenario. It may take many sessions over several days to several weeks to convince him that having Fluffy around is a good thing. You may – or may not – ever be able to trust him off leash around Fluffy. You might be taking a chance with your cat's life by keeping Fido around. You will need to decide if it's worth the risk.

Old Dog Meets New Cat

Chances are that if Fido has lived with you any length of time you already know how he is with cats. I would hope that if he were a confirmed cat-eater you wouldn't try to bring a cat into your home. So let's assume he is at least manageable around felines. If he is friendly but over-eager, you will want to use the methods described above to improve his behavior. Your challenge in this scenario is to help the new cat adjust to a new environment complete with predator.

We will assume that Fluffy isn't comfortable with dogs. Either she has never been around them, or she has had bad experiences. Even if she is comfortable with dogs, we want to give her plenty of time to adjust to her surroundings before she has to face the dog.

Have Fido already put away in a back room when you bring Fluffy home. Bring her into the house in a carrier (I assume she was in a carrier in the car!) and take her directly to a spare room that has already been set up for her with litter box, food, water, bed, toys and one or more scratching posts. This will be her home for the next several days. Close the door and let her out of the carrier. You can sit quietly with her in the room or leave her to explore on her own, but don't solicit her attention. Leave her alone unless she solicits yours. Once you leave the room you can let Fido out of his room to roam free in the house. We want Fluffy to get used to hearing and smelling him before she sees him.

Once she is relaxed and calm in her room you can put up the baby gate and open the door. How quickly you progress to this stage depends on Fluffy. If she is confident and adapts quickly, you can

move ahead. If she is still hiding under the bed on Day Three you will take it much more slowly. Be sure to give her at least a day or two in her room even if she seems quite at home.

Once you put up the baby gate your job is to monitor Fido and make sure he doesn't harass the cat at the gate or as she begins to make forays into the rest of the house. If you do this well, using down stays and time outs when Fido gets too enthusiastic about his new feline friend, you will soon see a peaceful relationship develop between them.

The Claws Clause

If you think there is any chance that Fluffy will launch an attack on Fido, you need to take steps to protect your dog's eyes. SoftPaws™, brightly colored plastic tips that are glued onto your cat's claws, can prevent damage to your dog's eyes while you work to improve the relationship. Ask your veterinarian about them.

When I sit on the sofa at night reading a book or watching television, Jackson vies for lap space with Dusty, my Pomeranian, while Gewürztraminer wrestles on the floor with Katie, my Australian Kelpie. I would hate to have to choose between the comfort of a cat's purr and the enthusiasm of canine kisses. Fortunately, dogs and cats *can* get along together, and I don't have to choose.

CHAPTER 31 ❤
Kids and Dogs

"Family Dog Mauls Toddler!!!!!!!!!!!!!"

We've all seen the sensational headlines about the tragic, unprovoked, and totally unexpected attacks on children by dogs. Yet dogs rarely attack without provocation, and in most cases the offending dog has been sending signals for quite some time that he was not comfortable with the presence of the child. If the parents had been better educated about dog behavior, the tragedy quite likely could have been averted through proper management of child/dog interactions. Better still, it could have been prevented through proper training and socialization of the dog from puppyhood on.

Early Training

Many young couples acquire a puppy early in the relationship, long before the advent of the first baby. The puppy is a surrogate child, and the couple dotes on him, taking him everywhere, allowing him to sleep on the furniture, even sharing the marriage bed. For several years the dog enjoys his status as an only child. The couple tends to socialize with other childless adults, and the dog rarely sees children. Then the couple decides it is time to have a baby. Now we have a problem.

Dogs are genetically "hard-wired" to absorb much of the information about their environment during a critical learning period in the first few months of their lives. During this time, usually somewhere between the ages of four weeks and four months, a puppy's brain files away information about which things in the world are safe and rewarding, which ones are painful and dangerous and should be avoided, and which are neutral, with no consequence. Anything not experienced during this critical period tends to automatically fall into the "dangerous" category. This is an important survival skill for wild animals. If they don't know for sure that something is harmless, the safest assumption is that it is not.

Herein lies the problem. If a puppy doesn't learn that children are "safe and rewarding" during those critical months, he is likely to assume, when he meets them later in life, that they are a threat. This assumption is often supported by the behavior of many of the children that a dog meets. Toddlers are likely to poke fingers into canine ears, prod them with pencils, hit them over the head with wooden blocks and pull tails or fur. They stare directly into a dog's eyes, and a direct stare is a threat in the canine world.

They compete for toys and food. They move erratically – running, tripping, falling, swinging their arms around – and make weird noises.

After weeks of supervised gentle handling by children and appropriate play (and sharing their snacks), these pups have learned to enjoy children for life.

In a perfect world, *every* new puppy would be thoroughly socialized to babies, toddlers and children while he was in his critical learning period. Despite many veterinarians' recommendations that their clients wrap their puppies in cotton wool and keep them strictly at home until they have been fully vaccinated, it is vitally important that your puppy have positive experiences with the big wide world during his first four months. Fortunately, this can be accomplished without exposing Buddy to life-threatening diseases.

Invite lots of people, including babies and children, vaccinated healthy puppies and friendly dogs, over to *your* house for puppy parties. Give everyone handfuls of really yummy treats to feed to Buddy. If everyone has Buddy sit to get his treats you will be teaching him not to jump up on people at the same time. Monitor your pup's interactions with children to be sure they are all positive. If Buddy acts fearful, don't force him to greet people. Ask your friends to toss treats from a distance until Buddy gains confidence and approaches them. Have children of all ages feed Buddy lots of treats and he will quickly decide that kids are a *good* thing, not dangerous.

You can also take Buddy out into the community to *safe* canine-friendly locations. Don't go to the local dog hangout and turn him loose to play, but do take him with you to places such as a well-run puppy kindergarten class, where you can monitor his interactions with kids and other puppies. Teach him that the world, especially the small humans of the world, are a source of pleasure and reward, and you greatly reduce the risk of "Dog Mauls Toddler" headlines in your family's future.

Too Late? Not Necessarily.

Maybe it's too late to socialize Buddy to children during his critical learning period because that stage of his life has long passed. Is it too late to teach him to live with children? Not necessarily. It is more difficult, but not impossible. This was the challenge presented early one summer when Kristin and Fred Wolf called Peaceable Paws and asked for help in preparing their two dogs, Helen and Charlie, to accept the imminent arrival of baby Molly, due to be born in late August.

Helen and Charlie, eight and five years old respectively, are both retired racing Greyhounds. As is often the case with rescued Greyhounds, they adapted beautifully to a life of luxury in a real home. The Wolf's hadn't demanded much of them, but the dogs were housetrained, slept on their own beds, didn't get up on the furniture, stayed in their fenced yard, and didn't remove food from countertops.

The dog *had* met babies on a few occasions. Helen was noncommittal, reported the Wolfs, but Charlie had exhibited what Kristin feared was an unhealthy interest, given the inherited prey drive that is encouraged in racing Greyhounds.

The expectant parents wanted to improve their dogs' manners in general, but understandably, their primary concern was for the safety of the baby.

Planning Ahead

I arrived at the Wolf home in Carmel, California, and was greeted at the front door by two lithe, leggy, brindle Greyhounds and a very pregnant Kristin. As soon as Kristin let me in, Charlie jumped up on me. I turned my back and stepped away, repeating the maneuver when he circled me and tried to jump up again. After three repetitions of this circle dance, Charlie stood still with all four feet on the floor. I said "Yes!" in a happy voice and popped a treat in his mouth. For now, a stand was acceptable. We would work later on getting a sit in place of jumping up.

Rather than banish the dogs once the baby was born, Kristin began preparing her dogs for life in a family with a baby months before the big event.

Kristin was impressed. So was Charlie. His teeth chattered with excitement as he thrust his chiseled head toward me in search of another treat. I pointedly ignored his pushy behavior, but gave him another "Yes!" and treat as soon as he backed off a step. Helen hovered in the background, and got a "Yes!" and treat just for being there. In this manner, we introduced the

Wolf household to one of the basic tenets of positive reinforcement training: *To the extent possible, ignore the behaviors we don't want, and reward the ones we do.* All living things tend to repeat behaviors that they find rewarding. The ones that don't get rewarded eventually go away.

Fred Wolf joined us, and we sat down in the living room to consider a training program. We started by listing the Wolf's concerns, questions and goals:

- Greyhound prey drive – threat to baby?

- Jumping on people (Charlie).

- Getting overly excited about going out for a walk (Charlie).

- Pulling on leashes; Helen with lots of sniffing, but especially Charlie, who would lunge at cats and other dogs.

- Shut the dogs away from Molly, or integrate them into baby routines?

- Goal: to keep the baby safe and maintain Charlie and Helen's quality of life.

I commended the Wolfs for thinking proactively and for wanting to continue keeping Helen and Charlie as full-fledged members of the family. Too many dogs are banned to the back yard, given away or surrendered to animal shelters when baby arrives. Others aren't given a second thought until it's too late and a confused and defensive Buddy bites the baby. All too often the trainer gets called *after* the bite happens, when Buddy is one short step away from euthanasia. I was pleased that the Wolfs were planning ahead, and committed to doing the right thing for the dogs and for Molly.

Managing Behaviors

We addressed the last question first. Given Charlie's intense stare at other babies he had been with, the Wolf's were naturally concerned about his prey drive. They had read in a dog-and-baby book that an intense stare was a serious red alert, a sign that the dog had dastardly designs on the baby. Would the baby ever be safe around a predatory animal that had been taught to chase down small animals?

I downplayed the threat of Charlie's intense gaze while emphasizing the need for constant supervision of interactions between dogs and young children. There is a huge difference between a fleeing rabbit and a stationary baby in a crib. Most dogs have no difficulty distinguishing humans from prey animals.

Perhaps Charlie was just intrigued by the sounds and smells of a human puppy. Still, no small child should *ever* be left alone with a dog even for a few seconds, no matter how trusted the canine companion. When something happens the dog always gets blamed, even if he has reacted in justifiable self-defense. If no one was present, who's to know if the toddler fell on top of the dog, or poked a finger in his eye? A dog who hasn't had many experiences with babies is certainly an unknown, but as long as Charlie and Helen were not given an opportunity to do the wrong thing, the Wolf baby would be safe. This is another basic tenet of positive training: *Manage the environment to prevent inappropriate behaviors from happening.* If you don't want your dog to counter-surf, never leave the roast on the counter when you leave the room. If you don't want your dog to bite your small child, never leave the two of them alone together. Ever.

I advised the Wolfs that it was important to implement any anticipated changes in the dogs' routine and privileges now, so the changes would not be associated negatively with the baby's arrival.

We scheduled training sessions twice a week for several weeks to work on improving the communication between the four current members of the Wolf pack, so the humans would be prepared to manage the behavior of the canines once baby made five.

The goal of our work was to ensure that when the baby arrived, the dogs would associate her presence with *good* things (lots of treats and attention), not *bad* things (when baby is here, dogs get shut away).

The Training

Charlie and Helen took well to reward-based training. Helen, older and a little arthritic, was slower to respond, but also less energetic than Charlie, so we focused much of our efforts on gently controlling the younger dog. We used "Yes" as our reward marker rather than a clicker, for two reasons. Charlie is very sound sensitive and would not have responded well to a clicker. Even if he had, we anticipated that Kristin, with her hands full of baby, would find it easier to use a verbal marker. We identified a number of behaviors that would be useful for the dogs to know:

- Sit
- Down
- Stay
- Wait
- Go To Your Rug
- Off
- Go First
- Over Here

We used a treat as a lure to get Charlie and Helen to offer the behaviors, followed by "Yes!" and reward. Initially we focused on "Sit," "Go to your rug" and "Off" – three key behaviors to master when there are new infants in the house. We taught "Sit" using the positive training techniques discussed in earlier (see Chapter 11).

"Go to your rug" would enable the Wolfs to send Charlie and Helen to a predetermined spot, such as a rug in the nursery. This would allow the dogs to keep Kristin and the baby company in the nursery instead of having to be shut out for always being underfoot – a common dog/baby management problem. We used the treat to lure the dogs to the rug and lie down, while giving the verbal cue "Go to your rug." Both dogs became proficient

The Wolfs were nervous about the rapt attention that the younger dog, Charlie, paid to babies. They taught him a special cue, "Over here," rewarding him when he turned his attention to them.

Anticipating that she will be spending a lot of time in the room, feeding and rocking the baby, Kristin sits quietly, occasionally praising and treating Helen for her "Down-Stay."

at this in a couple of weeks, and quickly learned to stay on their rugs until released with a cheerful "OK!"

"Off" (meaning "whatever you are paying attention to at this moment, I want you to leave it alone") has unlimited applications when dealing with dogs and babies. The object of the dog's attention could be the baby or a teething ring, for example, and you want to be able to refocus that attention whenever you want. With Charlie sitting in front of me, I offered him a treat in my closed fist, and said the word "Off" just *one time*. Naturally he was curious and inspected the fist, trying to get at the treat inside. I waited patiently until he got bored and glanced away, then said "Yes!" and gave him a treat *from my other hand*. In just a few repetitions he began glancing away from the fist as soon as it was offered with the word "Off." He was learning that he got a reward at least as good as the forbidden one, if he left it alone when he heard the cue "Off." We then repeated the exercise with the forbidden treat in an open hand (closing the hand into a fist if he tried to get the treat, but always saying the word "Off" only one time). Finally I placed the treat on the floor, using my hand or foot to cover the treat if he tried to get it. Like most dogs, Charlie and Helen learned the "Off" concept in one session.

Because Charlie had a dangerous habit of bounding down the stairs while

Kristin was descending, we decided to teach him "Go First" as well as "Wait." "Wait" means pause, and is sort of an informal stay that doesn't require the dog to remain fixed in one position. We could use "Wait" to ask Charlie and Helen to not go up or downstairs until Kristin had completed the trip. We also taught Charlie "Go First," so she could send him down the stairs ahead of her. This one was simple. We stood at the top of the stairs and told Charlie "Go First," then tossed a treat down the stairs. When Charlie charged down the stairs after the treat he got a "Yes!" His reward was the treat that was already waiting for him at the bottom of the staircase. The most challenging part of this exercise was fading the treat toss. Charlie tended to want to wait until the treat was tossed rather than going down the stairs on just the verbal cue, but he finally got the idea.

Pleasant Surprises

We anticipated that the hardest part of the training would be teaching Charlie to stop lunging at cats and other dogs on his daily walks. We were pleasantly surprised. Charlie was so enamored of the positive training method that it was easy to get him to focus on us (and a treat) instead of prey. We started with a head halter (see Chapter 36) for control, but quickly returned to a plain buckle collar when it became apparent that he didn't need the halter.

Since Charlie tended to get overexcited when Kristin picked up his leash to attach it to his collar, we tried a little negative punishment. Kristin picked up the leash and Charlie started leaping and cavorting about. Kristin put the leash down. Leaping and cavorting makes the good thing – the leash – go away. When Charlie calmed down, Kristin picked up the leash again. Every time Charlie got excited, Kristin put down the leash. In just a few repetitions, Charlie ran to the door and sat perfectly still – a behavior he had previously performed for Fred, but had never done for Kristin.

Once outside, we taught Charlie an "Over here!" cue, which meant "turn your attention back to me." We started by using it when Charlie was distracted and sniffing a bush, rewarding him with a "Yes!" and treat when he looked back at us. We had practiced a mere half-dozen times before we encountered a barking dog dashing back-and-forth on a deck. Charlie never gave the dog a second glance, he was much too interested in the treat in Kristin's hand. Mission accomplished!

Finally, we encouraged both dogs to walk on a loose leash by rewarding them with a "Yes!" and treat whenever they were walking without pulling. We did this with each dog individually at first, and at our last session Kristin tried walking the dogs together. That part of the program still needs some work, but it was a definite improvement!

Molly Wolf was born on Monday, August 23 – a tiny 5 pounds, 11 ounces. A week after her arrival, the Wolf's were delighted with the dogs' behavior around the new member of the Wolf pack.

Kristin Wolf works with her older female Greyhound, Helen, in the baby's room. When Helen complies with her request to "Go to your rug," Kristin gives the dog verbal praise and a treat.

After just a few weeks' practice, both Helen and Charlie would "Go to" and "Stay" on their rugs when given a cue, even when Kristin busied herself with other things in the baby's room.

"They're doing great," reported Kristin. "They were frenzied with curiosity the first couple of days, but we just kept rewarding them whenever they turned their attention away from Molly. At first Charlie was locked onto her like radar. Now, already, they are both so respectful of her space. If I am sitting on the sofa feeding her, Charlie will come in and lie down at my feet. Not too long ago he would have insisted on having his head in my lap."

"I am so pleased that we got help," Kristin continues. "We would have done all the wrong things – corrected them, told them 'No!' for looking at her, shut them out of the room – it would have been a disaster. We are very pleased."

I am very pleased too. It is always a pleasure to work with people who respect their dogs and truly have their best interests at heart. I expect that Kristin, Fred, Charlie, Helen and Molly Wolf will have long, happy and positive lives together.

PART FIVE

The Dog Owner's Toolbox

❤ A QUICK OVERVIEW

No matter how skilled you become at training a dog, having the right combination of equipment, training tools, toys and other resources can make it easier to achieve a successful relationship with your canine companion. In this section I will cover a variety of "tools of the trade" that will help you train and care for your dog. Also covered are topics like doggie daycare, the spay-neuter decision and finally, inevitably, the heart-wrenching euthanasia dilemma that most dog-lovers will eventually face.

CHAPTER 32 ❤
A Stitch in Time: The Spay/Neuter Decision

Most people respond with a warm fuzzy "awwww" reaction when they see a litter of puppies. After all, nothing could possibly be cuter than a bunch of roly-poly baby dogs tumbling and tussling together on the floor. Or could it?

Anyone who works or volunteers at an animal shelter for any length of time soon finds his "awwww" reaction tempered by the sobering knowledge that millions of unwanted dogs and puppies are euthanized in shelters around this country every year. I know. I worked at a humane society for 20 years. While I love dogs at least as much as the next person, to this day I cannot look at a puppy without also seeing syringes filled with blue euthanasia solution, needles inserted into furry puppy legs, and canine bodies piled up on gurneys outside the euthanasia room door.

For those who regularly deal with the hapless victims of our throwaway society, spay/neuter is a mantra. Rarely, in the shelter worker's opinion, is there a sufficiently valid reason for not surgically rendering a dog incapable of reproducing.

Arguments Pro And Con

The average dog owner, however, is more concerned with his own dog's well being than with the state of animal welfare in general. There are a whole host of commonly offered arguments against spaying and neutering. How valid are they?

"Surgery isn't natural. I would rather be responsible by keeping my dog home or on a leash than take the risks of surgery and alter my dog unnaturally."

There is some truth to this argument. Surgery certainly isn't natural. Neither are collars and leashes, prepared dog foods, fences, veterinary care, or the daily killing of healthy "surplus" dogs and puppies. Dogs haven't lived truly natural lives for centuries. If we are picking and choosing which parts of "natural" we want to recreate for our canine companions we are better off not choosing this one. If we truly wanted to be natural it follows that we would then let our female dog get pregnant and have puppies every six months, and no responsible dog owner advocates that.

It's true that every surgery carries risks, but the risks of spay/neuter surgery are miniscule compared to the certain death of overpopulation. Far more dogs die from lack of homes, from mammary tumors, prostate, testicular and ovarian cancers, and hormone-related behavior-problems, than ever die from spay/neuter surgery.

"Sterilization will change my dog's personality; She/He will get fat and lazy."

This concern seems valid. We have all seen spayed and neutered dogs who were, indeed, fat and lazy. But let's think about this for a moment.

Dogs, like humans, get fat if their caloric intake is greater than the calories burned off by exercise and other physical demands. It is true that sterilized dogs often get less exercise. Male dogs who are neutered no longer escape their yards and run for miles in pursuit of females in season, or nervously pace the fence line in sexual frustration trying to find a way to escape. Spayed female dogs no longer experience the immense drain on their systems caused by growing puppies in their bodies for 63 days and feeding them for another six to eight weeks. Nor do their bodies go through the stress of reproductive-related hormonal changes that result in an expenditure of nervous energy. It's true that sterilized dogs of both sexes are calmer and more content to stay home, but that doesn't mean they have to be fat and lazy. It does mean they are better companions.

You control the food intake. The dog doesn't open the feed bin and help himself to dinner. It's simple: if your dog is gaining weight it's time to cut back on food and increase exercise. I have owned a dozen sterilized dogs over the last 20 years, and not one was fat or lazy. If I noticed that one was starting to put on weight, I cut back on the food. Here are several tips for a simple canine weight-control program:

- **No free feeding.** Your dog should get *meals*, not all-day snacks. In a natural environment a wild dog makes a kill (along with the rest of the pack), gorges himself, and then doesn't eat again until the next kill. Dogs' systems are not designed for grazing. Besides, controlled feeding increases your dog's dependence on you, which will make your training program more successful.

- **Measure the food.** Use a measuring cup and dole out a specific amount. Eyeballing it isn't accurate enough; we tend toward generous. "He looks a tad hungry today...what's a few extra kibbles?" If you are measuring a specific amount you can instruct all family members to stick with the feeding program. A cup is always a cup. Two handfuls may be significantly different, depending on whether you are talking Mom's hands, Dad's, or Junior's. A measuring cup also gives an accurate gauge if Rover is looking a little too prosperous and you decide you need to cut back from, say, one cup, twice a day, to three-quarters of a cup, twice a day.

- **Weigh your dog.** If size permits, pick her up and stand on the bathroom scales, then weigh yourself alone, and subtract. Weigh her once a week so you will notice sooner, rather than later, if she is starting to put on the pounds. If she is gaining, cut back the kibble and/or the treats.

- **Use the feeding instructions printed on the dog food bag as guidelines rather than gospel.** Dog food companies seem to lean toward the generous side of meal rations. Perhaps they want you to use more of their product? I have *never* fed my dogs as much as it says on the bag. If I did, they *would* all be fat!

- **If you train with treats, be sure to count those treats as part of your dog's meal ration.** If he is sufficiently food-motivated you can even use his kibble as training rewards.

- **Give your dog plenty of exercise.** Since he is no longer burning off calories in his frustrated attempts to find females (or she's no longer making puppies), it's your job to make sure he works out. Throw the tennis ball, a stick or the Frisbee™ for him for 20 minutes a day. Take her jogging or swimming. Find a doggie playgroup or a local dog park (if there are none in your area, start one!) and let her work out by romping with her canine buddies. If you are a portly couch potato your dog will likely be one too!

"I want my (male) dog to have fun; I want my (female) dog to experience the joy of motherhood."

This is anthropomorphism (the projecting of human values and emotions on your dog) at its finest. It is usually a male human who insists on leaving his dog intact, perhaps in order not to deprive his four-footed friend of the joy of sex, or maybe out of the owner's own embarrassment at having a male dog without a full complement of male equipment. When you mention neutering, the human's eyes may glaze over and his hands often move to protect a highly valued part of his own anatomy.

Stop and think, men! If you have ever watched dogs breeding, you'll notice that they don't particularly appear to be having fun. They are simply driven by a powerful, undeniable, biological urge to reproduce. They rarely relax and have a cigarette afterwards! Unneutered male dogs are far more likely to escape their yards, run free, risk getting shot or hit by cars, get in fights with other male dogs, or get picked up by animal services officers. If the lack of visible equipment is your concern, ask your veterinarian about "Neuticles," artificial implants that are now available to help owners feel better about neutering their dogs.

On the other hand, if you are a responsible dog owner, you don't allow your dogs to run free and satisfy those mighty biological urges. Your choices are to neuter, and reap the benefits of having a calm, contented canine companion who stays home (and who no longer risks prostate or testicular cancer), or to keep your unneutered male strictly, safely and unhappily confined to lead a life of constant sexual frustration as he senses females in season for miles around.

The female dog, too, benefits from spaying. While many females *do* seem to enjoy motherhood, at least at first, by the time their babies reach the age of six weeks most mom dogs are eager to escape their persistently pushy pups. There are far more life-threatening complications from gestation and birthing than there are from spay surgery. The maternal instinct can also trigger behavior problems; a significant number of dogs develop protective maternal aggression during motherhood. For some dogs this behavior goes away when the puppies are weaned and placed in new homes. Others will continue to display seriously aggressive behavior even after the puppies are long gone.

"My dog is purebred/has papers. I can make money selling puppies. I want another one just like her. All my friends want one of her pups. I already have homes lined up for the puppies."

Certainly, if we are to continue enjoying purebred dogs, *someone* has to breed them. Why shouldn't that someone be

you? Maybe because there is a lot more involved in responsible breeding than just putting two registered dogs of the same breed in the same room together.

For starters, AKC papers are not an assurance of quality. Papers simply mean that both of your dog's parents were registered. Ostensibly. Every month, the *AKC Gazette* publishes names of breeders who have falsified records, or at least kept records poorly enough that the organization revokes their registration privileges. Even if your papers are accurate and your dog's parents were both champions, that doesn't mean your dog is breeding material.

The responsibilities of breeding should not be taken lightly. If done properly, it is an expensive, time-consuming activity. Prospective canine parents must be checked for hip displaysia, eye problems (such as progressive retinal atrophy), and any other genetic health problems specific to your breed.

Dogs intended for breeding should be outstanding representatives of their breed. If you plan to breed, you need to be willing to campaign your dog on the show circuit and have experts in the breed (judges and other breeders) confirm that your Labrador Retriever is one of the best around. Then you will need to do the research to find the "right" male to breed her to; one who complements her strengths and doesn't underscore her weaknesses.

Once you have gone to all the expense and trouble to be a responsible breeder, chances are your friends aren't going to want to pay the prices that you will ask for your well-bred puppies. Labs can have huge litters – as many as 12-15 at a time. You may not have all the homes for them that you thought you did. Many of these will be pet, not show quality puppies. They will sell for less than the show quality pups, and a responsible breeder will have them spayed and neutered before they are sold to ensure that they are not used for future breeding.

Don't forget to consider the additional vet bills; you want to be sure your female is in optimum health, and that the puppies get veterinary exams as well as proper vaccinations and worming before they are sold. A responsible breeder will also take back any of the puppies he has bred, at any time during the dogs' lives if the owner can no longer keep them. Not only may you be left with more puppies to place than you had planned, you may also end up with more adult dogs than you intended to own. Chances are excellent that this hobby will *cost* you a hefty sum of money rather than make you rich.

Here's some more food for thought. If you really want another dog "just like her," you are better off going back to the responsible breeder you got her from and getting a sibling from a repeat breeding rather than creating your own (this is still no guarantee that the new dog will be "just like her;" there is still genetic diversity among siblings, and environment plays a large part in your dog's personality and behavior). Any puppies that your own dog produces will have different genetics than mom because of the genetic influence from dad.

Finally, consider that every friend or family member who takes a puppy from you is a potential home for a puppy from an animal shelter or rescue group. Breed rescue groups exist for virtually every recognized breed, so if your friends have their hearts set on purebred dogs they can contact breed rescue groups or go on the breed request waiting lists that are now maintained by many animal shelters. Regardless of how many homes you have lined up for your pups, you are contributing to the pet overpopulation problem.

"I want my kids to experience the miracle of birth."

Understandable. When I was a kid I loved watching my dogs and cats have kittens and puppies. (Yes, we were an irresponsible pet-owning family.) But if you think this is reason enough to let your dog breed, knowing that "surplus" dogs and puppies are killed every day, then you have a harder heart than I. Your kids can watch videos that document the birth process.

If you want to let them experience the joy (and hard work!) of raising a litter of puppies, sign up with your local shelter or rescue group as a volunteer foster home. For many reasons, most shelters cannot feasibly raise litters of puppies in their kennels, and must often euthanize underage pups. Shelters are desperate for foster homes that can give tender-aged baby dogs a chance to grow up and return to the shelter for adoption when they are eight weeks old and able to withstand the rigors of shelter life. You can even solicit your friends to apply to adopt your foster pups once they have returned to the shelter. You get the joy of puppy raising and the satisfaction of providing a community service without the guilt of contributing to pet overpopulation. Win-win!!

"I live in a 'No-Kill' city. We have solved the pet overpopulation problem so it's okay to breed again."

"No-Kill" is a myth; it actually means "Someone Kills Them Somewhere Else." In San Francisco, often touted as the first "no-kill" city, more than 4,000 animals are still euthanized every year at San Francisco Animal Care & Control, one short block away from the "no-kill" San Francisco SPCA. While the SPCA labels these 4,000-plus animals as "unadoptable" in order to justify the deaths and claim their "No-Kill" city title, it is simply a matter of semantics, public relations and allocation of resources. In some jurisdictions, an upper respiratory infection (canine equivalent of the common cold) or a broken leg, both

treatable, qualify a dog as unadoptable. Even if San Francisco's 4,000 animals were truly not redeemable, surrounding communities in the San Francisco Bay Area continue to euthanize unwanted animals by the tens of thousands. Don't kid yourself; we are far from solving the pet overpopulation problem.

"My dog is old and my veterinarian says spay/neuter surgery is too risky."

Okay, you win. This is truly a valid excuse. At some point in a dog's life the benefits of spay/neuter are outweighed by the risks of surgery. There is no magic age when this happens; it depends on the individual dog. Follow your veterinarian's recommendation if she tells you that sterilization is not indicated due to your dog's age and/or condition.

My Opinion

I am very biased about spay and neuter because of my background both as an animal protection professional and a dog trainer. You don't have to watch very many homeless puppies and kittens die to get strident about birth control for our companion animals. After working with a few dozen dogs with hormone-related behavior problems that could have been prevented if the dog was "fixed" in the first place, you "get" the value of spaying and neutering.

The pet overpopulation problem is so serious that even state governments are getting involved in defining and solving the surplus pet problem. A California state law actually defines puppies under the age of eight weeks as "unadoptable," (thereby legitimizing the "No-Kill" approach of population control through word games). Another more positive California law requires all dogs adopted from animal shelters to be spayed or neutered before they go to their new homes, even puppies. The advent of pediatric spay/neuter – the safe sterilization of puppies as young as eight weeks – allows a law like this to be passed, and gives animal protection workers a powerful new weapon in the pet overpopulation battle.

I love dogs as much as the next person. I love them enough to believe that each one has a right to a lifelong, loving home. Pitifully few dogs get that in today's world. If we spay and neuter, encourage others to do the same, and take the time to teach our dogs to be well-behaved family members, maybe we will see the day when their lives are valued enough that they all end up in lifelong responsible homes, rather than dead by the side of the road or on the euthanasia room floor.

CHAPTER 33 ❤
Thought on Shots: New Vaccination Protocols

Modern-day dog owners enjoy the comforting certainty that their puppies can and will be given a series of vaccinations, so-called "puppy shots," to protect them from life-threatening canine diseases such as distemper, parvovirus and rabies. Most of us were indoctrinated in early childhood to take Shep to the vet once a year for his annual booster shots in order to extend that vital protection year after year. We accepted without question that a failure to do so was the height of dog owner irresponsibility. We wouldn't dream of leaving our beloved canine companions at the mercy of the multitudes of evil distemper, hepatitis, leptospirosis, parainfluenza, parvovirus, coronavirus, Lyme and bordetella germs and viruses that lurk in the environment. Faithfully following our veterinarians' instructions, we vaccinate our dogs year in and year out, confident that this is "the best thing" for them.

But according to some veterinary immunologists, we actually may be doing more harm than good by immunizing our furry friends. Many veterinarians and other animal care professionals believe that by injecting our dogs every year with what we perceive to be life-saving substances we are actually destroying their immune systems, condemning them

to a life of vaccine-induced allergies, behavior problems, encephalitis, epilepsy, cancer, and a laundry list of autoimmune diseases including Addison's disease, rheumatoid arthritis, Hashimoto's thyroiditis, systemic lupus erythematosus (SLE), hemolytic anemia, hepatitis, diabetes, Grave's disease, hypoparathyroidism, uveitis, and more. They insist that vaccines actually cause more problems than they prevent, and that dogs are dying by the thousands of "vaccinosis," a morbid reaction to vaccines. A few even go so far as to suggest that we should *never* vaccinate. Who are we supposed to believe?

What is a Vaccine?

According to *Taber's Cyclopedic Medical Dictionary*, a vaccine is defined as: A suspension of infectious agents or some part of them, given for the purpose of establishing resistance to an infectious disease. A vaccine's function is to stimulate the immune system to produce antibodies to the disease. If the dog is later exposed to the disease, the antibodies quickly react to attack and destroy the virus.

Vaccines come in two types: killed and modified live (or attenuated) virus

(MLV). Killed vaccines are mixed with a substance called an adjuvant to make them more effective. They often require more injections to accomplish immunization, and various adjuvants are suspected of causing allergic reactions. The modified live vaccines generally work more quickly, but are more likely to cause suppression of the immune system.

Many people assume that vaccines are 100% effective. Unfortunately, this is far from true. There are many reasons why a vaccine might not be effective. The first reason has to do with the animal, rather than the vaccine. The vaccine by itself does not confer immunity; it is the response of the vaccinated animal's immune system that determines the effectiveness of the vaccine. If the dog is sick, weak or malnourished his body may be unable to mount the proper defense. If his immune system is depressed due to previous disease, surgery, poor genes, old age or drug therapy, vaccinations are likely to be ineffective. Every vaccine package includes warnings against vaccinating any animal whose immune system may be compromised, and most veterinarians will agree that a sick dog should not be vaccinated.

Puppies present their own challenges to effective vaccination. If a puppy is young, his mother's antibodies may still be in his system and interfere with the pup's ability to respond to the vaccine.

This is why we give a "series" of puppy shots to span the period of time when he may, or may not, be protected by his mother's immunities.

In addition, if a vaccine has been improperly produced, poorly handled (for example, not kept properly refrigerated), incorrectly administered (i.e., given subcutaneously when it is supposed to be given intramuscularly) or given on a faulty schedule, it may be rendered ineffective.

Not Always Safe

Most veterinarians tend to reassure their clients that vaccinations are perfectly safe. This is not always true. A relatively small percentage of dogs can have an acute anaphylactic (severe allergic) reaction to one or more vaccines. When this happens, prompt administration of adrenaline, epinephrine, antihistamines or corticosteroids may be necessary to save the dog's life. Milder reactions, such as soreness and swelling at the injection site, lack of appetite, and general lethargy and depression can also occur within a day or two following administration of the vaccine. In addition, there is a growing body of evidence that vaccines are sometimes associated with immune system problems.

Off to the left side of the issue are vaccine alarmists who claim that, far from being safe, vaccines damage immune systems in a large percentage of dogs, causing more diseases than they prevent. In her book *What Vets Don't Tell You About Vaccines,* Catherine O'Driscoll says that vaccines are deadly poisons that disarm and unbalance the immune system, and suggests that they should rarely, if ever, be used.

Then there are the vaccine moderates, including W. Jean Dodds, DVM, a graduate of the Ontario Veterinary College. From 1965 to 1985 Dodds conducted comparative studies of animals with inherited and acquired blood diseases while working for the New York State Health Department. In 1986 she opened Hemopet, the first nonprofit national blood bank for animals, which she continues to operate to this day in Southern California. On behalf of Hemopet she consults in clinical pathology nationally and internationally, and is known as one of the country's leading experts on hematology and blood banking, immunology, endocrinology, and nutrition.

Dodds has identified a long list of breeds and families within breeds who are genetically predisposed to immune system sensitivities. The breed list includes Dobermans, Rottweilers, Yorkshire Terriers, Akitas, Standard Poodles, Great Danes, Weimaraners and American Eskimos.

"The vaccine," says Dodds, "is just a precipitating event. It does not create the weak immune system. For dogs predisposed to immune system problems, toxic exposure, overheating, poor diet or some other condition that stresses the system can also be precipitating events.

"For the last 20 years," she continues, "we have been increasingly aware that vaccines are associated with autoimmune disease. But vaccines have played a vitally important role in reducing severe infectious diseases in our companion animals. Because of this, we are seeing more adverse reactions than infections, and some people are tempted to cease vaccinating altogether. This is not wise. The diseases still exist, and it makes sense to vaccinate, when safe, in order to protect our pets and the pet population in general. A well-nourished, healthy animal should not have problems with the standard vaccines. We do need to identify high-risk animals and modify our vaccination protocols to meet their individual needs when appropriate in order to minimize their risk."

Dr. Susan G. Wynn, a private practitioner in Marietta, Georgia, who teaches classes in veterinary alternative medicine, co-edited a text for veterinary schools entitled *Complementary and Alternative Veterinary Medicine,* and completed a four-year post-doctoral fellowship in viral immunology. She agrees with Dr. Dodds.

"There is no question that vaccines are more beneficial than harmful," she says. "Distemper used to kill some 50%

of all dogs born. I have seen a total of three cases of distemper since my 1987 graduation. Vaccines have played a really important role in reducing the incidence of severe, infectious diseases. They have been so effective that today we do see more adverse vaccine reactions than the infections themselves, which may give the appearance that the vaccine is worse than the disease. This is simply not the case. Ceasing all vaccinations would be foolhardy. Our challenge is to reduce vaccines to the least needed to prevent harm, while maintaining our current high level of protection against infectious diseases."

Still, veterinarians have a legal and ethical obligation to inform their clients of the relative benefits and risks of vaccines so that pet owners can make informed choices regarding their animals' medical care. There are times when not vaccinating may well be the wise, educated decision.

No Ideal Frequency

Vaccine manufacturers have long counseled against vaccinating dogs who are pregnant or those who are not healthy. But they do promote annual vaccination protocols, and they clearly reap monetary benefits from the widely accepted United States Department of Agriculture (USDA) recommendation issued 25-30 years ago supporting annual vaccinations. It is disturbing to discover that the USDA recommendation is not based on any scientific evidence. In fact, only recently have scientific studies been initiated to determine the optimum frequency of vaccinations. The annual booster policy was instituted in large part so pet owners would be prompted to bring their dogs in for an annual well-pet check-up, allowing veterinarians to find and treat other conditions promptly.

Richard B. Ford, DVM, MS, Diplomate ACVIM and Professor of Medicine at North Carolina State University, is concerned over vaccine safety and the rapid proliferation of companion animal vaccines. In an address to the 2002 World Small Animal Veterinary Association (WSAVA) Congress, he argued that routine annual administration of an increasing number of vaccines was a disturbing trend, and stated, "We simply cannot continue to arbitrarily administer vaccines without regard for the number and type of vaccine antigens in the product and without realistic consideration of the risk of infection facing the individual animal.

Dr. Dodds agrees that we have been over-vaccinating our pets. "While there will probably never be a study to definitively identify the effective length of vaccines because of the immense cost involved, a recent study we completed of 1200 dogs demonstrated that one to two years after the initial immunization, 94.4% of the dogs still had adequate immunities to parvovirus, and 97.3% were still protected against distemper. Some dogs were tested as long as six years after the vaccination, with similar results."

Pressure from veterinarians including Dr. Ford, Dr. Dodds and other like-minded practitioners seems to have initiated change within the veterinary community. In a very significant move for the industry, the American Veterinary Medical Association (AVMA) has published several papers recently supporting a move to three-year protocols. In another, the 2003 "Report of the American Animal Hospital Association (AAHA) Canine Vaccine Task Force" recommends 3-year revaccination for commonly given rabies, distemper and parvovirus vaccines, following the initial vaccination series and 1-year booster. Many veterinarians and an increasing number of veterinary schools are rewriting their vaccination protocols to recommend three-year intervals between shots rather than annual boosters.

Vaccine Contraindications

Drug companies and veterinarians agree that sick and pregnant dogs should not be vaccinated. The definition of "sick," however, is left open to wide interpretation. Dr. Dodds and Dr. Wynn both advise not vaccinating in the following circumstances:

- If the dog is elderly.
- If the dog is pregnant.
- If the dog has symptoms of any illness, mild or severe, including everything from low-grade chronic

disease such as skin condition and allergies, to cancer.

- If the dog has any other medical condition including lameness.
- If the dog is undergoing surgery.
- If the dog is on any immune-suppressant drugs.

Clearly, this list encompasses a much broader range of animals than does "sick or pregnant." In general, if there is any question about the dog's health status, it is better to postpone vaccination until the dog is clearly healthy.

In addition to not vaccinating dogs in the categories listed above, there are a number of other ways to reduce the risk of vaccine-related problems:

- Measure antibodies through titer tests and only revaccinate when indicated by low titers.
- Reduce the incidence of booster shots to every three years after the first annual booster.
- Give individual vaccines instead of combined (such as DHLPP), and don't give several shots at one time.
- Watch your dog's behavior closely for several days following vaccination to look for any reactions that might influence your future vaccination decisions. ANY health problems following vaccination should be noted, whether the reaction is a hot spot outbreak, an ear infection, or something more dramatic, such as an

epileptic seizure. It may be wise not to administer the same vaccine at any time in the future to a dog who reacts to the shot one or more times.

- Don't vaccinate for Bordetella, corona virus or Lyme disease unless these diseases are endemic locally or in a specific kennel.

- Do not worm or otherwise medicate at time of vaccination, and avoid the use of toxic flea and tick control products.

- Only vaccinate against diseases for which your dog is at risk (usually rabies, parvo and distemper). There have not been any reported cases of canine hepatitis in a very long time, and the leptospirosis vaccine is not effective against current prevalent strains that produce this disease. It is the leptospirosis vaccine that is most commonly associated with acute anaphylactic reactions in dogs.

Little Support for Nosodes?

Nosodes are a homeopathic alternative to vaccinations, in which a small amount of the infectious agent is potentized in water (by vigorous shaking) and then diluted to such a degree that there is no longer any measurable amount of the agent in the liquid. Some holistic veterinarians believe nosodes to be effective in preventing disease. Others, including Dr.

Wynn, are reluctant to place much faith in them.

"While they are certainly not harmful and perhaps they are beneficial, there is no scientific evidence to support their effectiveness," says Dr. Wynn. "In fact, there is at least one study that clearly showed nosodes to be *ineffective* against parvovirus."

No Easy Answer

As much as we all want easy answers to the vaccination question, there aren't any. Even the revised vaccine protocols are general guidelines, not bibles for every dog. Here, at least as much as in any other aspect of our relationships with our four-footed companions, the holistic approach is critical. We must know our dog well and weigh all of the benefits and risks of vaccination in light of his unique self in order to be able to make the best decisions about what vaccination program is best for him.

Above all, whether in training, management or veterinary care, don't ever let anyone convince you to do something to your dog that you know is wrong. You are his guardian and he trusts you to make the right choices for his well being. As you wander through the forest of information and half-truths about vaccines and diseases, be sure to make your choices carefully and well.

Vaccination Schedule

❤ TRADITIONAL VACCINATION PROTOCOL

6 WEEKS – Temporary Distemper and Measles vaccination for puppies who did not nurse during the first hours after birth, or for puppies from a bitch who is not current on her vaccinations

8 WEEKS – DHLPPC (Distemper, Canine Infectious Hepatitis, Leptospirosis, Parainfluenza, Parvovirus and Corona virus)

12 WEEKS – DHLPPC Booster

16 WEEKS – DHLPPC Booster

6 MONTHS – Rabies (1-year vaccination)

14 MONTHS – DHLPPC, administered yearly from this date

18 MONTHS – Rabies (3-year vaccination), administered every 3 years from this date

Note: There is no single recommended vaccination schedule for puppies as there is for children. Suggested protocols vary among veterinary colleges, practitioners and vaccine makers. The sample schedule presented here is relatively conservative (for a traditional schedule) with 26-28 antigens given in 18 months, compared with Dodds' reduced protocol, with just 16 (min.) to 21 (max.) antigens given.

❤ DR. JEAN DODDS' VACCINATION PROTOCOL

EITHER...

6 WEEKS – Distemper and Measles

7 ½ WEEKS – Killed or modified-live (MLV) Parvovirus

10 ½ WEEKS – Killed or MLV Parvovirus

OR...

8 WEEKS – Distemper and Parvovirus. Maybe Hepatitis. Maybe Parainfluenza

10 WEEKS – Distemper and Parvovirus. Maybe Hepatitis. Maybe Parvovirus.

THEN...

12 WEEKS – Distemper, Hepatitis, Parainfluenza. (NO Parvovirus if possible*)

14 WEEKS – Distemper, Hepatitis, Parainfluenza, and killed or MLV Parvovirus*

18-20 WEEKS – Distemper, Hepatitis, Parainfluenza, and killed or MLV Parvovirus*

16-24 WEEKS – Killed Rabies vaccine

*During Parvovirus epidemics or for highly susceptible breeds such as Rottweilers newer modified live-virus (MLV) vaccines that provide more complete immunity and override maternal immunity are available or go to www.vth.colostate.edu/vth/ and click on "Small Animal Vaccination Protocol" from Colorado State University.

CHAPTER 34 ❤
New Choices in Vet Care: What's the Alternative?

Not long ago, acupuncture, acupressure, chiropractic, massage therapy, and homeopathy were regarded with scorn and suspicion by some dog owners and much of the veterinary establishment. Today, these healing modalities are becoming widely accepted and respected as viable companions to traditional Western veterinary medicine. As East and West form a working relationship, they are often referred to as "complementary therapies," as more veterinarians use them in conjunction with the medical skills and protocols they learned in veterinary college.

When their dogs present them with conditions that fail to improve with traditional veterinary treatment – things like persistent lameness, digestive ailments, training and behavior challenges, and many other mysterious canine puzzles – dog owners will try anything that they think will help. Frustration with a lack of results from the standard medical approach has led thousands of dog owners to try one or more of the complementary therapies. And everywhere you turn you hear success stories, cases where one or more of the complementary therapies improved a formerly hopeless condition.

But until recently, little controlled research was conducted on alternative therapies. Not until the last 25 years have the methods been scrutinized with Western scientific methodology and shown to be effective. Though the studies may mean little to people who have already seen the methods heal their dogs, the positive results have helped motivate the scientists and the veterinary establishment climb onto the complementary bandwagon.

And, suddenly, the bandwagon is starting to get crowded. Look in the classified ad section of any dog magazine and you'll be faced with a bewildering array of complementary therapy choices: canine massage, trigger point myotherapy, all-natural herbal remedies, homeopathic remedy kits. The variations seem truly endless.

The problem today is not finding alternative options for your dog and his health situation, it's figuring out which of the many alternatives will be most beneficial, and locating a qualified practitioner. How do you avoid the well intentioned but misguided or under-trained practitioners in the field, or worse yet, the scam artists who are riding the wave with glossy but unsubstantiated treatments? Dog owners are not alone with these questions. They are also on the minds of the responsible practitioners of the complementary disciplines.

Take heart! Education and guidance from well-schooled practitioners – whether they are veterinarians, practitioners who usually treat people, or skilled lay people – *is* available. Many of the alternative practices have formed national organizations that train and/or certify members, set training standards, and maintain a minimum level of quality control for practitioners of the therapy. You can contact these organizations for more information about the modalities or even referrals to certified practitioners. Below, you'll find a brief description of the most popular modalities and contact information for their national associations.

As you will discover, however, the demand for *qualified* professionals still outstrips the supply. Unless you're lucky enough to have one conducting business close to your home, you might need to rely on your local veterinarian for emergency and day-to-day health care for your dog, and complement that treatment with the services of a traveling "alternative" practitioner when available, or with the advice from one of the many holistic veterinarians who offer telephone or Internet consultations.

Holistic Medicine

Holistic practitioners differ significantly from those who practice conventional Western (allopathic) medicine, in which symptoms are treated in isolation. In Western medicine, diseases are believed to have one specific cause – a germ, virus or bacteria. By contrast, holistic medicine uses a matrix of treatments, addressing the entire, complex blend of body, mind and spirit that makes up each individual.

The goal of holistic medicine is to use whatever gentle treatments may be effective to bring all aspects of a being into balance, encouraging the body's natural ability to heal itself. Treatments may include conventional medicine, acupuncture, chiropractic, massage, and homeopathy. Practitioners contend that the strictly allopathic approach may be effective in the short term, but can also disrupt the body's intricate system, inviting long-term harm to the whole.

Organization: AHVMA

American Holistic
Veterinary Medical Association
2214 Old Emmorton Rd.
Bel Air, MD 21015
410-569-0795
www.ahvma.org

The American Holistic Veterinary Medical Association, established in 1981, does not offer any certification protocols or training sessions, but acts as a clearinghouse for anyone – veterinarians and non-veterinarians who want information about any of the therapies currently available. The association publishes a quarterly journal. Its largest endeavor is an annual conference featuring presentations on a wide range of health topics. For an introduction to the wide world of healing modalities, this convention can't be matched.

Acupuncture

Smile when you see acupuncture referred to as a new therapy. It has been practiced for at least five thousand years by millions of people all over the world.

Acupuncture involves the insertion of fine needles into the skin at specific points around the body. Acupressure uses fingertip massage instead, and in recent years, lasers and other electronic devices have been used on these same points as well.

The theory passed down from its ancient Chinese originators is that acupuncture can influence the chi (pronounced chee), or life energy, that constantly circulates throughout the body. Practitioners of Traditional Chinese Medicine believe that the chi comes in two complementary forms, *yin* and *yang*. When yin and yang are balanced, health results. When unbalanced, illness will follow.

Chi is believed to circulate through the body along invisible pathways called *meridians*. Each meridian passes close to the skin's surface at places called *points*. At these points, the insertion of needles or other stimulation affects the flow of chi.

Modern Western medical practitioners have a few problems with this explanation. How can you make sense of a system, after all, that you cannot see? One devoted researcher, George A. Ulett, M.D., Ph.D., director of the Department of Psychiatry at Deaconness in St. Louis, Missouri and clinical professor of psychiatry at the University of Missouri School of medicine, suggests that acupuncture works neuroelectrically. He postulates that the meridians may be motor nerves, the nerves connected to major muscles. Stimulating the acupuncture points with needles or finger pressure may change the flow of bio-electrical energy along the nerves and trigger the release of neurotransmitters – pain relieving and mood elevating chemicals such as endorphins – that allow nerve cells to communicate.

Obviously, the Western and Eastern theories that explain how acupuncture works are centuries and cultures apart. Both camps know it does work and the dogs respond positively as well. Does it sound too flippant to say, "If you need one, use whichever explanation works best for you?"

Organization: IVAS

International Veterinary Acupuncture
Society
PO Box 2074
Nederland, CO 80466
303-258-3767
www.ivas.org

It is interesting to note that the key organizing body for this group, the International Veterinary Acupuncture Society (IVAS), was founded by three veterinarians in December of 1974, 10 years prior to the creation of the National Commission for the Certification of Acupuncturists, which certifies human acupuncture practitioners!

IVAS offers extensive training programs that rotate through various locations throughout the U.S. and the world. Attendance at these programs is limited to veterinarians only. Many members also conduct local seminars and workshops and speak at meetings for other groups.

The group has about 1200 members. About half are veterinarians who have been certified in acupuncture through IVAS; the rest are non-certified veterinarians, associate members (lay people), and organizational members. Most of the 600-plus certified members are located in the U.S. To become certified, veterinarians must take a 100-hour course, pass a four-hour written exam and a practical exam, and complete a 40-hour internship with a certified veterinarian.

Homeopathy

This is the most difficult complementary modality to explain scientifically, and the one most likely to require a leap of faith from the recipient.

The word comes from the Greek *homios,* "like," and *pathos,* "suffering," to imply healing like with like. The founder of homeopathy was a German physician names Samuel Hahnemann, born in 1755. While translating a medical text, Dr. Hahnemann came across a description of a treatment for malaria, one that was made from the bark of a China tree *(Cinchona succirubra).* Out of curiosity, he ingested a bit of the bark. To his surprise, he soon felt a mild version of symptoms similar to those of malaria. More experiments led him to discover that extremely minute doses of the medicine sometimes reduced signs of the disease and cured the patient. From this work, he established the concepts of homeopathy.

Allopathic pharmaceuticals work by overwhelming and destroying the agents of disease. In contrast, homeopathic remedies mimic symptoms similar to those produced by the disease, engaging and strengthening the body's own disease-fighting defenses.

Homeopathic remedies consist of doses of the active ingredient substance, which are super-diluted, and then shaken vigorously or "potentized," following dilution. The shaking process, or potentization, causes friction between the water molecules and the substance, transferring the medicine's healing properties to the water. Most frequently, the active ingredients are plants used in traditional herbal therapies, although a few come from naturally occurring compounds.

Critics charge that homeopathic remedies are nothing but water, and that a placebo effect is responsible for any apparent improvement in a patient's condition – though the placebo effect is notoriously absent in non-humans! It's a seeming paradox that the greater the dilution, the more effective the remedy is believed to be, and some doses are so diluted that the solution may not contain a single molecule of the substance. This violates a principle of modern pharmacology, the "dose-response relationship", which predicts that the bigger the dose, the greater the effect.

However, it's a less-flashy principle of pharmacology thought to be at work in homeopathy. Dr. Richard Pitcairn, DVM, Ph.D., of Eugene, Oregon, was one of the first veterinarians in the U.S. to offer homeopathy for animals. He explains something called "Arndz law," in which weak stimuli excite physiological activity; moderately strong ones favor it; strong ones retard it; and very strong ones arrest it.

"In homeopathy, this principle has far more importance than it would in conventional pharmacology, where they are looking for what they call the 'therapeutic dose,' which is the largest dose the body can tolerate," Pitcairn explains. "The dose-response relationship doesn't explain all drug interactions. There are substances which have very different and sometimes opposite effects when given to patients in various dosages. When you remember that, homeopathy becomes easier to understand."

Homeopaths and their clients relate remarkable anecdotal successes, sometimes with almost immediate relief of symptoms in both human and non-human clients. And a growing number of studies indicate that the treatments are, indeed, effective.

Organization: AVH

Academy of Veterinary Homeopathy
751 NE 168th St.
North Miami, FL 33162
www.theavh.org

In 1992, Dr. Pitcairn began offering a five-session, 128-hour homeopathy training through his practice, the Animal Natural Health Center. The course is open only to licensed veterinarians.

Audios and videotapes of Dr. Pitcairn's seminars, written materials and remedy kits are available to lay people.

Very recently, Dr. Pitcairn and a small group of veterinarians he helped train have begun to organize an association to meet the needs of veterinarians who would like to use homeopathy. They have established a name for the association – the Academy of Veterinary Homeopathy (AVH) but are still in the process of defining their goals and curriculum. They do offer a short referral list of 32 veterinarians they have certified as qualified to practice veterinary homeopathy. Despite its newness, it looks as if the AVH is best positioned to become the definitive national association for veterinary homeopathy.

Chiropractic

The word "chiropractic" is derived from the Greek words *cheir* and *pratikos* meaning "done by hand." Since the nervous system controls or coordinates all the other systems and tissues in the body, any problem with the nerve function, whether caused by mechanical, chemical, or psychiatric interference, may cause pain and disease. Less noticeable, but perhaps more important, chiropractors believe that nerve dysfunctions can deteriorate or at least alter normal and optimal health and performance.

Chiropractors seek to improve the function of the nervous system by addressing it directly and indirectly through a variety of manipulations to the body, most often to the spine. Only after careful analysis are the precise and delicate maneuvers performed, chiropractors explain, and always to achieve a predetermined goal.

One of the earliest descriptions of soft-tissue manipulation was found in a Chinese document written around 2700 BC. Soft-tissue manipulation was also practiced by the ancient Japanese, Indians of Asia, Egyptians, Babylonians, Syrians, Hindus, and Tibetans. Hippocrates, the celebrated Greek physician born around 460 BC, wrote at least 70 books on healing, including several on chiropractic. One was titled "On Setting Joints By Leverage."

Modern chiropractic was developed in the U.S. in the latter part of the 19th century. Daniel David Palmer, a one-time grocer and teacher, studied the effect of physical manipulations on people and trained many of his friends and associates in the practice. By 1913 the first state law licensing chiropractors was passed, and by 1931, 39 states had given chiropractors legal recognition. Today, it is the most sought-after alternative health care for humans in the United States, and the practice of animal chiropractic is growing exponentially.

Organization: AVCA

American Veterinary
Chiropractic Association
623 Main St.
Hillsdale, IL 612567
309-523-3995
www.animalchiropractic.org

The American Veterinary Chiropractic Association (AVCA) was founded in 1989 by Sharon L. Willoughby, DVM, DC. The initials tell you that Willoughby is one of only a handful of professionals who have both a veterinary doctorate and a doctorate in chiropractic. The AVCA's mission statement includes a commitment to the continuing advancement of chiropractic as a health care choice for animals in the world community, and to bringing the veterinary and chiropractic professions together for a common and higher goal of the health care of animals.

While more than 600 veterinarians and doctors of chiropractic have taken the AVCA course, just over 200 have completed their certification requirements. The basic certification course consists of five separate modules, each with 30 hours of instruction (150 hours total). Written and practical exams are also required. Acknowledging the educational gaps in both groups' backgrounds, the course includes veterinary basics for chiropractors, and chiropractic basics for veterinarians. The modules can be completed in one year, and should be completed within two.

As with other alternative therapies, public demand for animal chiropractic has mushroomed, and practitioners can be hard to find. AVCA routinely makes referrals to only 230 certified animal chiropractors around the country.

Looking for Qualified Help

Be sure to ask about a practitioner's education, training, and experience, whether or not the person is credentialed by one of the organizations named above. Ideally, candidates will have an extensive history of practice, or, at least, impress you with their efforts to further their education.

Inquire about references. Every competent professional will readily share several names and phone numbers of satisfied clients. Follow up with at least one reference; your call needn't be an inquisition. Inquire whether the treatments proved to be of any benefit, and whether they would use that practitioner again.

Ask whether the practitioner is willing to discuss your dog's case with your regular veterinarian. Look for individuals who are willing to "be on your team," rather than those who insist on taking over management of your dog's case.

Make sure that you can communicate your concerns to the candidate, and understand his or her responses to you. Some practitioners are brilliant, but hard to communicate with. Ultimately, your dog will be better off if you fully understand what the practitioner is doing, why, and how you can help the process along.

Observe the practitioner in action, looking specifically for his or her rapport with the animals and their owners. Is the interaction pleasurable for all concerned, or anxious and tense?

If, after a fair trial, you determine that a healing art is not improving your dog's health, stop the treatments. Continue your quest for something that works, but don't continue to support a modality or an individual that is not helping. It doesn't mean the modality is useless or the practitioner incompetent, it just means it's not the right time or place for that treatment.

Dr. Jaggar, one of the founders of IVAS, adds a final note: "You know your own dog and your own dog care beliefs and standards. Don't compromise those," he says, "no matter how famous or forceful the attending practitioner is."

CHAPTER 35 ❤
Collar Choices Tell on You

Your dog's collar is more than just a handy place to hang an I.D. tag or attach a leash. Like a wedding ring, the collar is a symbol of the social contract between you and your dog, for better or for worse, until death do you part. Collars are a very important part of your training kit. The type of collar your dog wears says a lot about you as a dog owner and trainer, and about the nature of the relationship you have with your canine friend.

What's In a Collar?

It's important to select a type of collar that matches your own training philosophy. Some collars naturally go hand-in-paw with positive training methods. Flat collars that don't constrict a dog's neck, and harnesses that distribute pressure from leash-pulling across the dog's chest instead of her neck, are obvious choices. Because these collars don't punish the dog for pulling, you must make "not-pulling" a rewarding enough behavior that your dog doesn't develop (or continue) the habit of leaning into the flat collar or harness when you are walking her on the leash.

Some collars are specifically designed to be used as compulsion tools. The choke chain, prong collar and shock collar (also

called electronic collar) are all intended to deliver physical punishment when your dog does the wrong thing. If you are committed to a relationship with your dog based on positive training methods, you shouldn't be needing these.

There are also several other types of collars that serve various purposes. Some, like the Greyhound or martingale collar, tighten around the dog's neck in order to prevent her from backing out of it, but don't tighten enough to choke. Head collars and no-pull harnesses can gently restrain a dog who is committed to pulling. Combination collar-and-leads have leashes built in to the collar for owner convenience.

All of these collars come in an intimidating variety of styles, materials, and designer colors and patterns. How's a confused dog owner supposed to know which one to buy? Let's take a closer look at several different collars, and see if we can help you narrow the field.

Flat Collars

As an advocate for positive training methods, I recommend the flat collar as the collar of choice for most dogs. You can choose from nylon, cotton cloth, cotton web, polypropylene or leather. All are suitable materials – your choice may be based on personal preference and your dog's coat.

A flat buckle collar.

Nylon and cotton cloth and web collars are available with either buckle or plastic snap fasteners. *Caution: large strong dogs may be able to pop a snap fastener open with a hearty lunge. A solid collar with a sturdy buckle may be the better choice for a big strong dog who pulls with vigor.* Some nylon collars have a reflective coating that may be useful for owners who walk their dogs along roadways at night. Nylon is strong, durable, and sheds water better than cotton. It can also damage your dog's coat and skin, thus may not be a good choice for dogs with long, fine hair like the Maltese and Afghan Hound, or those with sensitive skin. If you choose a nylon collar, be prepared to pay a little more for a good quality one that will last longer and be softer on your dog's neck. Cheaper nylon collars are made of harder nylon and tend to have sharper edges. Cotton collars are less durable than

nylon, and absorb water more easily, but are usually softer. Cotton web is sturdier than cotton cloth. Cotton collars also come in a wonderful selection of colors and patterns. They may be less expensive than top quality nylon, but will probably need to be replaced more frequently.

Polypropylene collars are made of a soft, rolled, nylon-like material. These combine the durability of the nylon collar with a softness similar to cotton, and are also available in a wide variety of very attractive colors and patterns. The collar is narrow compared to the flat nylon and cotton collars, thus is a more subtle visible presence on the dog's neck. This is a fine choice for a dog who is not a dedicated leash-puller. The narrower the collar, however, the more pressure is put on a thinner band of the dog's trachea. Dogs who pull are safer with a wide, flat collar than a narrow one.

Leather collars probably run the widest gamut of quality and cost, from very cheap and cardboard-like to very high quality English leather. Avoid the cheap cardboard-leather collars like smallpox. Watch out for cheap dyed-leather as well – the dye can bleed onto your dog's fur. I also prefer to pass right by leather collars with metal spikes – that's not a fashion statement *we* care to make! Good quality flat or rolled leather collars are attractive and durable, and gentle to coat and skin. Leather collars need to be oiled occasionally to prevent drying and cracking, especially if they get wet.

Getting the Point

Choke chains, prong collars and shock collars utilize mild to severe punishment, called "corrections" by trainers who use them, to let the dog know when she has done something wrong. I don't recommend their use. Punishment can be difficult to administer effectively – timing and severity of the correction are critical to effective punishment training – and even when done properly there is a high risk of unintended and undesirable side effects, including aggression.

Overly enthusiastic jerks on choke chains have been responsible for countless collapsed canine tracheas, and there are documented incidents of dogs being killed by choke chains in the hands of overzealous compulsion trainers. Yet another drawback of compulsion collars is that they cannot safely be left on the dog all the time. Many dogs become "collar-wise," and will behave only when the collar is on and they know they risk punishment if they misbehave.

Prong collars are purportedly less likely to cause serious injury than are choke chains because the pressure of the correction is distributed around the dog's neck instead of just at the throat. Make no mistake, however, those prongs *do* cause pain – that's why they work. If you doubt that, slip one over your wrist and give it a solid yank. Then think about doing that to your neck.

Shock collars are in a class by themselves. The potential for abuse is extremely high, and it takes a high degree of skill to use them properly. Although they are commonly used to train hunting dogs, and unfortunately available for sale over the counter and through pet supply catalogs to the average Joe Q. Dog Owner, we strongly urge you not to fall victim to the "easy fix" promised by these collars. You risk irreparable harm to the relationship between you and your dog, and there is no need to shock your dog into correct behavior when there are kinder, gentler ways.

Head Collars and Head Halters

Head collars and no-pull harnesses utilize the principle of *negative reinforcement* to convince dogs to stop pulling. With negative reinforcement, the dog's behavior makes a "bad" thing go away. When the dog pulls on a head collar, it puts pressure on the dog's nose, which is uncomfortable. The dog's behavior (turning back toward the owner) makes the bad thing (the discomfort) go away. *Caution: because the head halter turns the dog's head sideways, it should never be used to give a physical correction, and care should be taken to prevent a dog from lunging forward and hitting the end of the leash with her full weight. There is some potential for damage to a dog's spine if the halter suddenly torques the head sideways*. Similarly, when a dog pulls on a no-pull harness, the device tightens around the dog's chest. When the dog stops pulling, the tightening sensation goes away. With both of these tools, the owner/trainer must consciously and consistently reward the desired behavior – the "not-pulling" – when it occurs, or remain forever reliant on the tool, rather than training, to keep the dog walking on leash without pulling.

Head halters are relative newcomers to the dog world. (For more details, see Chapter 36). They can be amazingly effective in controlling dogs that pull and lunge on leash. To the uninitiated they

The head halter is ideal for the dog who habitually drags his owner when pulling on a leash with a flat collar. The halter turns him back towards the owner when the dog pulls.

appear to be muzzles, but they are not. A dog in a head halter is able to eat, drink, breathe and bite normally.

Developed as part of the training profession's progression toward more positive tools and methods, they work physically on the same principle as a halter on a horse – if you can control the head, the rest of the animal follows. They also have a calming or subduing effect on many dogs, apparently from the pressure on the dog's muzzle, which may evoke a psychological submission response similar to that which sometimes occurs when a mother dog takes a pup's muzzle in her mouth as a reprimand.

Some dogs adjust to a head halter easily, others may need a few days to a week of gradual desensitization to accept it and associate it with yummy treats, and other good stuff. Some never do adjust to the feeling of a strap over their noses. For these dogs, the head halter is not an effective training tool.

The Gentle Leader™, The Snoot Loop™ and the Halti™ are the brands most commonly available. Each has its dedicated supporters within the dog training profession.

There are several varieties of no-pull harnesses. One is the Sporn™ harness, which is padded for greater comfort and designed so as to provide better control than many of the other brands available, with the leash attaching at the front of the harness behind the dog's neck, rather than at the back end of the harness. The Sense-Ation™ harness is a newer product that is receiving good reviews. Similar to the head halter in that it uses the dog's own power to effectively leverage her back toward her handler, this harness fits over the dogs barrel, shoulders and chest rather than the head, thus avoiding the resistance that some dogs display to the head halter. The leash attaches to a ring on the *front* of the harness, and uses pressure on the shoulders to turn the dog.

The martingale, or Greyhound collar, also known as the "limited-slip" collar, provides a greater degree of control in a different way. Dogs whose heads are relatively narrow (like the Greyhound) often discover that if they back up and duck, they can easily slip out of their collars. The limited-slip collar prevents this little maneuver by tightening just enough to prevent the collar from slipping off, without tightening enough to choke. While not a collar needed by every dog, the limited-slip is the perfect collar for the right application.

Yet another collar innovation is the Scruffy Guider™. Named after the inventor's dog, the SG is a double nylon collar, with one strap sitting high on the dog's neck, the other resting several inches lower. This can be a gentle and effective device for providing additional control. The upper collar gives more turning leverage than a regular collar – and while not providing the same degree of leverage as a head halter, it also avoids the resistance that the head halter can elicit in some dogs. The double-collar design distributes the pressure over a wider area of the dog's neck, so a dog who *does* pull hard is less likely to cause injury to his throat.

'Til Death Do Us Part

Finding the right collar is more significant than you might think. A 1998 study conducted by the National Council on Pet Population Study and Policy (NCPPCP) determined that 96% of dogs surrendered by their owners to animal shelters had *not* received any obedience training. Choose the right collar for your dog, use it in a good training program with a qualified instructor, and you just may find yourself fulfilling the lifelong commitment terms of your social contract with your faithful friend.

CHAPTER 36 ❤
Head Halters: Right and Wrong

Ten years ago, a new dog training tool hit the market. Known generically as the head halter (or head collar), it is a device similar to the halter commonly used on horses. It provides a greatly increased degree of control over the dog who is dedicated to pulling on the collar and leash, without the punishment or pain factors associated with choke chains and prong collars.

The head halter has a strap that goes around the dog's nose, and another that clasps around his neck, just behind the ears. The leash attaches to a ring below the dog's chin. Just like with halters on horses, bulls and other large animals, it works on the principle that where the nose goes, the body must follow. Rather than pulling against the dog's whole weight on a collar that rests just above his powerful shoulders, we simply put gentle pressure on the halter to turn the dog's head toward us. Almost like magic, the rest of the dog follows. It seemed like the answer to our leash-walking prayers.

The new tool was welcomed with open arms by many positive trainers. Indeed, some trainers started issuing halters to every canine student, and the first-night-of-class ritual was amended to include head collar fitting, just as many compulsion-based classes begin with choke chain or prong collar fitting.

Even from the beginning, however, some trainers were more cautious in their embrace of the new invention. They happily agreed that the halter had a place in the positive trainer's toolbox, but with a more limited application.

Predictably, now that positive trainers have had a decade to gain practical experience with the collar, it is becoming increasingly clear that the more conservative trainers were right. The head halter is the perfect tool for the right applications, but it is *not* the easy answer to every dog's leash-walking needs. In fact for some dogs, rather than being a positive experience, wearing the head collar is downright aversive. Let's take a look at the good, the bad and the ugly of head halters.

The Good

All of the positive things we initially loved about head halters are still true. Because it doesn't take great strength to use them, they can facilitate the control of a large or unmanageable dog, especially by children, seniors and people with physical disabilities. When used properly, the head collar does not depend on the infliction of pain to bring the dog under control. And for some dogs, the head halter has a wonderfully calming effect within moments of being placed on the dog's head. In the right circumstances, the collar can be a lifesaver. Dogs who might otherwise end up at animal shelters can be walked and enjoyed by their previously frustrated owners.

The halter is particularly appropriate for restraining and retraining dogs with aggression problems, especially dogs who lunge at people or other dogs. The halter provides the positive, non-punitive control that is vital for modifying aggressive behavior when we want to change the dog's perception of a stimulus from negative to positive.

With a dog-aggressive dog, for example, if you jerk on a choke chain when your dog barks or growls at another dog, you are inflicting pain, increasing his stress,

When walking a dog with a head halter, make sure that he does not charge forward and hit the end of the leash, forcing his head to snap and twist backwards.

and reinforcing his belief that having other dogs around is a bad thing. A head halter can gently restrain or turn him away from the negative stimulus (the other dog) so he can be rewarded for good behavior (turning away). If we can make *good* things happen in the presence of other dogs, we can eventually convince him that having other dogs around is a good thing too. The head halter is exceedingly effective at this.

When used properly, to elicit non-pulling behavior so that loose-leash walking behavior can be rewarded, the head collar can be an effective tool for teaching a determined puller not to pull on the leash. "Properly" means that the dog is frequently rewarded with tasty treats and other positive reinforcement (toys, petting and praise, for dogs that enjoy this) whenever the leash is loose, until he decides that it is more rewarding to walk near the owner without pulling than it is to constantly strain at the end of the leash. If the owner simply relies on the head collar to control the dog without rewarding for loose-leash walking, the collar is not being used properly.

The Bad

Trainers on the APDT (Association of Pet Dog Trainers) e-mail list have compared notes about head halter experiences. While most of the trainers used them on occasion and felt there were appropriate applications for head halters, they also agreed that tool could be misused. Here are some of the concerns:

- **Head halters can come off.** Some brands are more prone to this than others. This is disconcerting enough when you are using the halter for a simple pulling problem, but it is a disaster if you're dealing with aggression. Imagine having your collar pop off your dog as he lunges for a child walking by.

Some trainers now recommend using two leashes (or a "European" leash, with snaps on both ends); one attached to the halter and one to the regular collar, to guard against this. For those owners who already have difficulty handling one leash, this may be too much of a challenge.

However, while most dogs can eventually be conditioned to accept the halter, it *may* take more time and energy than it is worth, and some never do accept it. If the dog continues to fight, or acts very bothered or depressed when the halter is on, then it is very much an aversive for him, and not a positive training tool at all. Put it away and find a different positive tool for that dog.

- **The halter can be difficult to put on.** Especially with a very active dog (the kind most likely to need a halter), it can sometimes take two people – one to lure the nose into the loop with a treat, the other to snap or buckle the collar behind the dog's ears. Many seniors, children and others who could otherwise benefit from the collar's good points are physically unable to manage the complexity of the process. It helps to properly condition the dog to the haltering procedure, but sometimes it doesn't help enough.

- **The halter looks like a muzzle.** As the general public has more exposure to head halters this misconception is diminishing, but it is still a negative for many dog owners that their canine pal is perceived as wearing a muzzle.

- **Halter straps can rub**. If the halter is not fitted well or the dog has sensitive skin, nylon straps can rub the skin raw. This can often be mitigated by gluing moleskin on the insides of the straps.

- **It's an extra piece of equipment.** One of the beautiful things about positive reinforcement training is that the dog wears his regular "clothes" during training. It doesn't require any special equipment. When we add a special collar, we run the risk of teaching the dog that he must behave when the halter is on, but not when it is off. Compulsion trainers frequently encounter this phenomenon with the choke chain; the dog is great when the chain is on, but does whatever he wants when it is removed.

- **Some dogs are hard to fit.** Although some of head halter companies produce their halters in a variety of size and shapes, some dogs, especially those with flat faces like Boxers and Boston Terriers, can be very difficult to fit properly. The nose strap tends to rest against the eyes, which most dogs understandably find very irritating.

The Ugly

By far the most valid concern, and the one that is hardest to resolve, is that some dogs simply and absolutely hate them. Trainers who are familiar with behavior science understand that anything the dog doesn't like is an aversive. Just because *we* like the head halter (or petting, or praise, or treats) doesn't mean *the dog* does. If a dog reacts violently to the head halter, it *may* mean that you didn't take the time to properly acclimate him to it. If you start over and work with him more slowly you may succeed in getting him to accept it.

However, while most dogs can eventually be conditioned to accept the halter, it *may* take more time and energy than it is worth, and some never do accept it. If the dog continues to fight, or acts very bothered or depressed when the halter is on, then it is very much an aversive for him, and not a positive training tool at all. Put it away and find a different positive tool for that dog.

Any discussion of head halters is not complete without examination of the oft-repeated rumor that the halter, if misused, may cause damage to the spine. One of the complaints about choke chains is their very real potential for causing

serious damage to a dog's trachea, even when it is used properly. Dogs have been treated at veterinary hospitals for multiple puncture wounds caused by prong collars. If the head halter is used properly the chance of injury is so low as to be nonexistent, but some trainers express concerns that if an owner jerks on the head halter or allows the dog to hit the end of the leash at full charge, the halter can snap the dog's head sideways, risking damage to the spine.

I could find no documentation of any such injuries, and Dr. R.K. Anderson, inventor of the Gentle Leader, goes to great pains to attempt to confirm any alleged reports of head halter-related injuries. To date, he has not found any confirmed injuries.

While any training tool can be misused to potential injury, and despite the rumors, the risk to a dog from proper head halter usage appears exceedingly low. I applaud the head halter as a positive training tool, as do most of the APDT trainers who participated in the on-line head halter discussion. I also suggest that trainers and owners familiarize themselves with all of the possible pros and cons that accompany the halter, and make thoughtful, educated decisions about its use.

CHAPTER 37 ❤
King Kongs

I still have the very first Kong I bought 25 years ago for my Australian Kelpie, Keli. The indestructible black toy looks like it could have been purchased yesterday, despite years of intensely hard use by the typically obsessive herding dog. Pre-dating the popular sport of Kong-stuffing by more than a decade, Keli was dedicated to chasing the four-inch, hollow, beehive-shaped rubber object as it bounced and boomeranged erratically across the asphalt at the shelter where we worked. Dang, it was almost as fun as herding sheep!

When Kongs were first marketed, there was only one model. Today there are dozens of sizes and specialized features. The classic red Kongs are very durable, but the even tougher black Kongs provide gnawing opportunities for even the most maniacal chewer.

Twenty-five years ago the Kong, originally available in just one size and color, was a novelty. Today it is made in numerous sizes, colors and chewing densities, and it is a "must-have" staple in the tool kit of most dog trainers and many wise dog owners. Dog care professionals have invented an almost endless list of uses for the innocuous looking rubber object.

This amazing toy can distract a dog suffering from separation anxiety, entertain a bored pup who otherwise gets into trouble, help train an under motivated dog, and more. You wouldn't think that a mere toy could go so far as to help us cope with canines who might otherwise be labeled difficult dogs, or worse, end up on the discard pile at the local animal shelter, but the Kong can.

Top 10 Uses For Your Dog's Kong

1. **The Thrill of the Chase:** This was the original application of the Kong. Because of its unique shape, the Kong bounces every which way but straight, providing intriguing quarry for the prey-oriented pooch. I doubt I would have survived the Kelpie-owning experience without

engaging Keli in several intensive Kong-chasing sessions every day. Watching your dog bound and rebound after the elusive rubber prey is guaranteed to entertain you for hours on end as well as your dog. *Caveat: Herding breeds, especially, are known for literally running themselves into exhaustion. If you have a Kong-crazed dog, be careful not to induce heat stroke or physical collapse (as I inadvertently did with Keli on two occasions) with too much Kong fun!*

2. **Puppy Distracters:** Many of the more recent Kong applications involves Kong-stuffing, excellent for puppy distracting. Play-biting and inappropriate chewing are common complaints of new puppy owners. An ideal solution to perfectly normal but undesirable puppy mouth explorations is to provide an irresistible alternative to human

Most people use cream cheese, peanut butter, or yogurt to "glue" food into the Kong.

flesh or wooden table legs – a Kong stuffed full of tantalizing treats.

3. **Crate Training:** The crate, or kennel, is a vital dog behavior management tool, and one often slighted by dog owners because of an initial poor crate training experience. When Pal is trained to the crate properly and positively, the kennel becomes his den, a haven of security and comfort. A well-stuffed Kong combined with an appropriate training program can help your dog decide that his crate is a wonderful place to be.

4. **A Cure for Cabin Fever:** A few years ago, during a rain-soaked, endless El Nino California winter, my four dogs were getting seriously edgy with signs of a full-blown case of cabin fever. Stuffed Kongs to the rescue!! Silence soon settled over the troubled household as my snarling canine siblings settled into their separate corners, gnawing contentedly on their respective rubber pacifiers.

5. **Stress Reduction:** Stress is the underlying cause of most aggression. For a dog who is uneasy with houseguests, a Kong stuffed with doggie delicacies can help change the response to visitors from negative to positive. Stress is an involuntary response – the dog can't help it. The dog's brain reacts without conscious thought in the presence

of the negative stimulus, with an immediate "Visitor = BAD!!!!" response. We can use the stuffed Kong as part of a well-planned counter conditioning/desensitization program to change his involuntary response from "Visitor = STRESS" to "Visitor = GOOD!!!"

6. **Door Greeting:** Another great visitor-related Kong application is suggested by positive trainer Donna Duford. Dogs who want to greet guests too enthusiastically at the front door can be taught to fetch a toy instead. The knock at the door or the ringing of the doorbell becomes the cue to fetch the Kong, stuffed (if you know company is coming) or empty. Pal may then either retire to his rug to chew his treasure as your visitors enter, unmolested, or greet your guests politely at the door with his mouth filled with Kong instead of company. *Caveat: If your dog is a food or object guarder, this may not be a good Kong application for him.*

7. **Destructo-Dog:** Destructive behavior can range from simple high-spirited puppy fun to full-blown separation anxiety. By providing ample exercise for your dog, you can deplete the stores of excess energy sometimes that lead to ruinous house-romps. An intelligently Pal-proofed environment (crate, puppy pen, safe room) can minimize the destruction that occurs during your absences. And one or more stuffed Kongs might just keep your dog happily occupied and your home damage free while you are away. *Caveat: Crating is generally not recommended for true separation anxiety (SA) behavior. While Kongs can be a useful element of a complete SA behavior modification program, this complex and troubling behavior needs an in-depth, punishment-free behavior modification program, usually under the guidance of a competent dog trainer or behavior specialist.*

8. **Hide-and-Seek:** This game is an extension of the destructive behavior application of the Kong. You can occupy Pal's mind as well as his mouth by teaching him to look for and find his stuffed Kongs before he can chew on them. Start by hiding the Kong in plain sight and asking him to "find it!" Praise him when he does, and let him chew on it for a while. Then play the game again, hiding the toy partially behind a chair or table leg. Gradually make the hiding places harder and harder, until Pal learns to really search for his prize. Now you can hide two or three Kongs before you leave, tell him "find it" as you walk out the door, and your dog can keep himself occupied for hours, finding and emptying his Kongs. *Caveat: Hide*

your Kongs wisely. If you bury them in the sofa cushions or under the bedcovers you can expect to come home to an unmade bed, and strewn cushions...or worse.

9. **In The Swim:** Another good exercise application combines Kong fun with a favorite canine activity – swimming! While most Kongs sink, the company makes one model that has a polypropylene rope tied to it, and contains a chunk of buoyant spongy material inside, so it floats like a dream. The floating rope makes the "Cool Kong," as it's called, easy for owners to throw (swing it around and fling!) and easy for dogs who have trouble getting a whole Kong in their mouths to retrieve. It's a durable, ideal fetch toy for the dog who already loves to swim, and the perfect training tool for the Kong-loving dog who is a bit hesitant about getting his feet wet.

10. **Boredom Barking:** In my backyard, at this very moment, is Princess, a little stray beagle mix that my husband and I found on the highway. She is clearly an accomplished escape artist, as evidenced by her constant running of the fence line and her determined efforts to squeeze out between the fence post and the side of the house. Thwarted in her efforts to escape, she has taken to non-stop barking to express her displeasure at being effectively confined while we try to contact her owner. You guessed it – time to bring out the stuffed Kong! Princess is now happily licking cream cheese out of the Kong, and peace has returned to the neighborhood.

There's no doubt in my mind that this versatile toy deserves to be called "King" Kong. In fact, I'm betting that some of you have come up with some other very creative uses for Kongs yourselves.

CHAPTER 38 ♥
All in a Day's Care

The powerful Akita lunges at the Scottie, her mouth agape, teeth flashing. With a guttural growl, her jaws close around the neck of the little black dog. She pins the wiry terrier to the ground, where he struggles, belly up, in a fruitless attempt to sink his own teeth into his attacker's leg. As a handful of spectators laugh from a nearby doorway, the Scottie's struggles subside until he is motionless on the floor, the Akita pinning him to the ground with her superior weight.

What horror is this? Are we witnessing the awful blood sport of underground dog fighting? Far from it. Rather, this is a perfectly happy scene from a perfectly well managed dog daycare center. Shortly after the Akita pinned the Scottie to the floor, the little dog leaped up unscathed, chased the big dog around the room three times, and then took his turn pinning *her* to the floor amidst a reciprocal chorus of happy growls and snarls. It's all in a day's play.

Once upon a time, it was commonplace for groups of dogs to wrestle and romp together. Farmers and ranchers kept at least several dogs at a time: some to herd livestock and protect the homestead; some for hunting; one or two to kill rats in the barn; and maybe an unusually fortunate small house dog. The dogs had the run of the farm, romped and ran together, and led doggie lives. In a society more casual than that of today, even town dogs tended to roam freely in compatible packs, sorting out their differences with an occasional scuffle that rarely turned into anything serious.

In modern society, our dogs are more likely to stay at home, safely confined to the house or the fenced back yard, supplied with vaccinations, toys, and regular meals. As a result, while many of today's dogs live longer, healthier lives than their ancestors did, they also miss out on socialization and exercise with their canine pals.

Most dogs today also lack the stimulation of a real job – the herding, hunting, ratting, carting or guarding that they were bred to do. Left home alone all day while their families are at work and school, they are bored, lonely, restless and unemployed. Without the opportunity to interact regularly with others of their own kind, they even forget how to speak "dog," and when they *do* meet up with other canines they are socially inept and often fearful or aggressive. The sad result is a growing population of pets who exhibit inappropriate behaviors in the home, and who are "not good with other dogs."

Daycare to the Rescue

Enter the rapidly growing phenomenon of commercial doggie daycare. Our ancestors would have laughed heartily at the notion, but an increasing number of dog owners are realizing the benefits of paying to provide their dogs with a day full of activity and supervision. Imagine the relief of owners who realize, sometimes after the fact, the difficulty of housetraining the new puppy when no one is home to take her outside regularly. Now they can happily drop Puddles off at daycare in the morning, knowing that the staff can further the pup's understanding of proper potty behavior. Those who have separation anxiety dogs can stop administering tranquilizers (and stop taking them themselves), knowing that their house is not being systematically reduced to toothpicks in their absence.

In addition, in a well-supervised daycare program, Timid Tess can learn how to be a dog. She won't be allowed to run with scissors, and she will learn how to play well with others. Bouncing Bob, who now spends his days at home sleeping, storing up energy for wild greetings and demands that you pay attention to him when you get home, can romp with his pals all day and come home just as exhausted as you are after a tough day at the office. A tired dog is a well-behaved dog.

Many doggie daycare programs also offer training packages, grooming services, pickup and delivery, and will even transport Fido to his vet appointments for you. Others go above and beyond, including massage, aromatherapy and hydrotherapy in their service packages. Some provide you with photos to take home featuring action shots of Fido and Friends at play. Still others hold special events, such as holiday parties and outings to nearby dog-friendly parks, for you to socialize with your dog's pals and their owners. You might even find one that operates a retail pet supply store for the convenience of one-stop shopping for your dog's food, training tools, toys and other accessories.

Many Benefits

A dozen doggie daycare operators polled recently on a daycare e-mail list were in almost unanimous agreement that the top two benefits of their services were: exercise for Fido, which tires him out and promotes good manners; and the opportunity for him to socialize with other dogs, an important ongoing experience if Fido's owner wants him to be friendly with others of his kind.

They also listed numerous other benefits, including socialization with humans, relief from boredom, prevention of destructive behavior, a chance for the dog to have fun, and a lessening of owner guilt for those who feel badly about leaving Fido home alone all day. All of these benefits help to create a strong bond between dog and owner; a relationship that is vitally important in order to insure that the dog will be a beloved family member for the rest of his life.

Daycare operators offered words of wisdom to owners looking for a suitable facility for their dogs.

Jamie Lewis, of Zip A Dee Doo Dog Daycare, in North Hollywood, California, stressed the importance of having knowledgeable and caring staff, which can provide constant supervision and monitoring of the dogs. From responses to the poll, a ratio of one staff person for every 10 dogs seems to be the accepted norm, ideally with a second person on the premises at all times in case of emergency.

Cleanliness and safety, which go hand-in-glove with vaccination requirements and disease control, were also at the top of the list for almost all of the operators who responded. Several emphasized the importance of confirming that the staff's dog handling and training philosophies are in alignment with yours, and making sure that the dogs actually play together for most of the day, and are not simply stuffed into crates or kennels.

Amy Preston, owner of My Dog's Place in Mystic, Connecticut, voiced the feelings of many of the daycare operators regarding a comprehensive screening process for potential canine clients.

"Unfortunately, not all dogs are suited for daycare," Preston says. We screen three times: first over the phone. If nothing pops up there, we mail them an information packet that includes all the good stuff about daycare, as well as the risks and requirements, and a lengthy questionnaire that tries to uncover everything from food bowl aggression to grooming needs. If this doesn't scare them away, we make an appointment for an intake interview, where we carefully introduce the dog to our own dogs, one at a time, starting with the most mellow dog of the opposite sex. Although this may seem daunting, clients should see that this is in the best interest of their dogs. Careful screening will help create a safer environment for all."

Mary Watcher, of Animal Watchers and More, Inc., in Vermilion, Ohio, joined several of the other operators in cautioning owners to beware of overcrowding. A general rule of thumb is to allow 100 square feet for each large dog; 50 to 60 square feet for small to medium-sized dogs. This should be an enriched environment, offering toys to play with, obstacles for the dogs to run under, around and through, hiding places and beds for dogs who want a time-out, and matted floors for safety.

Robin Barbour of Puppy Playland L.L.C. in San Ramon, California, summed it up well in saying, "Use your own good judgment. If you get a bad feeling about the intake process, or anything just doesn't appear 'right,' don't leave your dog there. You are putting your faithful friend's welfare in someone else's hands. Make sure you are comfortable doing so."

The Right Stuff

Not surprisingly, doggie daycare centers have an endless supply of anecdotes that they are willing to share – some funny, others poignant.

Kellyann Conway, of Maritime Pet Kennel, Inc., in Tarpon Springs, Florida, tells of Alex, a Doberman client who had been coming to daycare religiously, once or twice a week, for the five years since they had opened. One day Alex's mom called the center to tell them that Alex had been diagnosed with a rare liver disease and, according to his doctor, probably only had a month or so left to live. Because Alex loved daycare so much, she wanted to continue bringing him for as long as possible. The Conways agreed, as long as the veterinarian agreed. Alex lived for another 15 months. Owner and vet were both convinced that the combination of exercise, fun and friends, as well as the anticipation of going to doggie daycare, kept Alex going. His blood counts taken the day after daycare were always noticeably improved, and he even ate all of his food on daycare days.

Just like us, having something in life to look forward to and enjoy can keep our dogs happier, healthier, and better behaved. Maybe it's time to look for a doggie daycare center near you.

❤ **CANINE DAYCARE RESOURCES**

Website for doggie daycare listings: www.doggiedirectory.com/daycare.html Daycare centers that contributed to this chapter:

Animal Watchers & More, Inc.
Vermilion OH   440-967-5436
http://www.animalwatchers.com/

Citizen Canine
Oakland, CA   510-562-1750
www.citizencanine.net

Every Dog Has Its Day Care, Inc.
Emeryville, CA   510-655-7832
www.everydog.com

The Good Dog Spot!
Bloomfield, CT   860-243-5500
mdogspot@earthlink.net

The Happy Camper Doggy Day Camp
Clearwater, FL   727-556-2676
www.doggydaycamp.com/

K9 Playtime, Inc
Medford, OR   541-773-2333
K9playtym@connpoint.net

Maritime Pet Kennel, Inc.
Tarpon Springs, FL 727-939-1089
www.dogdaycare.net/

My Dog's Place
Mystic, CT   860-572-7755
AmyDogsPlace@aol.com

Puppy Playland, LLC
San Ramon, CA   925-725-2300
www.info@puppyplayland.com

Paws Awhile, Inc.
Dubuque, IA   319-556-3800
pawsahile@lycos.com

T.L. Pets Doggy Daycare
Indianapolis, IN   317-631-DOGS
TLPets@aol.com

Zip A Dee Doo Dog Daycare
W. Toluca Lake, CA 818-980-7421
petguardian@earthlink.net

❤ HOW TO EVALUATE A DOGGIE DAYCARE

WHAT TO LOOK FOR:

- **Adequate staffing for supervision of canine clients**: Minimum of one staff person per 10 dogs, ideally with a second person on the premises in case of emergency. Staff monitors dog activity closely.

- **Knowledgeable, caring staff**: Staff is well educated and skilled in dog handling and behavior management, and employees obviously like dogs.

- **Clean facility**: No lingering odors. Dog waste is promptly removed and appropriately disposed of. Floors are routinely cleaned and disinfected. Facility is neat and free of debris and clutter. Canine clients are required to be reasonably flea-free.

- **Safe environment**: Matted floors (indoors), with no direct access of dogs to outer doors. Fences (outdoors) are high enough to keep dogs contained and are in good repair. Dogs are divided into size and play-style-appropriate play groups. Choke chains, if any, are removed prior to group play. Introductions of new dogs are done slowly and carefully.

- **Enriched environment**: Dogs have plenty of toys and equipment to play with, on, under and through, as well as access to safe and comfortable napping spots. Staff spends time interacting with dogs. Dogs are walked outdoors routinely (for indoor facilities) to maintain and encourage good housetraining habits.

- **Comprehensive screening process**: Owners are questioned as to dog's history with other dogs and people, and other potential health and behavior issues. New dogs are evaluated in an intake interview, and introduced to other dogs one at a time, starting with the most congenial.

- **Vaccination requirements**: Center maximizes protection for all canine clients by requiring proof of current vaccinations or, alternatively, satisfactory titer levels.

- **Compatible Philosophies**: Confirm that the center's dog handling and training philosophies are aligned with yours, and that the staff supports them.

WHAT TO WATCH OUT FOR:

- **Overcrowding**: A general rule of thumb is 100 square feet per large dog; 50 to 60 square feet per small to medium-sized dog. Overcrowding leads to aggression.

- **Limited access**: A center that has policies prohibiting owners from visiting their dogs at any time, with or without warning is unacceptable.

- **Unwillingness or inability to meet dog's needs**: Center should be willing and able to feed and medicate dogs as requested by owner.

- **Poor customer service**: Loving dogs is not enough; staff should also be courteous and friendly to human clients.

- **Dogs left unattended**: This should never happen. If a second person is not on the premises as back-up at all times, arrangements must be in place for someone to arrive quickly if an emergency requires the regular day care attendant to leave.

- **Anything that doesn't look or "feel" right.**

- **The opposite of anything on the "Things To Look For" list.**

CHAPTER 39 ❤
It's Okay to Cry

When you've spent a lifetime training, sharing and communicating with your dog, the relationship that you create is awesome in its intensity. It's impossible to explain to someone who has never experienced it. The joy of that relationship makes the inevitable end almost unbearably painful to even contemplate. But as much as we try to put it off, that end, and the accompanying grief and pain, will come. Our dogs' only real fault is that their lives are too short.

I have said painful good-byes to many of my beloved animal companions, and I know there are many more in my future. I'd like to share one of my own euthanasia experiences with you, in the hopes that it might help ease your pain, at least a little, when the time comes for you to say good-bye to one of your animal companions.

My Own Experience

It is now April of 2003. One year ago, we said good-bye to Josie. This is what I wrote then:

The sun is shining a little less brightly as I write this on a balmy April day. Just three days ago, we euthanized Josie, the beautiful canine spirit who led me on my journey from old-fashioned training methods to the positive training philosophy that I embrace today. My husband and I found Josie almost 15 years ago, while conducting a weekend undercover cockfighting investigation in San Jose, California. We had passed stray dogs all morning without pause, but something about Josie's adolescent terrier-mix presence compelled us to stop and invite her in when she darted across the road in front of our car. What a beautifully fortuitous stop for us that was.

We had fully intended to deposit Josie on Monday at the Marin Humane Society where I worked, confident that the top-quality shelter adoption program there would find her a top-quality lifelong loving home. But on Monday, I couldn't bring myself to leave her in the kennels. I brought her home again that night, telling myself that we would keep her just for the legal stray period, so she could go right into the Marin adoption kennels without risking exposure to kennel cough, or worse. Of course, I was kidding myself, if not Paul, who had already read the writing on the wall. A few more days in our home, and we both knew she had found her lifelong loving place in our hearts.

It was Josie who gently showed me the error of my force-based training ways when, after earning her CD and CDX, she slipped quietly under the back deck and refused to come out and suffer one more ear pinch as we struggled with the scent discrimination exercise for her Utility degree. It was Josie who taught me that dog training is so much more about relationship than it is simply about getting your dog to do a bunch of behaviors. And it was my relationship with Josie that led me to embrace the non-violent dog training philosophy that I teach in my written words as well as my everyday work.

We are each on our own journey through this life, and along the sometime rocky paths of our individual dog training experiences and philosophies. It is my hope that your canine companions are as skilled and gentle guides for you on your paths as Josie was on mine. It is my prayer that you all travel on positive pathways sharing relationships with your lifelong companions that are based on mutual trust and respect, and helping your clients to do the same. I have faith that the growing ranks of positive dog trainers will continue to spread the words of dog-friendly training to caring dog owners around the world. And I will consider it Josie's legacy to this world that she has brought me to a place where I can work to clarify and further this vital mission. I hope to see you all on that journey.

Euthanasia - The Last Kind Thing

I looked up from the front office switchboard just as the young woman stumbled through the front door. She stood blinded by her tears in the middle of the shelter lobby, immobilized by her distress. I quickly slipped from behind the counter and approached her.

"Can I help you?" I asked kindly, suspecting what she was about to say.

Instead of speaking, she thrust her hand forward. I removed the slip of paper from her clenched fingers and read it silently to myself.

"I have to put my dog Molly to sleep," she had written. "I knew I wouldn't be able to talk when I got here, so I wrote this note."

Tears welled in my eyes. I reached out to touch her shoulder in sympathy and she flung her arms around my neck, sobbing.

"It's okay to cry," I reassured her. I hugged her for a long moment, then with my arm still around her shoulders, gently guided her to a small room just off the lobby and sat next to her on the loveseat. With as much compassion as possible, tears spilling down my cheeks, I asked her the questions that had to be answered, and filled out the intake form. What kind of dog was Molly? (Oh, Pomeranians are wonderful dogs, I have one myself. I know how hard this must be for you...) How old is she? (18 years? How lucky she is to have had such a long life with you. Still, it's never long enough...) Why does she need to be euthanized? (Cancer. I'm so sorry...)

I worked at the Marin Humane Society for 20 years. Almost daily, owners brought their old, ill, injured and infirm dogs to the shelter so we could end their friends' suffering. It never got easier. Molly and her owner came to the shelter in the last month of my employment there, and the woman's pain pierced my heart just as sharply as the first owner request euthanasia I had experienced 20 years before. Anyone who has ever had to make that incredibly difficult decision to end a canine companion's life knows how all-consuming that grief can be – how deeply it penetrates your soul, and how close to the surface the pain lingers, even years after the loss.

Euthanasia literally means "good death," from the Greek words *eu* (good), and *thanatos* (death). Euthanasia by injection, the method considered by the AVMA and all major animal protection groups to be the most humane, is accomplished by injecting an overdose of an anesthesia drug, sodium pentobarbital, into the animal's vein or, in some cases, the abdominal cavity. When done properly, the animal lapses into unconsciousness within seconds, and death follows shortly. It takes a little longer if the injection is done abdominally instead of intravenously. If you have ever been anesthetized for surgery, you know what an animal experiences during euthanasia – one moment you are conscious and the doctor is telling you to count backwards from 100 – and then you're gone. The difference, of course, is that you wake up in the recovery room some time later remembering nothing of what happened while you were unconscious. The euthanized dog never wakes up.

We use euphemisms for the act of ending our pets' lives, because we don't want to say that we killed them. We put them to sleep. We send them to the Rainbow Bridge. We lay them to rest. But in fact, we aren't killing them. Webster's dictionary defines "killing" as *depriving of life*. When it's time for your dog to die because of old age, untreatable disease, injury or even serious behavior problems, we aren't depriving him of life so much as we are giving him a gift. We are relieving his suffering and easing a passage that every living creature will eventually and inevitably face. We are doing the last kind thing for him after a lifetime of loving kindness. We are giving him a good death. Euthanasia – it's a good word.

Quality of Life

There are a number of factors that enter into the decision to euthanize your dog, but they all relate to quality of life. This is a very subjective measure, and it is one that you, as the person closest to the dog, will know better than anyone else – as long as you can honest with yourself. We tend to be in denial about death in our culture – to prolong life at any cost, even at the price of pain and suffering. We have made great advances in medicine, so we are capable of prolonging life far beyond what was once imaginable. The fact that we *can* doesn't always mean we *should*.

When you are contemplating euthanasia, be honest with yourself. Is Molly still enjoying life? Can she still do the things she loves to do, like accompanying you on walks, sleeping on your bed, going for rides in the car? If she is in so much pain that she can't walk comfortably, or if her incontinence requires that she stay outdoors when she has been a house dog all of her life, she will be confused and miserable about the changes in her lifetime routines? An occasional bad day may not mean that her time has come, but if the bad days outnumber the good and the quality of her life is clearly deteriorating, you may be acting more in your own interests than hers by keeping her alive.

The quality of *your* life is an important consideration as well. The cost of some of the new treatments can be prohibitive. While it might be worth it to you to go into debt to pay for a treatment that will improve the quality of your dog's life for years to come, it may not be reasonable to pay thousands of dollars for cancer therapy that will give Molly a few more months under increasingly difficult conditions. If you can afford it and Molly is comfortable during the course of treatment, by all means, do everything you can for her. If you can't, or if Molly is suffering, then euthanasia is the right decision. It's your choice. It

is easy to feel guilty about not spending every last dime you have to keep her alive, but if doing so means neglecting your own needs, or those of your other family members – human *or* non-human – then it is appropriate to let Molly go a little sooner, rather than a little later.

Even a decision to euthanize a dog for behavioral problems is a quality of life choice. The two most common behavior challenges that lead to euthanasia are aggression and separation anxiety. Both can sometimes be resolved through appropriate behavior modification programs with a veterinary behaviorist or skilled behavior consultant. The programs can be long-term and costly and are often but not always successful. If you have the resources, by all means pursue behavior modification. If you can't, you may be putting the safety of family members and friends at risk, or your house may be systematically destroyed. Your quality of life is deteriorating, and so is your dog's. A dog with an aggression problem is frequently stressed beyond his level of tolerance, so he snaps – quite literally. Aggressive dogs tend to get banished to solitary confinement so their owners don't risk the moral and legal consequences of having their dogs bite someone. Dogs are pack animals; the more your dog is isolated from you and the rest of your family pack, the lonelier and more stressed he is likely to become. Fifteen years on a chain or in a pen in the back yard is not a quality life for a dog.

Separation anxiety dogs are extremely stressed any time they are left alone. Imagine having a panic attack so strong that you destroy things and even mutilate yourself. Not a quality life. If behavior modification combined with some of the wonderful new drugs now available for treating this disorder are not effective, and you can't find alternatives to leaving your dog alone – such as doggie daycare – then euthanasia is a reasonable alternative to the two of you spending the next 15 years in a constant state of stress.

Most importantly, when you know in your heart that it is time for euthanasia, don't let anyone talk you out of it. If your veterinarian tells you he can keep Molly alive for three more weeks with a new treatment but your resources are stretched thin and you have already mentally prepared yourself for her death, you don't have to succumb to the "life at any cost" temptation. If your best friend tells you that Molly doesn't look so bad, follow your own instincts. She doesn't know Molly like you do. She may not see how depressed Molly is, or understand how humiliated Molly feels when she soils herself. You know what's right for your dog. I personally choose to make the decision when I know that the end is inevitable, but when my dog is still enjoying life. I want her last days to be good ones. When I see the bad days starting to outnumber the good, I try to choose a good day for her final one, so that my last memories of her still have some wag in her tail, and some sparkle in her eye.

Be Kind to Yourself

Weeks, or even months prior to Molly's last days, take the time to plan ahead for the inevitable. As difficult as it is to do, it is even more difficult when her death is imminent. There are several different options for euthanasia. First, you need to think about whether you want to be present during the procedure or not. I have tremendous respect for owners who want to be with their dogs until the very end. It's not an easy thing to do, but I don't want my animal companions dying in the company of relative strangers. I want to be there for them. I also have great respect for owners who recognize that they can't deal with the trauma of watching their dogs die and that their very presence will be too upsetting for their dogs at a time when they need to be able to be calm and comforting to them. Either choice is right – so choose the one that is right for you.

Discuss euthanasia hypothetically with your vet long before the time is near, when you can be less emotional about it. Ask if he will let you be present. If he won't, and it is important to you to be there, ask him to refer you to someone who will. Many animal shelters and veterinarians do offer an "owner present" euthanasia service. Some shelters are exceedingly skilled and compassionate; shelter euthanasia technicians sadly must euthanize animals in far greater numbers than most veterinary staff, so they have ample opportunity to be good at it. Others are not, and some shelter environments are places where you might be less than comfortable taking your dog. Again, investigate well in advance, so you know whether this is an acceptable option for you.

Some vets will euthanize your dog for you at your home. This can be an appealing choice, especially if Molly isn't fond of the vet's office. That way you don't have to worry about driving in a distraught frame of mind, and Molly can die in the comfort of her own home, in her own bed. If you do take her to the vet's office or the animal shelter for euthanasia, take along her bed or a favorite blanket. That way, even if you don't stay with her, she will have something that is familiar to her.

Wherever and however you decide to have it done, the staff should take the time to explain to you what will happen. If you do this in advance, you will probably be in a better frame of mind to hear and understand. You will, of course, insist on euthanasia by injection – if anyone mentions the word "chamber," go elsewhere. If you choose to be present, a technician or veterinarian should explain to you in detail what you can expect to see: that death will come fairly quickly once the euthanasia solution is injected; that Molly may have involuntary muscle reactions after she is unconscious, including some vocalization – crying or

howling – and that this does *not* mean she is in pain; and that when she is dead she may void her bladder and bowels.

When the dreaded time draws near, be kind to yourself. Take some time off work. Surround yourself with people who understand and support your decision. Or take some time to be alone, if that feels better to you. Do one special last thing with your dog. A short walk to a favorite shady tree. A picnic. A long massage for her. Handfuls of her favorite treats. Whatever special things the two of you like to share the most. Take the time to say good-bye in a way that you would like to remember.

Your Final Farewells

After the euthanasia has been done, the vet or tech should use a stethoscope to confirm that the heart has stopped beating. You should be offered the opportunity to stay alone with the body for a time if you choose, to say your final farewells. If not, ask about that, if it is something you would like to do. You probably will have already been asked about disposal arrangements when you were making the appointment for euthanasia. Some dog owners opt for a general disposal of the body, which means it is either sent to a landfill site or tallow works, or sometimes cremated with a large number of other bodies. Many owners want their dogs' remains returned to them. If you have a suitable location on your own property (check with your local zoning laws) or have made arrangements with a pet cemetery, you can bury your pet's body. If you prefer, in many locations you can arrange for a private cremation, with the ashes returned to you in an urn. Some owners keep the ashes, others scatter or bury them. Private cremations tend to be the most expensive disposal choice.

It may be a comfort to you to have a ceremony for your pet, either by yourself, or with friends. Light candles, write a poem, scatter her ashes, bury her body, frame and hang a photograph, send a donation in her name to your local animal shelter... there are thousands of way you can honor her life after her death.

It's Okay to Cry

There is no question about it – the death of a close friend is a huge loss, whether the friend is human or canine. Sometimes people who have never known the joy of a close bond with an animal companion fail to understand the depth of that loss for us. They may try to downplay the importance, or tell you to get over it – she was "just a dog."

Pay no attention to those acquaintances and pity them their unfortunate ignorance. You have every right to grieve the loss of your friend. In fact, it is widely known that the loss of a beloved pet triggers the same stages of grief as those identified by Elizabeth Kubler-Ross and other psychologists in connection with the human death and dying. Those stages include denial (when we refuse to accept that Molly is going to die); bargaining (when we try to make deals, sometimes with a supreme being, if Molly can just live); anger and blame (why didn't the vet find the lump during her last checkup?); guilt (if I had a better-paying job I could have afforded that expensive treatment); grief – pure unadulterated pain; and finally, acceptance. You may go through all or only some of these stages. You may pass through some of them quickly, and linger in others for a long time. Know that they are all normal feelings, and if you feel yourself unable to cope, seek help. Find sympathetic friends who understand your pain and let them support you. Find a grief counselor who can help you deal with the raw emotions that emerge from your loss. There are now pet loss counselors in most communities who specialize in this field and are skilled at helping you endure and work through your pain.

Someone once said of dogs, "Their only flaw is that their lives are too short." How true that is. Yet, I tell myself that if they lived as long as we did, then we wouldn't be able to share our lives with as many wonderful dogs as we do. Every time one of my canine friends starts graying around the muzzle, clouding in the eyes and slowing down on our walks, I start to steel myself for the inevitable. I pray that she will die peacefully in her sleep, and I know that I will probably have to make the decision to do that one last kind thing for her. And always, I remind myself that it's okay to cry.

AUTHOR BIOGRAPHY ❤

Dogs and dog training have been a consistent thread throughout Pat Miller's life. Beginning at age six with the family Beagle, continuing on in her teenage years when she showed her Rough Collie and into her professional life, Pat has enthusiastically shared her world and her heart with dogs. She has titled her canine companions in Obedience, trained dogs in a wide variety of dog sports and built her career around animals. Pat is a columnist for *Whole Dog Journal, Whole Cat Journal* and *Your Dog Magazine* and she is the author of *The Power of Positive Dog Training*. Working now with people and their dogs, Pat has her own training establishment "Peaceable Paws, LLC" and is past President of the Association of Pet Dog Trainers, APDT, the largest professional organization for dog trainers in the world. As a 20-year veteran of the Marin Humane Society in California, Miller knows too well that when normal, healthy dogs aren't given the time and attention needed to become well-mannered family members, the results can be tragic. Pat recently moved to Hagerstown, Maryland where she will continue to build her training program.

Author Pat Miller and Josie.

RESOURCES ❤

I've mentioned several books, videos and other resources throughout the book and here are more favorites. These and other dog books and videos are available from *Dogwise, All Things Dog,* www.dogwise.com, 1-800-776-2665.

BOOKS

Aggression in Dogs: Practical Management, Prevention & Behavior Modification, Brenda Aloff, 2002. In-depth explanation of aggressive behavior in dogs.

Click for Joy! Questions and Answers From Clicker Trainers and Their Dogs, Melissa Alexander, 2003. Everything you always wanted to know about clicker training.

The Culture Clash, Jean Donaldson, 1997. Understand how your dog's brain works. Explore scientific principles of behavior and learning, and commonly held myths.

Doctor Dunbar's Good Little Dog Book, Dr. Ian Dunbar, 2003. Excellent puppy book; illustrates basic training using lure and reward methods.

Dog Whisperer: A Compassionate, Nonviolent Approach to Dog Training, Paul Owens, 1999. Thoughtful discussion of gentle methods of dog guardianship

Dogs Are From Neptune, Jean Donaldson, 1998. Case histories illustrate protocols for modifying aggressive behavior in an easy-to-read Q&A format.

Don't Shoot the Dog: The New Art of Teaching and Training, Karen Pryor, 1999. The book that launched the dog training culture's shift to positive training methods.

The Other End of the Leash: Why We Do What We Do Around Dogs, Patricia B. McConnell, Ph.D., 2002. Explores communication differences between humans and canines.

The Power of Positive Dog Training, Pat B. Miller, 2001. Explains positive training philosophies and methods; common behavior challenges; offers a 6-week, step-by-step training program.

Your Outta Control Puppy: How To Turn Your Precious Pup Into A Perfect Pet, Teoti Anderson, 2003. One of the best positive puppy-raising books on the market.

PERIODICALS

The Clicker Journal 1-703-777-2277
www.clickertrain.com/journal.html

Dog & Handler 1-802-254-1209
www.dogandhandler.com

The Whole Dog Journal 1-800-829-9165
www.whole-dog-journal.com

Your Dog 1-800-829-5116
www.tufts.edu/vet/publications/yourdog

WEBSITES

Association of Pet Dog Trainers www.apdt.com
This is a professional organization for dog trainers, with useful information for dog owners.

Clicker Trainers http://clickerteachers.travelvan.net/mainpage.php
Extensive listing of clicker trainers around the world. Search by state or by country.

Doggone Good www.doggonegood.com
Training tools, soft crates, jewelry, gift items.

Dogwise www.dogwise.com
Great source for dog books, videos, training products (Gentle Leaders), toys, food and supplies.

Karen Pryor www.clickertraining.com
Karen Pryor's website is a "must visit." Karen is the Queen Mother of clicker training.

The Kong Company www.kongcompany.com
Originator of the Kong, an exceptionally durable and versatile toy; other ultra-tough products.

Peaceable Paws/Pat Miller
www.peaceablepaws.com
Author's website. You can also join the author's email discussion list by sending a message to: peaceablepaws-subscribe@yahoogroups.com

Premier www.gentleleader.com
Source for the Gentle Leader head halter and various other *very* useful dog products.

White Pine Outfitters
www.whitepineoutfitters.com
Exceptionally well-designed leashes, collars, harnesses, hands-free belts and more.

INDEX ❤